Prologue

The horizons for today's Western women are broader than any of those who went before us. Three quarters of us are financially independent thanks to full-time employment, compared to just a third in 1985. Despite the overall gender pay gap (which has shrunk by about a third since 1997), women in their twenties are now taking home about £1k more than their male peers every year. Just under half of FTSE 350 directors are women, and we make up a third of the highest earners in the world – up from 10 per cent since 1970.

Recent years have seen the third British female prime minister take office, as well as a historic cabinet featuring the greatest number of female ministers ever. We can pretty much decide when we want to have kids, and how, thanks to medical advancements like egg freezing and surrogacy. Our football teams are finally being taken seriously.

What I'm trying to say is: today, our possibilities really are endless. In theory, anyway.

But whatever our professional endeavours, one life goal remains popular. And that is finding someone to do it all with you. Or at least be beside you. For many of us, this endeavour takes up a sizeable chunk of our late twenties and thirties;

be it via miserable dates with Hinge matches, or nights out hoping to bump into the hot guy or girl from the office who slid into your DMs for twenty-four hours, but ignored you in the post room.

We might not want to admit it, but a relentless quest shared by almost all of us is to find that person who irritates you a very little amount, isn't bad to look at, and loves you. When the hunt is over, you move to a flat or house in the suburbs and, in around half of cases, decide to get married. Eventually you'll stop bothering with contraception. At this point, according to contemporary society, you have *made it*.

You might think this picture of life's trajectory is outdated. It is true that far fewer people are choosing to make their union legal than they were forty years ago. But marriage is still a choice made by roughly half of adults in the US and the UK. Three quarters of people live with a romantic partner.

But what happens if that isn't the end of the story? What if the box you thought you'd ticked suddenly – and totally unexpectedly – reverts to blank? It's no secret that half of marriages end in divorce. It's assumed to be a problem for midlifers; children leave home and couples realise there's nothing left to talk about. But there's a new divorce demographic emerging. Young, bright things who are calling it quits before they can even celebrate a paper anniversary. These days, you're almost twice as likely to get divorced in your early thirties than you are in your late fifties. There's just as many people calling it quits after a year, as there are after twenty-five. And according to divorce lawyers, it's a growing trend: millennials fall in love, live together, get married and, relatively soon afterwards, get divorced.

Interestingly, in the majority of cases, they say, it's the man who pulls the plug.

I was introduced to this phenomenon in November 2022, when my once-adoring husband decided to call it quits after six months. I have since come into contact with a not insignificant number of women of a similar age who've experienced an adapted version of my same heartbreak. They too got married thinking this was it, only to find it wasn't before they'd had a chance to use their wedding china. What is happening?

Perhaps our current era of Hinge and Bumble is triggering mass newly-wed FOMO. Or maybe the immediate gratification granted by today's technological world makes the stability of marriage seem dull as hell. Perhaps our dire economic prospects make any type of commitment terrifying? Could it be because of Covid? Or Taylor Swift?

In *What She Did Next* I aim to find some semblance of an answer, by delving into the stories of twelve young women who've suffered similar shock marriage terminations, albeit in varied circumstances. Their stories explore all manner of themes as possible explanations for their relationships ending: children, financial differences, affairs, faith, race, emotional illiteracy, to name a few. Meanwhile, psychologists, relationship counsellors and divorce lawyers help unpick the conundrum too – offering insight collected from thousands of couples. Two thirty-something men reveal what it's like to be on the other side of the coin; one who wanted to be married, and one who really didn't.

These pages will also enlighten you as to the legal implications of marriage that many of us (including me) are initially naive to, and how to protect yourself from financial ruin. Once you sign a marriage certificate, half of everything you have is your partner's – which feels particularly unfair if you've only been legally bound to them for a year. There's plenty of advice to help you navigate proceedings – whether they have got ugly, or whether you just haven't a clue where to start.

But the ultimate purpose of this book is to show you that, while your life may not pan out exactly as you imagined it, it will likely be more fabulous than you could ever predict. The women whose stories you're about to read are a beacon of hope to the heartbroken; a smooth pile to keep you steady after the rug has left from under your feet. A flickering light at the end of the shit-filled tunnel. The assurance that, however fucked up life as you know it is, everything will be all right. In fact, it will almost certainly be much, much better.

The vast majority of names in this book have been changed to respect privacy – except for three women who wanted to be named, and the quoted experts.

Chapter 1

The Split

Pick up the phone, Sam, pick up the phone. It's 2.30 a.m. and I am starfished on the sofa, my heart exploding into my gullet. And I really, really need my brother to answer my call. I switch to loudspeaker and check the time in LA: 6.15 p.m.

'Heee-llo, sister!' My brother's voice transports me to our parents' loft room where we'd watch *Friends* reruns and compete in throwing the largest objects possible out of the Velux window.

But now I'm crying. 'I think Ben might be leaving me,' I say.

'Oooo-kay . . .' He either doesn't believe me or he thinks I'm being melodramatic. 'What happened?'

I tell him that Ben cooked my favourite aubergine pasta last night and then, out of nowhere, announced he wasn't happy – despite our recent second honeymoon in Mexico where we had romantic beach dinners and unprotected sex most nights.

When I'd asked if there was someone else in the picture he wasn't telling me about, he'd responded with silence. We'd been married for six months, together for eight and a half years. I ran to the toilet and vomited. I knew who it was. In the Mexican airport lounge I'd suggested we swap phones to look at each other's pictures of the holiday. 'Wait a second,' he'd said, bringing his phone towards his chest. At the time, I thought nothing of it. If Ben was one thing, it was trustworthy. After a couple of seconds he handed over the phone and, between pictures of me drinking margaritas and eating dimly lit shrimp tacos, was an image of a pair of earrings in the shape and colour of chilli peppers.

'Why do you have this?' I asked.

'Oh. Well, you know Lizzie in the office? She has the same earrings so I took a picture to show her,' he said. Lizzie was his friend. As far as I knew, she had a long-term boyfriend.

The whole exchange had been virtually forgotten until the Tuesday after we got back from Mexico, and Ben was home late from work drinks. I'd expected the familiar text to arrive at around 11.30 p.m., which usually read something along the lines of: 'Sorry babe, I've stayed out really late, on my way home now xxx'. To which I'd reply with a picture of our dog, Jez, modelling remnants of watermelon stuck in his beard. But the text never came. I went to bed feeling nervous and woke up to a frostier version of the 'I'm coming home' messages than I was used to, sent at 2 a.m. He was lying comatose beside me, the stench of stale beer radiating from his armpits. On the walk to the station in the morning I felt uneasy, and found myself drawn to a podcast I'd saved months ago about a woman who finds her husband cheating.

The next day, 10 November 2022, the night he handed me that bowl of pasta, he told me nothing had happened between them. 'If I had done something then I'd have been a total dickhead,' he said. 'We haven't even told each other we really like each other or anything.' The word 'really' felt stapled to the front of my brain.

Back on the sofa, my brother said this wasn't the end. 'The thing is, Eve, boys are stupid. And sometimes, we have our heads turned . . . We're thinking with our, well, not with reasonable logic,' he said in his best 'big brother' voice. 'He's just being an idiot and he'll forget all about it in a few days. Just take deep breaths and try to get some sleep.' When he felt anxious, he told me, he drew a mental picture of one thing in life that conjured feelings of unconditional joy and love, and this helped. For him, it was his two-year-old daughter, my niece, Laine. I put down the phone and wailed into the armrest.

Sam was wrong, of course. The following morning I left for work, expecting some sort of explanation or apology would arrive by 11 a.m. Ben was sorry, he was confused, of course he loved me and wanted to spend his life with me. At 2 p.m. I received this message: 'I am going to go out with the boys tonight so that you can have some space.'

Why didn't he want to beg forgiveness and explain the psychotic episode he was clearly having? I suggested we talk when I got back from work.

I returned to find him leaning against the kitchen counter, nervously smiling next to one half-filled glass of red wine. He was drunk. Or tipsy, at least.

'So, I've been thinking about our relationship,' he announced before I'd taken off my coat. I looked at the half-emptied bottle of wine beside him, and then at his face. It was one I didn't recognise.

The upshot of the conversation was this: Ben felt unfulfilled, ignored and fed up. Our relationship was boring, it had lost its spark, and he struggled to see how this could be remedied. 'The thing is, Eve,' he said, 'when you die, people won't remember you for the work you did.' This was an odd turn of phrase, seeing as I've spent much of my career writing health-related newspaper articles that expose wrongdoing towards patients. It's not *Spotlight*, but the last time I checked, articles on the internet last for ever.

He wasn't finished. 'It's like . . . they'll actually remember you for the way you treat your friends and family.' I frowned as if to say, What are you going on about? He waved his hands in the air and said, 'You know what I mean.'

Ben told me he wanted to take some time to decide if he wanted to try and make it work with the help of a couple's therapist. In the meantime, he refused to leave our house ('I have nowhere to go! You can't just kick me out on the street!'), instead suggesting that I sleep in the spare room and we 'keep out of each other's way'. He eventually relented, begrudgingly called an Uber to take him to a local Travelodge, and scoffed when I refused his valiant offer of a hug goodbye. He called the following morning to tell me he'd be coming back soon, and I ought to work out where I wanted to be. My answer was, in my house, with the husband I had a fortnight ago. Needless to say, I ended up in my mother's spare room, or, more accurately, pinned to the couch in a sea of sodden tissues.

Ben told me he loved me on New Year's Eve 2013, when we were both twenty-two. We'd been dating for two months – after meeting on our journalism master's course – and he said it first. We were drunk, but not hammered, after spending the evening at a soulless bar in Piccadilly, watching the fireworks – just us two. His words reverberated through my skull. It made no logical sense to me. Until Ben, my relationship history had read like a catalogue of silly men-babies whose idea of romance was texting you once every other day. Love, for me, felt like a pipe-dream fantasy. I told Ben I loved him too that night – even though I didn't feel it until a month later.

He loved the hell out of me. Most weekday mornings, for the best part of six months, he would arrive at university at least ten minutes early so he could wait at the top of the Tube station escalator for my arrival. He wanted to start his day with a five-minute walk together, he said. I was, according to Ben, the most beautiful woman he'd ever been with, and the person he'd prioritise every weekend – even early on – cancelling every plan to make room for our mooches round Soho, marvelling at leather goods we couldn't afford. Sometimes, on Sunday mornings, I'd tell him about my family, particularly my dad, who had died when I was twelve. He was, it seemed, the only person whose parents were still alive with a miraculous understanding of what it felt like to be a half orphan. He knew exactly what to say, and what not to, and when to say nothing at all. At Christmas, his mum bought him a stack of vouchers for fancy restaurants across the city – none of which we could afford as students. We spent three months dining on amuse-bouches and confit potatoes, and drinking nightcaps at hotel bars overlooking Hyde Park. We'd slump back into his flat, put a documentary on the laptop and interrupt it with sex halfway through.

*

The girls came with cupcakes on day one of the break-up. Mum got out the nice biscuits, and I could barely stand up. My face was dirtied with two days' worth of eyeliner and remnants of broken-up tissue. A best friend's romantic pain shoots through you like a freezing January morning. Their eyes were cloudy; they were so sorry he'd done this. But I was the one who had brought him into our circle of trust. I chose him – not them – and clearly I'd got it so very wrong.

I looked at Martha. 'I am so sorry you have to go through this again,' I said. Martha had been with John for eight years when he sat down one night and told her he was out. They'd shared a flat for five years and had been searching for a house to buy together. A week later, she went back to their shared flat to collect her belongings, and found a cork engraved with the words: BECKY'S FIRST DAY AT WORK. She would later discover that Becky was a girl John had been hooking up with for the past few months – and who would eventually become his new girlfriend.

'If it means I can help you navigate this, at least my heart-break wasn't for nothing,' Martha said. I licked a chunk of buttercream off my finger and thought about how lucky women are to be friends with other women.

It was clear, to everyone but me, that I'd eventually need to be admitted to hospital. It was August 2015 and I was critically ill with anorexia. Six months of weight-gain plans had failed to get me a pound heavier, and I was so thin that even my handbag strained my bones and muscles, which meant agonising back pain. Ben and I had been together a year and a half. He was anxious about my weight, but I'd always managed to convince him I was getting better. The doctors say it takes time, you have nothing to worry about, I'd say. But the threat of a section order, should I not agree to be admitted, wasn't something I could exactly hide.

'Mum, they're saying they want to take me to hospital.' I'd been told to take a minute to 'think' about the doctors' orders in the room where they did group therapy. Mum was surprisingly calm. She'd later tell me it was the call she'd been longing for – at least now it wasn't up to her to make me better.

'Ben will leave me . . . I know he can't do this,' I said to her. 'He's told me before, if I have to be in hospital, he won't be able to handle it.'

'Okay, let me call him and tell him,' Mum said.

Two minutes later, my phone rang. It was Ben. 'So you think I'm going to dump you?' he said. I reminded him of what he'd said months earlier about this very scenario. 'Nah, don't be silly,' he said. 'Do you think I might get to spin you round in a wheelchair?'

A fortnight later I was allowed visitors, and Ben showed up early, bearing flowers and seven newspaper supplements, as well as a USB stick loaded with all five seasons of *Breaking Bad*.

He climbed up onto my plastic mattress and cried into my shoulder. 'I miss you,' he sobbed. Visitors were only allowed twice a week and for ninety minutes per slot – one before dinner, and one after, as non-patients were strictly banned during meal times. Ben quickly adopted a new routine: he'd come for the first visit, walk twenty minutes up the road to the nice but cheap Turkish restaurant, eat dinner, and return in time for the second one.

Six weeks later I was fed back to health and discharged. Ben showed up at Mum's the following day, deliriously happy and showing me flats he'd found for us to live in together. We moved into our first home, in a part of west London we'd never been to, a couple of months later. But my illness hadn't relented. Three meals a day remained a challenge – as did pizza, chocolate and anything that wasn't made from mostly vegetables. Eating past 9 p.m. wasn't easy either. Over the following five years of our relationship, Ben helped me chip away at these anxieties. Once, when I was freaking out about our homemade chicken kebabs not being ready until 9 p.m., he googled the average dinner time in continental Europe; if eating late was good enough for the Italians, it was good enough for me, he said. He gently encouraged me to eat beyond my limits, but never pushed. He entertained my constant need for permission to spend my Sunday morn-ings on the sofa watching cooking shows. 'This is what most people we know are doing right now!' he'd assure me. He'd make dinner when he knew I couldn't – or wouldn't – and find ways to hide extra calories when my weight was slipping. Occasionally I'd notice and shout, but it never seemed to bother him.

It is likely that Ben saved my life. This fact characterised our relationship in the years that followed, for both of us. We subconsciously dismissed the bonds of other couples because no one had survived what we had: a near-death experience that welded us together for ever, whether we liked it or not. My illness was a recurrent theme in the emotional outpour-ing that was our wedding speeches. The guests said we were beautifully vulnerable, powerful, proof that love conquers all.

It's only now that I realise all this was a sign of dysfunction; evidence that our relationship had never got over the ordeal.

For instance, Ben's insistence on making dinner every night was, in hindsight, unusual. I'd notice his subtle panic when I'd choose a vegetarian meal at a restaurant. 'You should have something proper, something more substantial,' he'd say. The words were stuck in my head for years afterwards. Had I gained enough weight for him to fancy me again? Ben wasn't humble about his leading role in my recovery. My illness wasn't my fault, he'd say, but thank goodness he was there to direct my portion sizes. He'd dismiss the efforts of my best friends, and even sometimes those of my mum, in helping me make my peace with food. 'We did it together,' he'd say. 'You and me.' And at times, it did feel as though it had been that way.

By January 2020 I was virtually recovered. Apart from one detail: I was yet to have a period. My disordered thoughts had all but disappeared and I was stuffing my face most weekends. My weight was creeping up. But, infuriatingly, not enough for my hormones to kick back into action. I just wanted my recovery complete – once and for all. Ben came up with a plan. 'I think you should get high,' he suggested one night during the series finale of *Curb Your Enthusiasm*. By the following morning, Ben had found some high-strength skunk-infused chocolate. That Saturday, we stocked up on three different ice-cream flavours, biscuits and tubs of Celebrations – as well as an entire rotisserie chicken, in preparation for the expected munchies.

We started with half a square of chocolate each, and settled down to an episode of *Line of Duty*. It took twenty minutes to kick in – at which point I could feel my face starting to melt. 'I'm talking but I don't know if the words are coming out,' I said to Ben, who, by this point, was red-faced and dribbling.

'I think this might be a bit strong,' he said.

I looked down at my legs, which were now shaking uncontrollably – bouncing, hilariously, in all different directions. 'I NEED A WEE!' I shouted, and attempted to lift my bottom from the sofa but instead fell sideways into Ben's lap. He pushed me off and held my hips, steadying me on my feet. 'HOW DO I GET TO THE TOILET?' The bathroom was about five metres away. My legs were now bouncing from the knee. I made it, somehow, before running to the bedroom, telling Ben he should probably call an ambulance. He followed me in and drew the curtains shut.

'This will help,' he said, stroking my hair. 'Lie down on the bed and try to close your eyes. I'm here beside you, and you're fine.'

The rest of the evening is a blank hole. But Ben later told me I patted him on the chest every ten to fifteen minutes, asking if he was still alive.

Ben took just over a week to consider whether or not he wanted to try and make our marriage work, during which time I saw him twice. Once, to discuss intermediate plans: who looked after the dog; whether or not I kept paying the mortgage. The second time was for him to outline a catalogue of my flaws, and explain why, in agonising detail, he'd realised I wasn't right. It was a thousand tiny nails lodging into every part of my body's tissue.

'First of all, our families are very different. I'd say yours is loud and close, and mine isn't.'

My breath was suddenly short, staggered.

'And you prioritise work way too much. It's not normal to want to work on the weekend. I'm never at the top of your list. Some people would be perfectly happy with that, but I don't think it's right for me.'

I fixated on his face, which was angled towards the back wall of the living room, avoiding my eyeline. Maybe if I caught his eye he'd see the woman he loved, and realise he was making a terrible mistake. But the list didn't stop. I'd failed to make enough effort with his friends and family. It was fine to be ambitious, but I was too ambitious, at the expense of the people I loved. I hadn't given him enough attention or praise when he'd got his new job. I felt a bruise forming inside my gut.

In the end, I asked him to stop – if he wasn't offering a conclusion or decision, I didn't need to hear it. 'Can we just decide what we're doing about the house? Are you moving out?'

He did that unrecognisable face again. The one I imagine he'd use if someone accidentally trod on the back of his shoe, or refused to give him a refund. 'We've talked about this. I don't have anywhere else to go. It's my house and I want to stay here. You've been living at your mum's, so I don't see what the problem is.'

I thought back to Martha's advice. On break-up day one, she'd told me: Whatever you do, don't leave your house. She'd been so traumatised by John's admission that she'd fled the flat within the hour, dragging her belongings onto the Tube in bin liners. 'It was the most humiliating moment of my life – and I would die before I let you do the same,' she'd said. I already regretted last week's decision not to insist Ben remained at the Hertfordshire Travelodge. This time, I'd listen to Martha.

I stood my ground. 'This is my house, and I want to come back. You're the one with doubts. If you want to separate for a while, then you need to come up with a plan and go somewhere. Why is this my responsibility?'

He didn't get it.

The following Monday, he messaged to say he wanted to talk. He'd made a decision.

'Do you want a cup of tea or anything?' he asked as I walked in the door. Was hospitality a sign of wanting to make a marriage work? The place was cleaner than usual and he looked surprisingly good; the fleece he wore for tennis was zipped up to the top, hugging his broad shoulders, and his hair had fallen into that tangled curl thing that I liked. Was this all for my benefit?

We sat on his side of the sofa – the spot where he used to lie flat with his legs dangling, leaving enough room for me to nestle into the side of his torso. But now we were sitting like colleagues, nervously watching our knees in case they accidentally touched. It would be a ball ache to move this gigantic sectional sofa out the front door if we had to sell it. I fixated on the round patch of Jez's piss that marked our white mohair rug, which reminded me I needed to take it to the dry cleaner. Although, maybe now I wouldn't have to. I thought of Jez wiggling his lumbering backside through the hole in the gate at Ben's parents' house, where he was being looked after. Whatever comes from this conversation, at least Jez will be happy, I thought.

'I'm a bit nervous . . .' Ben said, before taking three – very intentional – long, deep breaths. He wasn't going to say what I wanted him to. Vomit was rising in my gullet. My legs went numb. The grey area – waiting for his final decision – had kept me cushioned. But now all I could see was black.

'Just spit it out.' The words escaped me so quickly I got lightheaded.

'I don't think I want to try.'

There it was. The ultimate fear: alive and kicking. I opened my mouth to respond but couldn't. My legs were ten steps ahead, launching off the sofa and running past his feet to the front door. I opened the door and turned to see him standing with his hands in his pockets, bewildered. I blinked to let the tears run down my face, looked him dead in the eye, said, 'I think you're a scumbag' – and bolted out the door.

A week later we put the house on the market, and I emailed him to confirm that I'd get a larger share of the profits, given that my mum had gifted us £25,000 towards it. I asked for half of the £800 we'd paid for our dog Jez, who we'd since decided would stay with Ben's parents. He refused, telling me Mum's money was a 'shared' gift and, anyway, we'd spent most of it on house renovations. I muffled something about giving me whatever was left, knowing that this still wasn't fair. It then dawned on me that I'd made a catastrophic mistake. For the entirety of our relationship Ben had overseen our shared finances. Not just finances – just about everything practical a person needed to do to live in a house or flat. I had transferred money to him every month for bills, mortgage and anything else household related. When we had saved for a house, we'd pooled the deposit money – including the £25k from my mum – and put it into his savings account. I couldn't even tell you which water company we used.

Now he'd had a shock metamorphosis, I was fucked. Not only had I no leg to stand on when it came to fighting for my family's savings, I was clueless about how to stand on my own two feet. It took all of twenty seconds for me to realise that I would now, aged thirty-one, have to learn how to be an independent grown-up. I'd moved from home to a life with Ben aged twenty-three and, apart from a brief stint at university – which had involved me driving back to London from Brighton every weekend with a car full of dirty washing – I'd never had to fend for myself. Not really.

All I could think of was the internet. In all three homes we'd shared, Ben had set up the utilities, and in every place it had been a struggle. Engineers couldn't find the right fuse box, or Ben had to buy one of those cable extension leads for the ... bandwidth? Our first weeks of living in every new place had been punctuated by me yelling, 'BEN, INSTAGRAM WON'T LOAD AGAIN!' from the bedroom, while he put our pictures up. How the fuck was I supposed to do this all alone?

In the weeks that followed I bombarded Ben with heartfelt pleas, reminding him that this was his doing. My mother was a widow and pensioner who had gifted all her savings under the belief we'd be together for ever. I told him he could stay in the house. I wouldn't fight him for the dog. He could have whatever furniture – all of it. All I wanted was my mum's money.

His responses read like they'd been sent by my Year 8 form tutor. Phrases like 'as we discussed previously' and 'I would advise' made me feel as if I were married to my accountant. He wasn't budging. The money was gone, and he was not interested in finding a way to make it up to me. It was then that I learned of the legal fuckery that is marriage. One of my pathetic begging-for-money letters triggered a response sent by Ben, but clearly written by a lawyer. It callously reminded me of all the assets he'd have access to in the eyes of the law, should I attempt to pursue him for my mum's £25k. My savings, pension, property in the family name and any other investments were all, technically, shared. He assumed that I wouldn't want to engage in such negotiations, but he thought it important to remind me that I'd be forced to, should I begin legal proceedings or push for mediation (the independent, middle man in divorce that helps you negotiate finances when you want to rip each other's heads off).

About a month later I went back to our house to box up my life, in preparation for its transfer to a storage facility on the outskirts of London. I walked into the dining room to find every birthday gift he'd ever given me with Post-it notes beside them that read BEN'S.

I've hated Christmas for as long as I've been a person with a dead parent. Actually, any occasion in which the entire world and its mother are frolicking in family fun time makes me want to hide for at least a week. It's like the whole of Instagram is saying: 'Don't forget your dad is dead!'

One year, a couple of weeks before John Lewis put up its tree, Ben handed me a present. He knew it was early, but he couldn't wait any longer. It was a framed Paul McCartney record – a little-known album from his back catalogue called *Flaming Pie*. Ben had spent months trying to track it down and eventually found a second-hand pressing from an obscure vinyl store in Athens.

It was the album Dad had played relentlessly in his car in the year before he became too ill to drive. Sam and I would laugh as he banged along to the drum solos on his steering wheel, and joined in with the harmonies on 'Young Boy' (pretty successfully, actually). I'd completely forgotten that I'd told Ben this earlier that year, one morning when a song from the album came on Radio 6 and I'd started crying. He'd remembered. 'When you told me that story all I could think of was how happy you'd have been in that car with him,' Ben said as I hugged the record sleeve, using the bottom of my pyjama top as a tissue to dry my eyes. 'Now you can look at the record on the wall, and take a minute to think about those times, about him.'

Another idiotic divorce fact you may not be aware of is that you must wait to have been hitched a full year before applying to officially end your marriage. Ben was annoyingly punctual. On 16 April 2023, a year to the day after we'd picked confetti out of our hair at Islington Town Hall, an email arrived in my inbox from His Majesty's Courts and Tribunals Service.

'Dear Eve Simmons, your husband has applied for a divorce,' it read. All I was required to do was click the link enclosed and select if I agreed or disagreed, and whether I supported his claim that we had no children.

I ticked the box titled 'agree', bit off a chunk of my nail and looked at the screen, thinking, now what?

Chapter 2

The Blindsided

Most official definitions of a traumatic event involve two fundamental words: *unusual* and *unexpected*. According to one NHS description, it is not the size of the event that makes it traumatic, it's what the person who experienced thinks about what happened, and what it means to them.[1] Notably, a traumatic event 'shatters the basic beliefs we hold about life'.

This is also a neat description of how it feels to experience an episode of what is known among divorce experts as *blindsiding*. There is no extended crescendo, no summer of discontent, not even a period of sexlessness. In fact, it often occurs scarily close in time to some form of evidence that you're still in love – be it a wedding, all-inclusive holiday or, God forbid, a pregnancy. It is a disturbing phenomenon that, while not novel, is, I'm told, increasing in prevalence – especially among younger married couples.

'What happened to you is not uncommon,' says Aina Khan OBE, London-based divorce lawyer and international law consultant. 'We see people living together for long periods of time and they seem to be happy. Then they get married and things seem to go downhill. One of them changes their mind.' Anyone can be a victim of blindsiding. But these days, the woman is more likely to get burned.

Sandra Davis, a partner at Mishcon de Reya specialising in family law, has noticed the same pattern: 'It is almost as if men get caught up with the excitement and pomp of the wedding and it serves as a distraction. When all that's over and they wake up to the reality of the day-to-day of the relationship, they realise they don't want it after all.'

It is this element of my break-up that I've found myself most simultaneously alarmed and fascinated by, and that I've spent the past two years endeavouring to comprehend. The desperation to slot together the pieces isn't just for my own warped sense of security; if I know what caused it, I can stop it happening again. It's also in aid of the astonishing numbers of women I've come across since, who've faced almost exactly the same horror. A bit later on in this chapter, you'll hear from psychologists and relationship counsellors who will offer a window into the mind of the blindsider, and what possesses them to do it. But first, the phenomenon: how common is it, and what about it makes it so earth-shatteringly shit?

Six months after the split I told my humble Instagram following what had happened. The messages came pouring in from other women who'd suffered similar experiences, almost all honing in on the element of surprise. I realised that, while they may not have been marriages, this has also been true of pretty much all of the break-ups I've seen involving twenty-nine-to-thirty-something straight couples: best friends, extended family, colleagues. In almost all cases that I have come across, there's been a (usually male) blindsider.

One newly-wed told me her husband had recently encouraged her to come off contraception so they could start the family they'd longed for. The following week he'd announced he was 'too young' to settle down and wanted a divorce. Another had recently become pregnant with their fourth (!) child when he'd revealed his secret affair. One twenty-nine-year-old said her new husband just got up and left one day. No warning. No explanation. More on these depressing tales later.

Social media forums like Reddit offer further evidence. There are endless break-up subreddits (I scrolled through 80 per cent of them), each attracting several hundred comments. I noticed only a handful of men revealing they were the victims of blindsiding. The vast majority noted that they were the ones doing the break-up, and their female partner was 'surprised' (more on the hormonal enclave that is Reddit later).

All break-ups are hell. But shock adds a special sauce, leaving the victim not only rudderless, but forever tortured by the knowledge that what you believe to be safe may suddenly not be. So what is it about the element of surprise that feels so mind-numbingly dreadful?

Shock is an interesting emotional state. When we enter into emotional shock, adrenaline is pumped through the body and brain as a result of the 'fight or flight' mechanism that is intended to protect us from sabre-toothed tigers or gunshots.

This activates our limbic system, which is responsible for both emotions and memories, meaning the sensation of panic is stored alongside fragments of the event. Hence, future triggers of the memory also spark the unpleasant feelings that whacked you over the head at the time of the emotional crash.

Simultaneously, the frontal part of the brain involved with reasoning and logic – the prefrontal cortex – temporarily shuts down. This means the memory isn't often captured in an ordered, articulated fashion, and you may find yourself unable to speak, write, do and think properly in the moments immediately after the event. But soon comes the psychological aftermath. Because the memories are stored in a state of confusion, the mind begins a particularly tortuous psychological process: it tries to write a story that makes logical sense. A story that fits with this outcome.

Could I have been more enthusiastic about our shitty neighbourhood? I should have bought him dinner when he got his new job, or written him a card at least. I should have backed off from talking about babies, and done more of the grown-up house stuff. Plenty of people work long hours and still manage to arrange a cleaner and a handyman (or woman) to come and fix the leak in the roof. Then there was my lack of physical effort; it was a wonder he wanted to touch me given that I thumped around the house most nights wearing my mottled fleece and sweatpants, which I let the dog rip holes in. I cringed thinking of the leopard-print fleece dressing gown, stained with tomato sauce, that I was wearing the night he broke up with me. I was a selfish, inconsiderate slob who had carelessly passed the vital minutiae of our shared life to him, using the pathetic excuse that I was always at work. I had pushed him to the sympathetic ear of another woman and who could blame him for developing feelings for her?

This was my daily torment, swimming around in my brain until I went to sleep at night. And when I didn't sleep, which was often, it became darker. I'd use this assumed narrative to predict the future. Why would anyone want to come within an inch of me?

These thoughts remained deafeningly loud for three weeks. Telling my therapist exactly what was going on in my head helped. This was a natural reaction to being in an unfathomable situation, she said. She also challenged my destructive beliefs by asking insightful questions such as, 'Don't you think nine years is a long time to spend with someone who is, as you say, a disgusting, lazy troll?'

Relationship counsellors tell me this unhelpful story writing is a common experience in people who are blindsided by a break-up. 'It's your brain's way of trying to process the traumatic events, but without the help of the other party, who holds a lot of the answers,' says relationship therapist, Deborah Hill. 'It's common that, in the absence of explanations, you end up in a cycle of extremely damaging thoughts.'

My original plan for this chapter was to pick one woman with the most attention-grabbing blindsiding story and dig into the illuminating details. Perhaps she'd since realised a litany of red flags that would help me to join the dots of my divorce. Maybe he had offered clues as to why he – and so many others – had kept such deep misery secret for so long.

But my research taught me two things. First: usually, the life explosion is virtually impossible to predict. Excavating your memories in search of clues will only lead to madness. Or at least a lot of crying. Secondly: far too many women have experienced a blindsiding break-up for me to choose one to dig into in detail. Far better to have a collection of tales, involving various scenarios, to illustrate my point: that this can happen to anyone. Yes, it's terrifying. But I've come to learn it is possible to harbour trust while also accepting that a sacred bond could, theoretically, end at any moment (psychologists are on hand later in the chapter to tell you how to get here too).

Sally, 33

I got married at twenty-eight, and three months later, my husband said he didn't want to be married any more. I later found out he'd been having an affair. But, in hindsight, I know he did me the biggest favour. I'd never felt secure in the relationship, to the extent that I would constantly hold my tongue for fear that he might leave. It meant that I'd somehow lost my ability to communicate.

After the break-up, it was as if I found myself in a world I didn't understand. I threw myself into doing things to excess, like getting drunk a lot and over-exercising. I started dating but couldn't trust anyone, and I felt constantly judged for being divorced.

Eventually, I bought my own flat and designed the interiors with my mum, turning it into my very own girly palace. On the night I got the keys, I sat on the floor drinking champagne out of a mug with my mum. I allowed a lot of my healing to happen in that space.

Quite soon afterwards, I met a new man who would become my husband. He was very patient with me because I wasn't able to trust anyone for a long time. When he proposed, I said no. But after a while I started to think, what's the worst that can happen? I couldn't let my divorce define me. So I did it. Now, four years down the line, I am happy and fulfilled.

I honestly believe if I could get through that, I can get through anything.

Jess, 29

Two weeks ago, my partner of twelve years and husband of two years decided he didn't want to be with me any more and left with no explanation. I turn thirty this month and I don't know where to start. Despite his desire to exit our relationship, he's saying he doesn't want to do the legal bit of our divorce just yet, but I don't want to wait around.

I am panicking about starting my life again as 'damaged goods'. Hopefully I will feel better in time and stop crying every day, but I guess I have to take it one day at a time. I've changed his name on my phone to 'I DESERVE BETTER' just in case I feel the temptation to text him.

Rachael, 33

We'd been married for a year when, three months ago, my husband and partner of eight years started acting weird – like he was off with me and I'd done something wrong.

Then one day, he confessed he'd fallen in love with a woman at work and didn't know what to do. He said he wasn't sure he wanted a divorce, but he was pretty sure he wanted to be with her.

I thought, what the actual fuck is going on? I'd come off the Pill and we were trying for a baby. He'd watched me take pre-natal supplements. I couldn't understand why he was throwing away everything we'd built for a woman he'd known for five minutes. It was wildly out of character. He's a decent, kind and loving man who had confessed his undying love for me at our wedding.

I became obsessed with knowing everything about this girl. It turns out she's married too. She's got her own husband – why did she have to take mine? I managed to get hold of her number and sent her texts begging her to stop doing this and get out of our lives. I was a woman possessed.

Within a month my husband had moved out of our flat to live with a friend. But he still wants to be close to me. Sometimes he'll come over, we'll talk things through, he'll cry, I'll cry and he'll hold me like he used to. Once we ended up in bed with barely any clothes on, but he drew the line at sleeping with me because it 'wouldn't be fair'. Odd how he'd suddenly stumbled across his moral integrity.

In a few weeks my best friend is going to move in with me and we'll redecorate to eliminate signs of my married life. I'm excited, I guess. But it still feels like this is happening to someone else.

There were no red flags. But I have to admit, there is a whisper inside my head already telling me that he was always the wrong guy. The volume increases as each day passes. It's not just the atrocious way in which he's ended our marriage and long partnership. I've always had concerns about his excessive drinking and didn't like how sloppy he'd get on nights out. On a few occasions he'd stumble home at 3 a.m. on a work night and throw up all over himself. I turned a blind eye to it in hope it would stop at some point. But it never did. Well, that's someone else's problem now.

Martha, 34

We'd had an argument the night before that was so inconsequential I can't even remember what it was about. That morning on the way to work I messaged my boyfriend of eight years to say sorry and that I thought we should talk that evening. I also said I was struggling with my mental health and was feeling delicate, so could do with a bit of love and support.

When I got home after work he was already waiting in the living room. 'Do you want to go first or shall I?' he said, to which I replied, 'You go'. He said: 'I don't think we should do this any more.'

My first thought was that I hadn't heard him properly. I told him I didn't understand, and he began a spiel about how it hadn't been right for a long time and he didn't think either of us were happy. I struggle to remember those words because I couldn't absorb them. The roaring in my ears was deafening. I asked if there was someone else and he immediately said no.

The blindsiding was a physical sucker punch to the gut and the heart so violent that it knocked the breath from me and felt like a groaning train within my chest. I ran to the bathroom, locked myself in, and suffered my first ever panic attack.

Shortly afterwards I felt an urgent need to escape our shared flat. I grabbed as many of my belongings as I could, threw them into bin bags and dragged myself onto the Tube home to my parents' house. It was perhaps the most humiliating part of the ordeal – and the reason I told Eve to stay put when Ben did the same to her. It's their decision to leave and it's their responsibility to figure out how to do so. In the weeks that followed I asked him numerous times if there was someone else in the picture, and he always maintained there wasn't. Ultimately I learned that this was a lie.

I'd be lying if I said I was truly happy in my relationship. In all honesty, I don't think I'd ever felt so low. Deep down, both of us knew it wasn't right and neither of us were okay. But the shock of a break-up from out of the blue – when he hadn't so much as even hinted at it before – has left big, emotional scars. Now, even five years on, I suffer self-doubt, mistrust and am wary of taking people at their word.

Despite this, I surprised myself recently by opening up to a kind and understanding man, who I met at a friend's wedding. He is now my boyfriend, and we live together. My insecurities haven't vanished, but he's helped me to see that sometimes the risk is worth taking for love.

Abbie, 40

We'd been together seven years and married for almost two when it happened. It's important to know that, throughout our relationship, I struggled a lot with anxiety. In fact, around the time we broke up I was suffering through a period of acute anxiety that had pretty much stopped me leaving the house alone for the best part of a year. But he looked after me. He was the only person who could pull me out of it and make me feel brilliant. I relied on him and felt like he was always there when I needed him.

My family arranged a party for me on my thirtieth birthday and, bizarrely, he spent the entire night standing with the barmaid and laughing away with her. When I got upset, he told me I was paranoid and ungrateful to my parents who had thrown me this big party. A few days later he called me from work about something menial and I realised he was being particularly unkind. I didn't understand why and made some comment about him replacing me with another woman.

He got angry and said I had a problem with paranoia and should consider taking antidepressants for my anxiety. That night he came home and was still acting odd. A bit like he didn't want to be around me. I asked him again: 'Are you cheating?' He went silent, and then nodded. I said, 'Do you have feelings for her?' and he nodded again. I was flabbergasted. I felt like I'd been punched in the stomach, like my whole world had collapsed. He said he wanted to break up, and I am embarrassed to say that I begged him not to. He left that night.

The following week was horrendous. The doctor prescribed tranquillisers and sleeping tablets because my body was wired with terror. I couldn't work or do anything. Meanwhile, he was playing games with me – calling up and saying he wanted to come over, referring to me as 'babe', telling me romantic songs he'd heard on the radio that day had made him think of me.

But then, about a week in, I started doing things for myself – connecting with old friends and going for walks on my own. I grew a new-found confidence that made me realise

I didn't need him. Within two weeks I'd signed up for adult swimming lessons, and walked there and back on my own. Six months later I'd even started my own Meetup group for people in the local area and ended up making a bunch of friends for the first time in years.

Miraculously, my anxiety vanished. Slowly but surely I realised the reason I had felt mentally unwell over the years was him. He'd lie to his friends and family all the time about stupid things and was always very secretive about his phone and his iPad. I'd find out that he'd lied to me about where he was on some evenings. But I'd always convince myself he'd done nothing wrong and I was just paranoid. All of that nervousness was bubbling under the surface with me that whole time.

A year and a half after the divorce, I met my current partner, who I've been with for eight years. I assumed I wouldn't be able to trust again, but with this relationship, I felt secure from day one. I have never felt paranoid or untrusting – and we've always been on the exact same page about everything. And because of that, it all moved very fast; we said 'I love you' within three weeks, moved in within two months and were married within two years.

There's no drama; we've never had a fight that's ended in us nearly breaking up. It's just happy, and great, and he's a very, very good person. There are some good eggs out there. It might just take you a while to find one.

Why are men more likely to blindside?

... or are women ignoring realities that are too painful to process?

Psychotherapist and relationship counsellor Susanna Abse says it is often the case that male life explosions appear out of the blue, because of the different ways in which men and women deal with inner turmoil. 'Women are much more likely to complain when they feel unsafe or unsatisfied, which means their male partner will be aware of their unhappiness. They might make an argument or get upset,' she says. 'But men tend not to do that. Instead, they withdraw.'

She says this withdrawal might not be so obvious. Sometimes it is as blatant as sulking off to another room and disengaging in conversation, but, more often than not, it's emotional withdrawal. And symptoms of this mostly appear outside of the house. I'm talking about affairs, extra-marital flirtation, forgetting notable dates, spending more and more time away from a partner. Behaviours that, if you're very busy, you might not necessarily notice.

'Their only way to deal with their unhappiness is to act on it and move away from the situation,' says Abse. In younger men, a reluctance to air dissatisfaction could be partly explained by an anxiety about acting 'too aggressively'. 'I don't think we recognise men's nervousness about coming across as angry or aggressive enough,' says Abse. 'We bring up our boys telling them not to push, not to shout, to sit nicely. So, if you're a man who is not particularly assertive, and not the type to say "I won't put up with this or that" and have blazing rows, what do you do? This can lead men to express their aggression in underhand ways, like lying, or leaving out of the blue.'

Female social circles prevent women from getting stuck in the same silent trap.

From the age of about eleven, I've used the phone or, spe-cifically, the person answering it, as a source of inconspicuous emotional support, as well as a vehicle to talk out important plans. Important, aged ten, meant who in a particular friend-ship group would be tasked with the 'big twirl' at the end of a dance routine we were set to perform in assembly. Aged eleven, it was what to wear on non-uniform day. Aged twelve, it was to tell my three best friends that my dad had died, and feel validated by their muffled cries. By fifteen, I'd actioned a schedule: I'd watch one episode of *Friends* before calling Felicity to debrief on the annoying things that annoying girl of the month had done that day. Then another episode, followed by an hour talking to Kelly about her ongoing fight with Felicity. If Mum didn't need the phone I'd wait an hour before calling Grace to plan our next move in our master plan to follow (stalk) the band McFly around the country.

Among the mindless crap were pillars of companionship and a forum to explore who we were and what we needed at any given time. We aired our fears and perceived inadequa-cies which, most of the time, were met with reassurance. At the very least, we took comfort in our shared cluelessness. The phone calls kept me afloat throughout university, to and from lectures, reminding me that I was worth more than the idiot on the football team who slept with me and then ignored me for the rest of the year. A couple of years back, when I was fully immersed in suburbia, I became struck with an odd sense of disconnectedness. My head felt noisy, rattled even, and I struggled to get to sleep. Then, one morning, my best friend called. She'd realised our collectively hectic lives had thrown off the loose phone call schedule we'd had for a number of years: twenty minutes, once a week – usually Mondays – on our way to work. We picked it up again on Thursday mornings. Within a couple of days my sleeping pattern had returned to normal and I felt myself again.

I am afraid to say this DIY therapy is dying out,[2] with the number of phone calls dropping by 20 billion in the UK over the last decade, thanks to other forms of instant communication. Most men, especially those born in the '90s and '00s, aren't the telephoning kind. Susanna Abse says women's constant communication with friends means they're often well aware of how they feel about a partner's fuck-ups, and are therefore able to communicate it better. Sometimes a friend's validation is enough to squash the disappointment or resentment that lingers after an argument. We realise it's not so bad. We move on.

'And other times, female friends can work us up,' says Abse. 'They'll say he shouldn't have done that, I wouldn't put up with this, etcetera. We then go along to our partners and tell them what we think, so there's no surprises for them.' But while this might benefit women, it can be 'disempowering' for some men, particularly the ones who lack assertiveness.

'Some men don't really know what to do with all of that, and they haven't learned how to do the same. Often they haven't had the same type of conversations with their friends so they're unsure about how they feel.' And so, it all comes out in one big explosion that appears, to the outside observer, to make no sense whatsoever.

What do men say about all this? After realising I wasn't likely to get much out of my embarrassingly small number of male friends (all of whom are serial monogamists), I did what any online journalist would do: I turned to Reddit.

There are hundreds of 'I broke up with my partner and now I am sad/feel guilty' posts written by men, which detail a kaleidoscope of break-up circumstances, usually involving a 'heartbroken', 'devastated', 'torn apart' woman.

The anecdotes appear to echo the observations of Susanna Abse, who says men are far more likely than women to come to a sudden, solitary decision. Male dumpers rarely document details of the cogitation that led to the dumping, i.e. airing discontent, suggesting therapy or even talking to a best mate. Well, apart from one dude on Reddit who said he decided to end his 'bad' relationship after a, erm, long and meaningful (?) discussion with his best friend, who advised that he pretend to be a character in a film, and act accordingly.

Admittedly there's a small pool of female Reddit dumpers to choose from. But the ones I found spoke often of an extended crescendo, featuring a series of desperate grasps to resuscitate the relationship. Their partner has long been well aware of their unhappiness, they write. 'When I tried to resolve our problems I felt like I was bugging him,' wrote one thirty-five-year-old woman planning to ask her husband of fifteen years for a divorce. 'I asked for couple's counselling which at first he said yes [to] before changing his mind. I tried everything!'[3] Another woman wrote that she'd 'finally' reached breaking point with her husband of six years after a decade of difficulties (such as his tendency to flirt with other women) that she'd long 'put her foot down' about.

'He finally told me he wants to work on his issues. Still can't say "I'm sorry" though. The problem is, I've heard this before. I've given him so many chances to fix things. He's acting like it's all coming out of nowhere, when the truth is I've been trying to talk to him for years and years ... How many times did he watch me cry and do absolutely nothing?'[4]

(Side note, my favourite Reddit dumpee has to be the angry woman who was furious that her partner had spent her pay cheque on Funko Pop Figures (figurines with exaggerated features, many of which resemble celebrities or characters). To add insult to injury, he had purchased all of his favourite characters – and said that they were a gift for her.)

My Reddit sleuthing proved that blindsiding is not necessarily an exit strategy reserved for men. Nestled within the comments are a few tales from men about textbook blindsiding committed by women. One man said his partner of three and a half years broke up with him via text two hours after sending him a nude. No explanation, no apologies. He had been planning to propose.

Another said he came home one day to find his wife of eight years announcing she wasn't happy and wanted a divorce. It had come completely out of the blue.

I am not denying these experiences are true and traumatising. But divorce lawyers and others in the field have told me men tend to be less observant when it comes to signs you're making your partner miserable.

Rebecca – who is one of the divorced women we will hear from later – has coached hundreds of men and women through divorces since her own marriage ended a decade ago. She said that, no matter the circumstances, in her experience, a man is 'always' surprised when his wife ends it.

'Men tend to ignore the fact a woman has been expressing

her unhappiness throughout the relationship and likely has pointed out specific needs that aren't being met multiple times. So they'll often say it was a shock, when really it wasn't.'

Much is written about the impact of infidelity on the future relationships of the person cheated on (including in this book – see Chapter 5). The crumbling of self-worth that leads you to assume you are only worthy of a partner with eyes for someone else. But you don't often hear much about the impact of the unforeseen break-up.

I can't quite shake the ingrained assumption that eventually, a romantic partner will leave me. While I've got pretty good at suppressing my anxieties, I wake up at least once a week expecting the arse to suddenly fall out of my world for no logical reason. Sometimes, it is really quite debilitating. It makes every communication with an important person a source of anxiety. You avoid disagreements like a hot potato. You put your feelings at the back of a cupboard in a desperate attempt to keep peace. So what can you do about it?

Recovering from blindsiding is a long and excruciating process. So don't expect it to be easy. Remove all pressures driven by imagined timelines, self comparison and other external meddlers. You cannot foster healthy connections until your faith in humanity is at least somewhat healed.

Psychotherapist Deborah Hill says restoring confidence in both confidantes and strangers is key. 'You need to believe there is good in the world and that most people are kind and well-meaning. Otherwise, your tendency to expect the worst will curse future relationships – and maybe even present ones – with a toxic undercurrent of anxiety.'

Practical ways of doing this include writing down examples of kind-hearted acts gifted to you by those you know and love. And maybe even some you don't. As embarrassing as they might sound, gratitude lists can be helpful too. Every few days, remind yourself that someone once walked half a mile to get you a coffee, spent three hours cooking you dinner, invited you on holiday, waited until your Uber arrived, called to see how you were feeling, told you they loved you – and definitely meant it. Working with a therapist through all this is ideal, if you have the means to.

Deborah's work with hundreds of couples over the years has left her convinced that there are plenty of decent, loving people who are 'desperately searching' for a committed relationship – both men and women. 'For a little while, you might feel as though you're not worthy of happiness and everyone is out to harm you in some respect,' she says. 'But think of how different life could be if, instead, you told yourself: "I am valuable and good things are coming my way." You'll get there. Give it time.'

Chapter 3

The Legal Alien

North Finchley is a two-mile strip of north London high road nestled between the Hertfordshire-bordering region of Barnet and well-to-do, artsy East Finchley. It is where my mother moved months before my husband decided he no longer wanted to be married, and round the corner from where I grew up. It is also where I fled to in November 2022, when my life exploded.

When I was a kid, it was your standard middle-class area; vital suppliers like Woolworths and River Island nestled between accountancy firms and family-run Italian restaurants with big pots of free lollipops by the door. Today, it's the embodiment of Britain's economic downturn – and a really fucking depressing place to be when you're already quite depressed. A triplet of almost identical cafés now dominates the north tip of the high road, which have become a sort of meeting spot for a group of shifty-looking, bald, large-bellied men, who govern the pavements and hurl insults at each other.

The remainder of the street is a series of boarded-up clothing boutiques and hardware stores that sell everything from shredding machines and non-stick pans, to teeny tiny hair bobbles. There's still a few old staples left: the Wetherspoons pub where we'd drink entire Blue Lagoon pitchers and come home to spew turquoise vomit all over our parents' bathrooms. The Boots where we bought Danielle Anders a pregnancy test in our free period. The Subway where I sat nervously beside my teenage boyfriend and cringed at the remnants of wafer-thin turkey stuck to the corner of his mouth.

Needless to say, I never imagined I'd end up back there. But after a week of refusing to veer from my walk to and from the station, I went for a wander. It was a Saturday morning and I thought getting my nails done might ease my crushing sense of hopelessness.

Familiarity is a strange thing. It creates one of life's most common contradictions. A place, a sound, a feeling – even a person – can feel totally misaligned from your present, something no part of you seeks out or desires. But the mere fact that you've seen or felt it before makes it comfortable, if nothing else.

By the end of the year at Mum's I would realise that that place, unchic as it may be, had been exactly what I needed to bring me back to myself. It gave me a much-needed reminder of who I was before Ben, and who I wanted to be afterwards (not living in North Finchley). Sure, I'd wake up every morning, see the collection of family photos Mum was 'temporarily storing' on my windowsill, and be reminded of my gigantic leap backwards. But at least I was home.

A couple of my oldest and best friends still lived round the corner, and a few others who I'd lost touch with were a twenty-minute drive away. We'd meet at the same mediocre restaurants we went to at nineteen, and I'd talk about how I had no plan and no hope, without fear of dominating conversation or judgement for not being 'okay'. I revelled in Mum's joy at a house once-again filled with a group of silly girls who told her she looked fabulous and offered to help install her shelves.

I even found a relatively normal coffee shop and a yoga class within walking distance. And the Aldi at the top of the road came in handy.

I can't imagine how I would have done this so far away from home. I came across Sutanya Dacres on one of my prolonged Instagram trawls, in which I searched for other youngish divorcees who were happy and fulfilled despite life-ruining heartbreak (or at least appeared to be, on Instagram).

Sutanya, now thirty-eight, split from her husband of three years in 2016, at the age of thirty. Sutanya is from New York – where everyone who knows and loves her lives. Her ex-husband is from Paris, where she relocated her life soon after they got married.

'At first I thought, I have to go home, but I told myself I'd at least try and do six months here, so I booked a flight home for that summer, assuming I was going to sort all of my stuff out to eventually move back for good,' she tells me when I call her at home: a Parisian 'lady castle'.

Seven years after her divorce, this woman is not just okay – she is her very and absolute best. And, most remarkably, in a country she barely knew, without the familiarity of home. How did she do it?

The break-up, she says, was not altogether surprising, in

hindsight at least. 'It didn't take long before our incompatibilities became glaringly obvious. It was the little things you only realise when you start living together.'

Up until then, every meeting over the course of their three-year relationship had been 'like a holiday', with the couple arranging to meet in each of their respective home countries roughly every six weeks.

'The long distance meant we were living in a place that wasn't reality. Still, we were both aware of that and believed we were supposed to be together for ever. No one gets married thinking they're going to eventually break up.'

A key issue was Sutanya's husband's inability to grasp her experience as a black woman in a predominantly white, ignorant Parisian neighbourhood. 'I guess it was never something I'd ever thought of because I grew up in ultra-diverse New York. I guess I was in a bit of a bubble and then coming to Paris, that bubble sort of burst.'

Sutanya encountered a number of microaggressions at the hands of friends of friends, waiting staff and other service people. She describes one incident at a hair salon in which the hairdresser said 'several derogatory things' about her afro.

'I felt so disrespected. I was made to feel ugly,' she says. 'And he [her husband] just didn't get it. It was about him not understanding that my blackness is a problem for a lot of people. Me being in certain spaces leads to a reaction that I have to manage. He just couldn't get it. We'd sort of assumed me being black and him being white didn't mean anything, but there were occasions when it did, and I needed him to see it and try to understand.

'He was a straight, upper-class white man, the world was his oyster, and it just wasn't the same for me.'

One night Sutanya's husband came home from work and told her he didn't want to be married any longer. 'Our relationship was grating and it was becoming harder and harder,' she says. 'But I was like, well, we can go to therapy and sort it out. I really, really wanted it to work. I practically begged him to stay. I made all the promises; I'd change, I'd do what he wanted. But he was already out. He just said I can't do this and he left that night. I was devastated.'

He moved out permanently two weeks later, but it took about three months before he collected the last of his things. Eventually, the apartment was free of virtually all of her husband's belongings. 'My bed and an ugly coffee table were the only things left. The place was completely bare.' The pair shared no assets so opted for a low-admin no-fault divorce, all more or less completed online. She never heard from him again.

Interestingly, a wealth of studies suggest that straight, interracial marriages are more likely to end up in divorce compared to marriages between those of the same race.[1] However, the effect seems to be far stronger when the woman is white and the man is black.

It's not entirely clear why this is, although a group of family therapists based in California published an analysis on the trend in 2022, which featured some interesting observations. One of the lead authors, Dr Sarah K Samman, a family therapist based in San Diego, wrote of her own relationship with her North African husband.[2] 'He is spoken to slowly when we are out and about. He is also commonly ignored in social situations and asked about by others who appear to feel entitled to learn about him without directly speaking to him,' she wrote. 'I'm a European, American and Arab/West Asian white woman, and often feel put on the spot and uncomfortable when others, often perfect strangers, ask invasive questions about our interracial/multinational relationship.'

She goes on to say that acknowledging and processing these 'hardships' is critical for maintaining a healthy relationship. In other words, the ignorance and judgemental attitudes of others can literally tear your marriage apart – unless you face it as a united front, and discuss how you feel about it.

A study from 2016 showed the extent of racist attitudes towards interracial couples that still exists. Published in the *Journal of Experimental Social Psychology*, cognitive neuro-scientists Caitlin Hudac and Allison Skinner conducted a series of experiments on volunteers, designed to test their reactions to images of interracial couples. Not only did the participants show preferences for white couples, brain scans showed increased activity in neural regions associated with disgust when looking at the interracial weddings.[3]

It only took a month in her hometown of New York before Sutanya began to miss the quiet charm of her old Parisian neighbourhood. 'I really didn't expect it, but after a little while in New York I was like, I kinda want to go back to Paris now.

'I guess I thought, if I'm going to be a sad, divorced woman, I may as well do it in Paris.'

She went back to the same apartment she'd lived in with her ex and gradually started filling it with 'odd, random things like kitsch ashtrays that I love.'

Sutanya was luckily relatively well-equipped for single

life, having collected an army of girlfriends throughout her three years in Paris (some of which she knew through her ex-husband). Hers is a valuable lesson to all lovebirds: always be as prepared as possible for the arse to fall out of your world. And that means having lots of friends.

'I threw myself into a bunch of things,' she says. 'I started doing improv which, well, was weird. I also volunteered at a local cooperative supermarket. I ran half marathons; I took up guitar lessons. Oh and I also went out, got drunk and hooked up with some terrible men. In the end that's what volunteering became helpful for – I made sure I picked up shifts on the Friday and Saturday nights to stop me going out.'

A note on the endlessly drunk post-divorce phase
Mine lasted all of a month. For some it lasts much longer, even up to a year. In the aftermath of having your heart put through a mincer, you are perfectly entitled to do whatever the fuck you want to do (so long as it doesn't injure you or anyone else and is legal). This includes swigging from a bottle of corner-shop Prosecco while dressed as a cat, overtly flirting with colleagues (maybe even sleeping with them), kissing a random guy on the bus, kissing a randomer on the Tube, raiding your mother's cupboards for snacks at 3 a.m. before vomiting said snacks into her toilet – and giving a hand job to a guy you met on Bumble forty-eight hours previously. Perhaps you spend £400 on bougie tablecloths for a dining table you no longer own. Whatever it is you're into, it's all fine. FYI I did some, but not all, of the above.

It is equally true, however, that you do not have to do any of this. Many will feel they don't want to. Going from committed relationship and domestic life to single debauchery in a matter of days can feel just as discombobulating as the break-up itself. I forced myself to try on a new identity – maybe now I wasn't married, I'd return to twenty-two-year-old Eve who went on drunken, impromptu trips to Brighton and spent the weekends dancing in Watford clubs. I imagined I'd cling to my single, heavy-drinking girlfriends like a desperate boyfriend, and convince myself that going to that new year rave in Stratford was necessary to push me out of my comfort zone. When you go through a break-up, people will talk a lot about 'discovering who you are'. Some of it has value; it's likely that some of your identity is still wrapped up in your relationship, and disentangling it is the first step to regaining your confidence. But that doesn't mean you have to try everything and anything. And you probably – actually, definitely – won't gain confidence somewhere that you spend every moment praying you were doing anything else. The experience of a committed and adult relationship changes us, it teaches us maturity and unique forms of compassion, and it is unlikely you will feel comfortable slotting back into traditional 'single' life, whatever that means. And that is okay.

My identity crisis was eventually soothed by one of my life's constants: writing. My words on a page were the only way of recognising myself, my voice. Part of this was achieved through work – I'm lucky enough to have a job that pays me to write both important, fact-finding reports, but also more narrative, personal prose. And on the weekends I wrote about Ben, and the break-up. I'd read back the words and think, okay, maybe it's not actually all my fault.

*

When Sutanya's period of organised fun came to an end, she also landed on a familiar, healing activity to get her through. She started cooking. 'My ex and I loved to throw dinner parties,' she says. 'And then, after the break-up, I found cooking for myself was the hardest thing to do. But once I got back into the habit of it I found a sense of peace, like a reminder I was capable of caring for myself. I'd tell myself: As long as I can do this, it will all be okay.'

Her dinners became more complex, each one bringing up another buried emotional detail relating to her heartbreak. Sometimes she'd call friends and explain the epiphany that had crept up on her while she was breadcrumbing a chicken leg, other times she'd muse to herself. And that was when she thought all of this might make a good podcast.

Dinner For One is an account of the aftermath of Sutanya's break-up, with each episode centred around a recipe that represents the theme of the week. A virtuous salmon, avocado and fennel salad marked the end of her period of 'excess' – drinking, smoking, going out, as she puts it. Meanwhile, an ostentatious vegetable tarte was an ode to Sutanya's new-found fearlessness. 'One year ago I would have been too afraid to make it,' she wrote in the blurb. The podcast eventually became a book, and Sutanya now spends her days writing professionally; a career she always dreamed of.

Recently, she's been having random, single women over for dinner. 'I started out wanting to find women with similar stories to mine: American women who had moved to Paris for love, [but] it hadn't worked out. But it's become so much more than that.

'I bring a different group of women to my apartment every

month and we just eat and share stories and talk. It's like we feast on our fabulous lives together.' Sutanya tells me she's still recovering from last night's soirée – the final guest didn't leave until 3 a.m.

I say I'm amazed it's not awkward, given that these women have never met before. 'Well, everyone knows me, right? And it's automatically cosy because you're in someone's home. I also try hard to curate the group so that there will be things to talk about. I pick people who I think will get along. For instance, last night was a group of writers, so we spent the first hour just talking about books and stuff.'

Romantic relationships inevitably come up in conversation, she says. 'But what's refreshing is that it's only a very small part, because it is not the driving force of these women's lives. So we talk about men in the context of their lives. Men do not create the context of their lives. They're interesting outside of who their romantic partner is. I think it's great to have that validation and reassurance that you are a whole woman without a partner.'

I am a little jealous of Sutanya. She exudes positivity and self-assurance, and it seems she recalibrated into a more confident version of her former self in relatively little time. Unlike me, she doesn't see her coupled-up twenties as a complete waste of time, or grieve her long-lost prime years.

'To be honest, just knowing who I am, I am not sure if I would have left my twenties unscathed if I was single. I would have been so broken and beaten down [by dating]. I don't know if I would have even had faith in relationships by the end of it.'

I think of my friend, whose twenty-something boyfriend

broke up with her because she wouldn't have a threesome. Or the swathes of friends left baffled after a seemingly lovely man goes cold and stops texting back. Sutanya's got a point.

Sutanya and I differ wildly in our interpretations of our short marriages. As much as I try to fight it, I think of mine as a reflection of my poor judgement of character – as well as my cowardliness. In my heart of hearts I knew it wasn't great, but I clung on for fear of the alternative: being alone.

Sutanya, on the other hand, says: 'I think of it as a positive thing that you were able to make that commitment to some-one, and also find someone willing to make that commitment to you. And that's amazing. It basically says nothing is wrong with you, in the context of a relationship. Okay, it didn't work out, but the truth is you don't really know anyone really, really, really well, even if you've been with them for a very long time.

'No one can predict how a person will act in a certain situation. So you can take an educated guess at how they will respond to things, but at the end of the day, you're not in their head.

'No one truly knows what's going to happen. You could be the one that surprises yourself, and ends up doing something horrible that puts your relationship into question. You can never tell.'

We move on to dating, and Sutanya tells me she's only had one semi-serious relationship since her break-up, which ended after a year.

'I think I was trying to replace my husband, and obviously I couldn't. So it didn't work out,' she says. 'I've been dating on and off since then. I haven't really been in anything serious. I dated a DJ for a couple of months.'

That sounds fun, I say.

'Nooo. If a DJ comes your way . . . just run. No one has stuck just yet, which is fine.'

This leads me on to another fear of mine: running out of time, biologically speaking. Does Sutanya want children?

'I try not to think about that too much,' she says. 'It'll make me spiral into places I don't want to be . . . I really want kids one day. And I want love. I feel like it's going to happen. I don't know when or in what format, or like, how it's going to come to me, but I'm relaxing and doing everything in my life to make myself prepared for that.

'I could be being really delusional and maybe I'll look back and think I should have done this and this. But what can I do, right? I mean, the universe sees that I want it and will bestow it upon me.'

Three and a half years ago the president of the all-female Murray Edwards College at the University of Cambridge, Dorothy Byrne, announced she planned to give fertility lessons to all students.[4] She said she wanted to make sure women who were focusing on their career didn't 'forget to have a baby'. I read this seething with anger.

With eight years of health journalism under my belt, I am not naive to the facts of nature that Ms Byrne is referring to. It is generally believed that it's much harder, and takes longer, to fall pregnant in your late thirties.

But quite frankly, Ms Byrne: what are we supposed to do about it? It's not as if we're not trying – why else do you think we endure the boring men on dating apps? Or force ourselves out on a Friday night when we'd really rather have a bath and order fried chicken? Or stay in relationships that make us miserable and unfulfilled, telling ourselves we ought to feel grateful we've at least found someone?

As Sutanya says: 'If they want us to hurry up and have babies, they should just make men a little better.' Aside from freezing eggs (costly, time-consuming, not guaranteed to work), there is really little we can do to ensure we make it on time. I'd also argue that most women are already well aware of their ticking clock. Or at least society's pressure to find a man – and quickly.

(While we're on the topic I'd like to take this opportunity to inform women that, although fertility does decline at thirty-five, the dip is only marginal. Really, it's only when you reach thirty-eight to forty that the reduction in conception after a year of trying significantly drops. Still, there's always the next year – and the year after that. More on this in detail in Chapter 4.)

'It's just another thing for us to worry about, for us to put on our shoulders,' says Sutanya. 'And that we can't control. The implicit message is that we're not doing enough.'

At the time of Ms Byrne's announcement, my anger mostly stemmed from empathy for friends who desperately wanted children but had shit luck in relationships. I remember talking about the subject on a podcast and being deeply aware of my privilege: who was I to talk? I'd be married in a few months and straight on the baby train.

Of course now my anger extends further. I found a dependable man and got married. I made every effort to 'try' reasonably early, aware that I wanted two children. And look where I am. Sutanya stops me when I venture into regretful sentiment. 'Your ex-husband did you a favour,' she says. 'You do not want to be with someone that would do anything to put their relationship with you at risk. If someone is truly in love with you and wants to be with you, there's nothing that they would ever do to ruin it.

'That doesn't mean that your relationship is not gonna go through ups and downs, or that it will be perfect. But there will be no doubt that the person wants to be with you. And they will never blindside you like your ex did.'

I am hopeful that she's right.

Chapter 4

Children

In 2019 I went for an ultrasound scan of my uterus. I'd not had a period in five years – a result of my old eating disorder that had left a low-key reluctance to outgrow my size six wardrobe. I had, until then, made a conscious decision to bury my concerns about what my missing cycle meant for my childbearing abilities. But Ben and I were recently engaged – and I'd developed a pattern of lying awake at 2 a.m. panicking about a future without a family. I'd conjured a deeply ignorant and frankly offensive image of life without children: miserable Christmas dinners for our parents, sat across a massive dining table making pleasantries about the size of my tablecloth and what time the *Call The Midwife* special was on. A vibe totally void of the joyful silliness that kids radiate, and that I'd always dreamed of.

The gynaecologist's first disconcerting remark was that she 'couldn't find' my ovaries. Wait, what? Had my lack of periods made them so redundant they'd evaporated? She explained that doctors see your ovaries by detecting the follicles – small, fluid-filled sacs that sit on the surface of ovaries and house the egg that is released every month.

Most women of fertile age will have around six to seven follicles growing on each ovary,[1] one of which will mature and eventually send its egg off for fertilisation. I, unfortunately, had no follicles. And no follicles make for 'hidden' ovaries.

It meant, the doctor explained, that my chances of natural pregnancy were slim to none. I was crushed. I delivered the news to Ben in our bedroom, where we both lay and cried. He told me, worst comes to worst, we'd adopt. Ultimately, if we couldn't have kids, so be it. All he wanted was to be with me, he said.

Ever since that day I've believed that my path to motherhood would be extremely difficult, if not impossible.

This is despite the fact that, in the years since, and thanks to significant weight gain, my menstrual cycle has kicked back into action and, according to subsequent scans, everything appears normal. Side note: my revitalised ovaries are testament to the incredible resilience of the human body – as well as the good that comes when you don't starve yourself. All my uterus needed was another stone of fat to do its thing.

Even so, at the time of the scan I'd been stung by a sense of urgency. If I was married at thirty, I could be pregnant by thirty-one. And if it didn't work and we needed help, I'd have a few years to do at least two rounds of IVF and *still* have a couple of years to play with before making a second child. I didn't want to be an old mum.

The Covid pandemic delayed our wedding a year, which meant we were already behind schedule. The sooner we tried, the better. And we did, ish, in the months before the break-up.

In the days after I moved back to Mum's, 'the plan' was the only thing I could think about. Ben had destroyed whatever slim hope I had of a family with the time it would take for me to meet a man who wasn't a) taken and b) a psychopath, build up a rapport, live together, and get him to agree to get me pregnant.

This also made me feel weird about comments made by 90 per cent of people I told about the break-up, who offered me the same maddening 'silver lining': Well, at least you didn't have children.

Clearly, it is impossible to know which is more horrific: losing what might be your only chance of having a child, or having one that you now must look after alone. I think the answer is probably neither situation is worse than the other; they are just different.

Although, from my experience, the child-free panic eases with time. Within two months of my break-up, I'd forgotten all about my stupid plan. It was as if I'd suddenly been handed extra time. I have a theory that your brain adapts to whatever situation you find yourself in and makes peace with it, simply because you have to. And maybe that's what happened here. Of course I still get pangs of urgency. But they soon pass.

These days, I find myself feeling surprisingly grateful for my child-free status. There are even moments – when I relished buying an absurdly expensive cream-coloured sofa, and on Sunday morning lie-ins – when I question if a family is really what I want. I never imagined I'd feel lucky for my childless divorce. There is freedom in realising you can't predict the future.

*

Kristina, now thirty-seven, had four kids by the time she was divorced in 2014, five years after she got married. Her story is unique because of the unusually young age she was when her doomed relationship began – just fifteen. When we speak, I tell her that I'd just about learned how to use an oven aged fifteen, and couldn't imagine entering into an adult – and potentially lifelong – relationship.

'I guess I just got thrown in at the deep end,' she says. 'We just really loved each other. But obviously we lived in separate houses and were both still in school, so it was pretty much a normal teenage relationship.' At seventeen, she got pregnant. 'I had plans to go to university and get a great job and all of that stuff, and then suddenly there was a big spanner in the works.' Her first instinct was to terminate the pregnancy. 'But the more I thought about it, the more I knew I'd struggle with that memory for the rest of my life.

'I am very pro-choice and believe everyone has the right to choose. But I guess, at the time, I thought the right choice for me would be not having to live with the memory that I'd done that.' Her parents were disappointed, but too distracted with their own divorce to give much of a shit, she says. By eighteen, Kristina was married. And by twenty, pregnant with her second child. 'I look at my kids now, who are about that age, and think, my God, how did I do it?' She admits there's pangs of jealousy. 'They get to do all the normal teenage stuff and I missed out on all of it. I was just this mum and wife. That was my job.'

Four years later, a third child came along. At this point, perhaps, the potential for divorce may not seem any great surprise to an outsider. Three kids at twenty-four, with most of the domestic responsibilities shouldered by one partner, would, you'd have thought, been a recipe for resentment and misery before the age of thirty. Kristina had never worked, instead dedicating her time to looking after their growing family.

But for the best part of a decade, she says, they were 'pretty happy'. 'We would bicker like most other couples but we never really argued or anything. There was nothing drastic about our relationship at all.' In August 2014, when Kristina was twenty-seven, she found out she was pregnant again – for the fourth time.

'We hadn't intended to have any more children,' she says. 'In fact, he was booked in for the snip.' Her husband wanted Kristina to terminate the pregnancy, pushing her to pursue a procedure so they could continue with their current project of furnishing a newly purchased house.

Kristina said she wanted time to think about it. And by September, she'd decided she'd continue with the pregnancy. In December, out of nowhere, her husband announced he was no longer happy in the marriage. 'But he still loved me and he wanted to try and get through things,' she says. This dedication lasted for all of three days.

'He came home one day and said he wanted to leave. That was it – he was leaving. The marriage was over.' Despite 'swearing blind' that there was no one else in the picture, a few weeks after he moved out, Kristina found out he'd been having an affair for at least two months with a woman from work.

'We lived in a very small village and so it didn't take long for me to find out that he'd been walking around the supermarket with another woman, holding her hand, for months. A friend told me she'd seen them picking up takeaways together and that sort of thing.

'I was completely blindsided. I didn't see it coming at all. There wasn't even the smallest inkling. I knew the woman quite well. And she knew I was pregnant and that we had three other children. She knew everything about our lives, really.'

I have heard some extreme scumbag stories since I began researching this book. But walking out on your pregnant wife of a decade and mother of your three (about to be four) children while engaging in a very public affair is perhaps the most heinous.

'I guess it was sink or swim,' says Kristina. 'I had four kids. I had no choice but to swim.'

To begin with, swimming was a case of getting through the pregnancy. 'It was all very up in the air to start with. I chose my friend to be my birth partner, but he was around towards the end of the delivery, mostly looking after the other kids when they arrived.' She says she noticed him texting his girlfriend during some of her contractions.

Within a few weeks, the troop of extended friends and family disintegrated, and Kristina was left alone with her new reality. And four children, aged between zero and ten.

'When I look back, I just think: How the hell did I survive that? Somehow, I did.'

Financially speaking, benefits payments and a 'pitiful' maintenance allowance from her ex kept her just about afloat. She kept the house thanks to UK law that can allow some single parents to remain in the marital home until the eldest child finishes full-time education.

'I didn't have a clue how anything worked, having never done any of the bills or anything before. I didn't even know how to set up a direct debit. I remember sitting down with my dad and going through everything. I was clueless. I'd gone from only really having to worry about the food shop to having everything on my plate.'

As if her ex-partner's behaviour couldn't get any more deplorable, he grew attached to his 'child-free existence', choosing to see them only on alternate weekends.

'It hit the children very hard that he suddenly wasn't around. They were too young to be particularly angry; I think it was more confusion as to why he didn't always want to spend time with them.'

Even so, she made a point of saying not one bad word about him, so they could make up their own minds.

Today, she describes their relationship with their dad as 'strange'. 'It's been up and down over the years. I wouldn't say that there is a usual type of closeness there with any of them.'

Something that struck me about Kristina's adaptation to single motherhood is the automatic life that comes with children. The school runs and pick-ups, the mum friends from after school club, the distraction of folding PE kits. For some women, this autopilot can grant a sense of relief. No matter the eruption unfolding in the rest of your life; with kids, regular service must resume. In the short term, anyway.

'I've never been very good at making friends,' says Kristina. 'But the nursery mums started coming to the house for coffee after dropping the kids off, or they'd be in the park with me during the summer holidays. The friendships just grew from there really.' Kristina said this group of women 'latched on' and 'didn't ever really let me go, which was very nice'.

'It meant that on the weekends I didn't have the kids, I could say to the girls, let's go to the pub for a drink or something. It gave me a few hours to think about something other than the children and the housework. Even now, those friendships are some of the most important to me.'

How to know that you definitely want children

I was introduced to Emily through a friend earlier this year, when she was seven-and-a-half months pregnant with a baby girl.

She was stirred and excitable, telling me of the 'alien' that was bolting about in her uterus and chuffed about the free dental care she gets for a whole other year. About a year ago, at the age of thirty-five, and following the end of another disappointing relationship, Emily decided she was 'done with trash men'. Concerned that she was running out of time to have the family she'd always wanted, she opted for a choice that's becoming increasingly popular with millennial women – she got pregnant all by herself. Well, with the help of a sperm donor and an eye-wateringly expensive round of IVF.

Pregnancy without a partner has mostly been a doddle; 'the only difficulty has been lifting things by myself with the bump, but I've managed', and she's 'chilled' about the idea of raising a kid without a significant other. Her dad left when she was six weeks old – single parenthood is pretty much all she's ever known. But as empowering as it might be, aspects of Emily's situation make me jittery. First there's the minefield that happens when the child reaches sixteen, and is legally entitled to make contact with her sperm donor father. What if he's fathered twenty-five other children? Or slams the door in her face? Or likes watching *Mrs Brown's Boys*? Then there's the rigmarole of the fertility treatment itself which, for Emily, involved two fertility MOTs (£500 each), £3,500 worth of donated sperm she ordered online, a procedure to check the health of her fallopian tubes, a (failed) procedure to inject said donated sperm into her uterus (£3,000) followed by a successful cycle of IVF, which cost £18,000. Then there was the £2,000 worth of oestrogen pessaries she had to insert into her vagina three times a day for three months to increase the chances the pregnancy will be sustained. All in all, producing her much-longed-for miracle cost around £28,000. And that's before she's got to childcare.

On a PA's salary, Emily won't be able to afford a mortgage and nursery, so she'll be on a (notoriously risky) interest-only deal until she can balance the books. We talk about how she'd love to give her child a sibling ('I grew up an only child and always prayed for a brother or sister') but says the likelihood is she'd 'have to pay for one, and I can't afford it'. I sat listening to all this and thinking about the time my two-year-old niece screamed in my face because I sat next to her in the car, and later brazenly took a piss on a ping-pong table. Is it really worth it?

The truth is, it's impossible for women to truly know the extent of their desire for children. The expectation that you, as a woman, will bear children, is transmitted before you learn how to sit on the toilet. Go to any toy shop with a display 'for girls' and you'll find an assault of fake babies dressed up for their Holy Communion, willing two-year-olds to adopt them. My niece's doll, which she imaginatively named Baby, went everywhere with her between the ages of two and three, carted around in a toy pram that she often flung across the pavement, leaving baby Baby with a series of traumatic injuries to her plastic skull. Now five, she's recently discovered make-believe games, in which she likes to cast me as her child. I oblige for ten minutes before distracting her with sweets.

But *how* we get to the point of craving babies – and whether it is engineered by society – is sort of irrelevant. You want what you want. Having said that, I do think a modicum of curiosity about the roots of this particular yearning might be helpful for quelling anxiety about not fulfilling it just yet.

Last year, I found myself having the same conversations with my girlfriends in their early thirties re: fertility and kids. All of them were acutely single and psychologically as far from parenthood as you could possibly be. They all thought they wanted to have kids at some point, but were, for the first time, faced with the question: what happens if I don't?

Their most common concern was that of regret – what if I get to forty-five, realise I made the wrong decision, and spend the rest of my life feeling as if there's a gaping hole in my soul?

I decided to write about the subject on my Substack, and called a child-free woman in her sixties to help foster an idea of what such a lifestyle might look like. I also looked at the research on the mental health and life satisfaction of child-free women and was interested to find that the vast majority of studies find no difference in self-reported happiness between sixty-plus women with children and those without.

Sally, 60s, works in IT, single

I both regret and don't regret not having children.

When I was alone or struggling with work, I'd think about how having children might have been a buffer to absolve me from having to focus on my job. I'd envy my friends who had children in a supportive marriage set-up and whose children kept them busy at weekends. They had other mother friends through their children and I envied this shared experience.

I was also very conscious, however, of being able to go where I wanted, when I wanted and with whoever. And ultimately, at the time in my life when I could have had children, I knew I was not ready or emotionally mature enough to have children. I also had a real fear of perpetuating the mistakes of my own family. Most of the sixty-year-olds I know have fantastic lives, whether child-free or not.

The assumption was always that I would have children. I often babysat for my parents' friends' children and did work experience at a nursery in secondary school. There were few real opportunities for work experience, and I think all girls were expected to do theirs at the child-care/nursery anyway. I think I always wanted children in an abstract way, never really thinking about what it would entail.

In my mid-twenties I was with an older partner who was wrong for me and quite aloof. My career wasn't going anywhere and I remember saying to him, 'I might as well have children if I can't get on the career ladder.' I can distinctly remember the look of horror on his face at this, and we, not much later, broke up.

For the next ten years I did not actively seek a partner or

think about having children, though I was getting (and being made) increasingly aware of the clock ticking when both siblings settled down and had six children between them. But still there was no right time or urgent need to have children.

Then at thirty-six I had breast cancer and as part of my treatment, was offered egg preservation. I was only 'allowed' one round of harvesting, due to the risks. There was a sense of relief when the process failed; I was unable to undergo another round and I began chemotherapy. There was a sense that it had been taken out of my hands in some way.

I have enjoyed so many opportunities in my life without children! I have spent a long time working on myself, studied postgraduate courses and have established a career. If I'd had children I would have subjugated my needs to theirs, and prioritised them over work or friends.

Living in London, I have been able to avail myself of all that the big city has to offer, taking myself to the theatre/cinema/concerts/dinner/clubs whenever I wanted to without having to worry about babysitters or even the need to get home before 3 a.m.

I travel when I want and am very grateful I did not have to experience that afternoon dread when the kids are back from school, the door is closed and you're all in the house for the night, before it starts all over again next morning. I felt a real claustrophobia and impending doom if I found myself in a suburban area around 3.30 in the afternoon.

I was lucky enough to have a number of friends who would invite me on holiday with them and their family, which has meant I enjoyed numerous free holidays in villas overseas, although I am aware that it was often in the capacity of an extra pair of hands, an extra adult, babysitter or 'outsider' around whom the kids would have to behave.

I am financially stable on my own terms and this allows me to be generous in contributing to friends' children's school trips and university accommodation or postgrad study. I doubt I would have this had I had children of my own.

As for the downsides: I envy my friends' ease with their children now, how shopping trips and holidays come with ready-made companions.

While no one has ever said so out loud, sometimes if I'm with a group of dance or school mums, there will be a frisson of not being 'one of them'. It's not something I can pinpoint explicitly, but with some who are not close friends there's either a sense of pity or resentment.

Ironically, as I am the only one who didn't have children, I am now expected to take sole care of my elderly mother. I spend most of my time working from her home, as well as acting as her unofficial full-time carer. I resent my siblings for having a built-in excuse (children) as to why they are unable to help.

I'd tell women in their thirties to spend a lot of time thinking about whether or not they truly want to have children. Do as much as possible while you're still young to establish strong financial foundations. This way you'll have choices when, if at all, you have offspring.

I believe children act as a buffer against loneliness later in life, especially the much later life stage. On the whole, I think we are not yet set up, as a society, to accept women without children. The notion of 'having it all' has now been debunked. The issue for me is that we are still living in a society and working structure that is primarily set up for, and benefits, unencumbered males.

I do worry about who will look after me in my old age, which of my nieces or nephews would be willing to sacrifice their working life for me. I find the idea that many people have children so that someone will be available to look after them in their old age abhorrent, but at the same time it allows the burden, in theory, to be borne by many instead of just one.

It's worth saying my opinions are based on being single and childless. I have friends who are couples who have decided, for whatever reasons, not to have children, whose opinions will very likely differ hugely from mine.

Three years after her husband left, Kristina began to pick up odd jobs here and there, in between school and nursery runs. 'I worked in a café, did admin for local businesses, and worked cleaning jobs. I helped out in a garden centre for a bit. I did all sorts of little things; whatever I could get, really.'

When the pandemic hit, she started looking into writing jobs in the hope of getting paid for the extra-curricular activity she'd always loved. She was surprised to find the work wasn't as hard to come by as she'd imagined.

'I predominantly worked from home so it was easy for working around the kids and homeschooling during the pandemic,' she says. 'Eventually I started going off to meetings and various trips. For the first time in my adult life, I had a sense of purpose other than the children. And now I have a career that I absolutely love.'

A few years ago she came across a Christmas list her son, then ten, had written in preparation for the big day. 'There were all these other gadgets and stuff and then, in big letters, "a boyfriend for Mummy".'

At thirty-seven, Kristina would like to imagine that she won't spend the rest of her life without a romantic partner to help share the load. But for now, dating seems a step too far. 'The idea of letting someone into my life again is utterly terrifying,' she says. 'I still have relatively young children, which comes with an overwhelming desire to kind of protect them from everything.'

If and when she dips a toe in the dating pool, potential suitors will be kept well away from her kids, until she's absolutely sure he'll stick around for ever. Even then, she says, you can never really be truly sure.

'How do you know if you've found a good one? I thought I did and he turned out to be, well, not so great.'

I ask about the extent to which her kids have been affected by the sudden collapse of their parents' marriage. Perhaps it's wildly different for some of the children, given the difference in age. Her youngest, for instance, will have no memory whatsoever of her father as a factor of everyday life.

'The eldest two have been offered therapy, but they didn't want it,' she says. 'But we've always talked openly about what happened and how they feel about their father. But sometimes going over difficult memories over and over again isn't helpful. At some point you just have to get on with it.'

Thankfully, so far, so normal.

'They're moody, hormonal and only really bothered about their friends and their own lives. To me, it seems like they're perfectly normal teenagers.'

Perhaps, Kristina suggests, it's because the marriage ended

before the inevitable fights about suspicious voicemails and credit card bills. All four kids were safeguarded from conflict. 'Children are far more impacted from seeing their parents unhappy than they are by seeing a parent cope alone,' she says. 'And this is coming from someone who grew up with parents who argued a lot. That had a huge impact on me.

'Now, as an adult, I massively avoid confrontation. I'm a people pleaser – and not in a good way – because I do anything I can to not argue. I hate it. My parents were a terribly, terribly matched couple, and it was horrible. Hearing them argue was terrifying to me as a child.

'One of the things I'm working on in therapy is how to know the signs of a good, healthy relationship – because I've never seen one. My marriage felt like a great relationship when I was in it, but behind the scenes it clearly wasn't because he turned out to be unhappy. So what examples do I have?'

Having said that, given the choice, she wouldn't have changed the course of her life. Oddly – and perhaps promisingly – this has been the case for everyone featured in this book; no matter how horrific and unplanned-for their story. Myself included.

'I've realised in recent years that he was actually quite controlling and, when I look back, I wasn't as happy as I could have been,' she says. 'He didn't want me to have friends he didn't know. Sure, it was nice not having to worry about all the finances and stuff, but I think he liked being in control of the admin stuff and denying me a say in anything. It wasn't good for my independence or confidence.'

Perhaps it's surprising given the number of mouths she has to feed, but Kristina feels being alone is 'infinitely better' than being in a relationship that clips your wings. 'Even if you're struggling financially. Even if you're sitting in bed every night and feeling lonely. It's still better than a relationship that doesn't make you particularly happy.'

A note on your biological clock

Four years ago I wrote a piece for the newspaper I worked for at the time in response to warnings about leaving baby-making too late.[2] Gynaecologists said the wave of celebrities giving birth to healthy kids in their late thirties and forties was misleading, giving the impression that it's easy to conceive after thirty-five.

But just how difficult is it, I wanted to know. I went on a fact-finding mission for the article, raking through large-scale studies on fertility and talking through the data with some of the country's leading gynaecologists.

I hope my findings offer you the relief that I felt when I filed the article. They are as follows: in a nutshell, fertility doesn't fall off a cliff at thirty-five.

It is true that, after the age of thirty, the rate of decline in the quality of eggs we have picks up steam, increasing the risk of DNA mutations, which cause genetic abnormalities, or miscarriages.[3]

However. We are born with around 2 million eggs, so we can afford to lose a few. Studies show that in an average woman's twenties, she has around a 30 per cent chance of conceiving with every cycle. By thirty, this drops to 20 per cent. But remember this is *per cycle*, rather than per year.[4]

By forty, the odds of getting pregnant are one in twenty per cycle, or 5 per cent.[5]

When it comes to how likely you are to get pregnant over the course of a year, the data is a little cloudy. Most of it is based on studies from the 1700s on birth rates among French churchgoers. Scientists have suggested that the sample is uniquely reliable because of their aversion to birth control.[6]

The results showed 70 per cent of women over thirty-five got pregnant after a year of trying, compared to 80 per cent of those in their late twenties and early thirties. But subsequent research hasn't found the same results.

Later studies have actually suggested a more positive picture. A 2004 analysis of 700 women in seven European countries found 86 per cent of twenty-seven-to-thirty-four-year-olds conceived within a year, compared with 82 per cent of thirty-five-to-thirty-nine-year-olds.[7]

One gynaecologist even told me 'very few' women will have problems getting pregnant even into their forties. He said there is 'no line drawn in the sand' when it comes to age.

Having said that, it is right to be cautious about pregnancy in your forties. The risk of serious problems like gestational diabetes and high blood pressure is up to four times higher, compared to your thirties. Half of pregnant women over the age of forty-five will miscarry. One in 100 women who give birth over forty will have a baby with Down's syndrome, due to genetic malfunctions related to maternal age, more than ten times the risk of a twenty-five-year-old expectant mother.[8]

Arguably, the medical establishment has only got stuck on the age of thirty-five because of IVF success rates. Experts say they are relatively stable until a woman reaches thirty-five, at which point they start to decline.[9]

But there's another element to this conversation that is rarely explored: the father.

One leading gynaecologist I spoke to, Dr Geeta Nargund of CREATE Fertility in London, said in half of her cases, it is the man's sperm that is the reason for the couple's lack of baby.

A man over forty takes five times longer to conceive than one in their twenties, regardless of the woman's age, according to research.[10]

In 2019, US scientists at Rutgers University reviewed forty years of fertility research[11] and concluded that fathers over forty-five were associated with an increased risk of premature birth, late stillbirth, low birth weight, newborn seizures and birth defects such as congenital heart disease – all regardless of the mother's age.

A 2013 study of more than five thousand men[12] aged up to seventy-two found the proportion of normal sperm started to decline at thirty-four, dropping significantly after forty.

The TLDR is that you don't *really* have to worry hugely about fertility until you're approaching forty. Sure, it might be more challenging – and take longer – to get pregnant in your late thirties compared to if you were twenty-five. But it's probably worth waiting for a partner who is capable of raising another human being.

Chapter 5

The Affair

One Sunday morning in the winter of early 2022, Ben and I were rushing into the car, chucking dog poo bags into the back seat and pleading with the furry maniac to stop gnawing at our ankles. I can't remember where we were going, but it was a route complex enough for me to need Ben to provide directions. He hadn't yet passed his driving test.

'I'm going to be a bit distracted because I'll be on my phone texting Lizzie,' he said. 'She's supposed to be going to the New York office today, but she had her passport stolen on the way to the airport, so I'm trying to help her work out what to do.'

I hid my childish irritation about sharing his attention, and instead focused on his admirable dedication to his friends.

About eight months later, Lizzie came up again. We were in a restaurant in Mexico. Ben said I'd like Lizzie; we had a lot in common. She occasionally read my articles. We'd probably get on well.

After our break-up, he told me nothing had happened between them. I believed him. I still do. But their relationship was still significant enough to elicit silence when I asked if he'd met someone else. He maintained that the decision to end our marriage wasn't a case of him leaving me for someone else. I still don't know the truth of what happened. And that's probably for the best. The thought of Ben entertaining a crush was enough to splatter my brain into a million tiny, dead pieces. I could not, and still cannot, imagine the development of their relationship. I can't even begin to imagine the paralysing betrayal of discovering a full-blown affair.

In preparation for this chapter, I stumbled on Zoë, an interior designer. In February of 2021, Zoë, then thirty-four, received a message from an unsaved number one night while lying in bed beside her husband of three years, and partner of a decade. The text was from her husband's colleague. Said colleague informed Zoë that she'd been sleeping with her husband for the past eight months.

'I was very, very calm,' she tells me when we speak on the phone. 'I said, what have you been doing? I want you to just tell me what's going on so I don't have to read it in a text from somebody I've never met.' What was going on was this: Zoë's husband had been feigning depression for the last year in a bid to mask his dwindling interest in his wife. Rather unsurprisingly, his sexual desire for the woman he had married dropped significantly around the time he started sleeping with his colleague.

Were there any signs?

'That question is the thing I get asked the most,' Zoë says. 'And sometimes I feel myself almost wanting to ask other people who knew us, like, were there any signs? It's impossible to know. But if you are an open-hearted, trusting person, you are not looking to doubt your partner; you are not looking for signs of betrayal or lies or a shift in feeling.

'I'm a very emotionally in-tune person. So it made me really doubt myself. I was like, how am I not seeing these signs? Am I this naive and stupid? But actually, when you build a life with someone, it's very easy for them to deceive you; they know exactly what to say. They know exactly how to frame things. They know exactly what to leave out. They know exactly how to console you.'

While she never suspected a third party, she knew her husband was miserable. His withdrawal from the relationship was so obvious. The 'shift' in his attitude had begun during the Covid lockdowns, making it especially hard for Zoë to ignore.

'It was a year of him treating me like shit,' she says. 'He'd go out for a walk to "clear his head", but really he was just pushing me away. This was the pandemic, so we were stuck in our basement flat a lot of the time. I'd be cooking all his meals and asking if he wanted to eat together, shall we sit in the garden? I'd lay it nice for dinner and all that stuff, and he'd be like, no I'll sit in the other room. I'd go to hug him and he'd push me off. I was trying hard every single day to find some kind of common ground with him, to find some kind of remnants of connection. And he was pushing so hard to distance himself from me.'

As far as she knew, he was in the midst of a mental health crisis. 'I thought, this is my opportunity to be a fantastic wife and put my needs aside and prioritise him. And so that's what I did for a year. While he was cheating on me.' Zoë's sympathies began to wear thin as Covid restrictions loosened up, when she was offered the most exciting opportunity of her career to date – to compete on a televised interior design show – and he, quite clearly, could not give a fuck.

'I started to realise while I was filming that this person wasn't really a partner to me.' Preparation for the show meant littering the apartment with boxes of embellished fabrics and upcycled armchairs. 'He was moaning about it a lot, because the extra deliveries coming to the house were disrupting his life. He was like, why are the boxes everywhere, can you just move the shit out the way, it's really pissing me off. It was like that.

'Meanwhile, there were nine other people in the competition who were all saying things along the lines of, my partner wrote me a different card every day to open for encouragement, or my kids are baking me a cake. Most people's partners helped them load up the van.

'It was then that I thought, wow, my husband could not give less of a shit. He is not interested. He's not impressed. And he's not supportive.'

So perhaps her chilled vibes on the evening he divulged the affair can be explained by the fact she'd somewhat checked out too.

'Deep down I knew that depressed people are not unkind. And there had not been any glimmer of kindness in him towards me for a really long time.'

The cheating revelations came to light on 19 February 2021 – just after Valentine's Day. 'We'd had a big argument on Valentine's Day because he didn't want to have sex with me,' she says. 'I wanted to prepare an amazing meal and was saying, let's cook it together – we were still in the Covid lockdown.

'I got him a gift, I laid the table beautifully and he just turned to me and said: "I think I'll just cook by myself". He was like, it will just be annoying if we do it together. So I just sat at the kitchen island watching him do it on his own.'

His reaction to her Valentine's gift killed the mood entirely. 'Full disclosure, I bought him a sex toy. He opened it and then pushed it to the side, and then we both ignored it. I tried to circle back and say, can we talk about the fact that you don't want to have sex with me, and he just started an argument. So it just made me feel ashamed for wanting to have sex with my own husband.'

The debacle was followed by four days of what can only be described as ghosting. 'He just iced me out for a bit. So that was fun.' On the fifth day, he announced he was going to stay with his parents for a while. 'At that point I just thought, fine, go. I've reached the end of my patience and I don't know what else I can do.'

The universe has an odd way of gifting us cultural moments that somehow align with a partner who is just about to tell you they want to fuck other people. For me, it was a podcast host who described a mysterious feeling of 'something not being quite right', shortly before she decided to end her marriage. I remember listening to it as I walked back to our house the day before the break-up, thinking surely if I felt like that, I'd have done something about it by now. But I couldn't get the conversation out of my head. I put it down to my anxious, overthinker predisposition.

For Zoë, it was an episode of the Netflix scripted reality series *Selling Sunset*, based on the tumultuous and often seedy inner world of a real estate firm in the Hollywood hills. 'That evening I was watching the episode where Chrishell finds out her husband is cheating on her and she's thinking she's going to get a divorce. I remember watching that and thinking, hmmm, I think I might be about to get a divorce soon, too.'

Then at 1 a.m. the next morning, lying in bed next to her husband, she received the text that joined the dots. 'As soon as it was clear what he'd done, he was a totally different man from the one who'd just told me he wanted to go and stay with his parents. It was all, "You're my world, I love you, you're the best thing that has ever happened to me."

'I just thought, this is manipulation. Several hours ago, you couldn't stand the fucking sight of me. You didn't want me near you, or in the same house as you. I was looking at him and listening to what he was saying and just thinking, no, I don't believe your denial.' She made her decision there and then: that was it. She was out.

'I think people can work through affairs if they both really want to make it work. But what clinched it for me was the way he had treated me and the extent of his lies. I'm a very understanding person, and if he'd come to me and said: Look, I'm not happy, I've done this thing and I'm sorry – I probably would have worked through it with him. I wanted the marriage to work.

'But he didn't. Instead he let me believe he was struggling and desperately unhappy when in fact he was off having a lovely time.'

I've become fascinated by the behaviour of a cheating person at the height of their affair. Several women who've fallen victim to male partners' affairs have described a similar extreme withdrawal that Zoë saw in her ex. It's almost as if they're serving you the punishment they expect for themselves.

Thankfully, I was only subjected to a week of sudden disinterest in anything I did or said in the lead-up to my break-up. And it should be said that my husband did not have an affair (as far as I know). Either way, those days were not pleasant. On the Sunday before, I'd invited my mum and aunt and uncle over for brunch. Up until a few months before, I had precisely two members of my family living in the same country, which often made me feel panicked and sad. My aunt and uncle's recent emigration from South Africa had offered a sense of kinship that I'd always craved. Not least because it meant there was someone else to worry about Mum.

Ben did not care for the family brunch. And he made no secret of it. Mum gave him a card to congratulate him on a new job and to wish him a belated happy birthday. He opened it without grace or thanks, and pushed it to the other end of the kitchen table. He barely looked up from his eggs, occasionally whipping out his phone in case we had any doubts about his capacity to give a shit. I made several attempts to involve him in conversations, banging on about the wine he'd liked on our recent Mexican trip, or his talent for teaching the nutbag dog totally useless tricks. I got nothing.

Shawn Smith, a psychologist specialising in male relationships who is based in Colorado, says this is a scenario he sees often with men he comes across in therapy. According to Smith, a lot of men are 'naturally geared towards keeping others comfortable and squashing their own desires', and think keeping quiet about misery will achieve this. I tell him I know a lot of women who would respectfully disagree.

'It's their belief that they just need to suck it up and tolerate things. Complaining a lot is not seen to be helpful because it doesn't make the situation better.'

I'm not entirely sold on this theory, although I can very much relate to the tendency for some men to self-identify as 'good guys'.

Ben took it upon himself to master the most complex of tasks – both inside and outside the house. I said I'd quite like a walk-in wardrobe one day, so he built me one, despite his total lack of construction experience. He insisted on setting up Mum's new computer and gave her strict instructions to cancel the subscription to the emergency tech helpline that bailed her out when the screen did that whirring thing, or when she accidentally stuck the recycling bin in her download folder. He said she shouldn't waste her money; he'd take care of it for her. I considered myself extraordinarily lucky to have a partner who was generous with his time and skills, and wanted to do whatever he could to help.

But. Ben's usual 'I'll help' attitude began to shift in the couple of months before the bomb dropped. I am only alive to this now, of course; it was perhaps the first glaring red flag that I managed to skirt over. He threw what I can only describe as tantrums about taking the dog to the vet while I was at work. Suddenly, he wanted me to take more of an interest in the bills and our mortgage (which was very fair). And his patience with my mother's technology debacles grew wafer-thin. After the break-up it came to light that his attempt to fix a tilted drawer was so angered that he'd broken said drawer – but never mentioned it.

'I've seen many, many situations which illustrate the harms

of containment of concerns and problems,' says Shawn. 'You suddenly see an outburst, when somebody gets very upset.' Smith explains an age-old psychological concept known as the 'hydraulic model of emotion', which essentially means feelings act similarly to a pressure cooker; always one bit-lip away from exploding.

Research for this book involved listening to more episodes of 'man talk' podcasts that any woman should ever have to endure. One of my most frequented themes was explorations of why men cheat. The same interesting phenomenon was highlighted over and over, something I like to call the 'Susan Sarandon in *Stepmom*' effect.

When I was eleven, I became obsessed with the 1998 movie *Stepmom*, starring Susan Sarandon and Julia Roberts. The premise is basically this: a sexy, effervescent Julia Roberts (stepmom) is forced to adapt to her unlikely maternal role and compete with the children's dreary, boring – and eventually, cancer-stricken – mother, played by Susan Sarandon, for the kids' affections. The children's father, played by Ed Harris, is a sort of handsome go-between, in charge of the distribution of power between the two women. As a teenager, I saw it as a heartfelt exploration of mother-daughter relationships – and a fail-safe for a good old cry, if that was what you were after. I watched it again aged twenty-five and saw something different. The male director has leant into a tiresome narrative that has blighted Hollywood films for decades. It presents the idea that women fall into two distinct categories. We're either Julia Roberts – professionally exceptional and ready to fuck at any minute – or Sarandon – a miserable nag who spends her days knitting personalised throws until she eventually suffers a gradual death from a devastating disease.

Several of the men's interest podcasts I listened to presented a similar picture of how men view the women they date – and even marry. Men are binary thinkers who like to separate ideas into neat categories, it is often said. And this presents a fundamental problem when selecting a partner for a long-term relationship. Potential wives must be loyal, dependable and, to a certain extent, predictable – satisfying the male ego with consistent security. How, then, are said 'wives' able to satisfy the men's deepest, darkest sexual desires which, by definition, are risky and unforeseeable? Experts have long concluded that the most exciting element of sex is mystery.[1] It's a dilemma that's otherwise known as the Madonna–whore complex, the idea, first posited by Sigmund Freud, that men see women within two defined categories: either marriage material or a sexual conquest. (Madonna, in this scenario, is the virgin Mary, not the singer, in case there was any confusion.)

One of the podcasters I listened to said something along the lines of: men find it difficult to see the women they deeply care for in a hyper-sexual capacity, so when they want to scratch that itch, they'd rather do it elsewhere.

Honestly, I think this sounds like bollocks.

Shawn Smith presents a theory that gives credence to this line of thinking, which I'm also suspicious of. Research, he says, has shown that the key factor for securing male attention is *variety*. 'Sexually, biologically, we want more variety. And this explains why men might be drawn to affairs more than women are,' he says. 'You can have variety in relationships by making things different from the norm, in sexual and other ways, but generally we see that women who do less of that are more likely to be treated badly. It tends to be one of the things that men and women really struggle to understand about each other, mostly because women just don't have the same experience.'

So if you're not into the dressing-up box he'll start playing away?

'No, you have to have a combination of factors,' Smith says. 'Whether or not someone chooses to participate in an affair is also to do with their personality. He has to be a guy who is willing to hurt people, or who doesn't consider the consequences of their actions.

Men are more likely than women to fall into the latter category, he adds. 'Men are, for want of a better word, more antisocial than women. We break more laws, we get drunk more often. We're just a little more reckless. So if you put all those big factors together, it explains the impetus behind a lot of affairs.

'As far as I know, we don't choose our predispositions or urges, but we are each entirely responsible for our decisions.'

My concern is that this theory somewhat excuses awful behaviour and attributes blame to an amorphous higher being (evolution), as opposed to the idiot who couldn't keep it in his pants. As a good friend once said to me: 'I hate it when men blame evolution for stuff. It's like, MOVE ON.'

Relationship psychotherapist Deborah Hill vehemently disagrees with biological theories of gendered behaviours. 'Quite often I see that it's the woman who gets bored with the tedium and repetitive nature of married life, while the man feels comfortable in the routine,' she says.

Although Hill, a member of the British Association for Counselling and Psychotherapy, admits men are more likely to have affairs, on the whole. 'Most often a man strays away because he doesn't feel seen, loved, and thinks he's being rejected. They then try to seek all those things from outside the relationship.'

She adds: 'But all the same themes apply to women. There isn't much of a gender difference.'

Hannah Dillon, a Leicestershire-based lawyer, had been married for three years when she started an affair with a man she met at work.

'He wasn't attractive at all,' she says. 'And he was horrible to me. In fact, I went to his house to meet him once and saw him through the window having sex with another woman. He was truly awful. It's proof that it could have literally been anyone. I was just looking for a way to get out.'

The affair lasted for about four months, and began as a way of 'escaping' her 'miserable' life with a man she didn't love.

Hannah, now forty-four, and her husband met in their late teens at university, when they were drawn together by the power of youthful passion, despite having very little in common. 'There was nothing particularly wrong with my ex,' she says. 'We just weren't right together. He was very, very emotionally repressed. Looking back at our whole relationship, I never really knew how he felt about anything. I kind of learned that I can't be with somebody like that. I think the difficulty was that we'd been together for such a long time, we'd become different people who wanted different things.'

By the time they were in their late twenties, and chatterings about marriage hung in the air, they'd become 'friends who didn't really ever have sex'.

'But it was that thing of, like, either we stay together and get married, or we break up. And I felt all this pressure from everyone around me, from my parents and family. I guess I was sort of afraid of letting everyone down, which is silly, really.'

Hannah says she was never happy in the marriage. 'I remember the day before the wedding I spent most of the time sitting alone in my bedroom. Why wasn't I running around with my girlfriends and getting all excited? I think it's because, on some level, I thought there wasn't much to be excited about. I spent about a week crying after we got married, too. I'd speak to my friends who were married and ask if they were tearful afterwards too, and they'd try to tell me it was happy tears. But I knew this was something different.'

Hannah says her husband was, 'never really that nice to me ... I always felt like he never really had my back. He treated me as if I was second to his friends. He was always so bothered about what they wanted to do, and wasn't very interested in my wants or needs.' She tells me about one occasion, at a friends' wedding, in which he announced to an entire table of guests that she was 'on the blob'.

'I'd dread going to events like weddings with him because it would mean I'd have to sit there with him all night. He'd belittle me quite a bit. It was always in a subtle way that just made me feel unwanted.'

And then came the 'awful bloke at work'.

'I would call him a predator, who sort of shagged anybody that was going. And obviously I was a prime target because I was in an unhappy marriage and gave off those vibes of being desperate for male attention.' She feels quite sick talking about it, even a decade later.

'It happened slowly. We'd been friends for years because we worked in the same legal chambers but, well, he was horrible. In fact, he had a girlfriend when the whole thing started. The flirting had been building for a while and then, one night, he came over to my flat to go through some papers and he ended up kissing me. I remember thinking – and this is so bad – oh, I've done that, so I may as well carry on.'

Hannah and the awful man met up in local hotels on 'too many weekends to count' over the following few months. 'I'd say I was staying late at work to finish some stuff off. It was pathetic. Really, really awful.' One evening, Hannah came home to find her husband sitting at the kitchen table with several papers splayed out in front of him. They were her bank statements.

'He'd seen the hotels and questioned me about them. I can still remember the fury on his face; he was sweating. I denied it, made up some excuse about how the hotel bills weren't mine and they'd made a mistake. It was pathetic.' The next morning he called Hannah at work. He'd called one of the hotels and asked for a receipt – and the receptionist had obliged.

'He said, "You've got three seconds to tell me what's going on." So I said, "Yes, I've been having an affair." He told me I disgusted him and put the phone down, and I ran to the toilet and was sick.' Later that night she came home to find him sweating with fury. 'He spat at me,' she says. 'And I don't blame him. I deserved to be found out.'

Interestingly, the change in her behaviour towards her husband was remarkably different to the torment Zoë's partner subjected her to.

'Ironically, I probably treated my husband far better during this period than I ever had before – to his face, at least,' she says. 'I would come back from an evening with that awful man and feel so horribly guilty that I would be so nice to my husband, like I was acting out some sort of alternate reality. It was obviously to ease my own guilt.'

Immediately after the break-up, Hannah moved out of the couple's flat and back in with her parents. She owned the London flat they lived in, and he didn't fight her for it, which meant no hairy splitting of assets. The following six months saw her endure a constant stream of activities – mostly suggested by her parents – that would serve as either punishment or potential absolution. She volunteered in a charity shop on weekends and accompanied her parents on a geriatric cruise at the age of thirty-three. 'It was like I was a wayward drug addict who needed to make up for the cash I'd stolen or laws I'd broken.'

Even today, Hannah struggles with this underlying yearning for redemption. 'Sometimes I think I'm on a constant mission to prove to the odd person that I'm not a total bitch,' she says. 'There's that little voice in there that says I am not a nice person because I was able to do what I did. It's like I constantly have to atone.'

Second – and perhaps more upsetting – was the desperation to return to her miserable relationship after it all fell apart, for fear, as she says, of 'being all alone'. 'I managed to convince him to meet up about a week later in a pub so that I could beg him to take me back. And that's what I did. I got down on the floor on my knees and literally begged. I said, please have me back, please have me back.

'He just said, no, you're disgusting, you're disgusting. And I believed him. It's astonishing to me now that I was so pained by the idea of being alone that I was willing to go back to a man I didn't love, who made me so sad and unfulfilled that I was drawn to having an affair – something I'd always judged other people for doing.'

I am aware of the difference in tone I've taken when re-counting these two affairs. I'll admit I have more sympathy for Hannah than I do Zoë's husband, most likely because she is a woman. But I am sure that Hannah's husband suffered much of the same unimaginable pain that Zoë did, leaving scars that may muddy future relationships and destroy faith in loyalty. No affair is justifiable. Plenty of people manage to leave unhappy relationships without fucking someone else first. Honesty is no magic trick.

As someone fortunate enough to have never been a victim of cheating, my understanding of the extent of the impact of adultery is limited. So I wanted to give some space to this, by asking experts exactly what happens to someone's psyche when the one person who is supposed to have your back knowingly stabs you in it.

A wealth of academic literature shows the significant, long-lasting impact of infidelity on the mental health of the person who is cheated on. Affairs, particularly in long-term relationships and marriages, are associated with increased lifetime risk of depression and anxiety in the person betrayed. In fact, one 2000 study by New York psychologists found that women who'd been cheated on in the past had six times the risk of depression than those who hadn't.[2]

According to one California State University review, affairs can trigger PTSD-like symptoms, as well as feelings commonly associated with grief.[3] Detroit-based psychologist Dr Dennis Ortman even invented a term for the unique set of emotions that last decades after the event; he called it 'post-infidelity stress disorder'.[4] Interestingly, research consistently shows that men are far more affected by physical infidelity, while for women it's emotional cheating.

'It is well recognised that people who experience infidelity suffer a trauma response,' says therapist Deborah Hill. This is more likely to be the case if the unfaithful party has left you to find out, rather than admitting it, because it adds to the feeling of betrayal.

'Traumatic memory acts a bit like if you've left clothes in the washing machine for several days and it starts to smell. Usually, when clothes are clean they go in the drier before they are all folded up and put onto their individual shelves. Memories are the same – they all get stored in their rightful places in the brain. But if there's a trauma, the smell lingers and, eventually, spreads to other areas of the house, where it has a sizable impact.'

Memories of betrayal can help to form unhelpful beliefs – you're not good enough, for instance – which then informs the way you behave, your choices and the goals you set for yourself. Hill says many of the couples she's worked with have recovered from an experience of infidelity – and are still happily married. But it takes work – and time.

Hill explains an approach from relationship expert Esther Perel. Perel says (to couples who have experienced infidelity): 'Your first marriage is over. Would you like to create a second one together?'

'It involves both parties taking full accountability for their actions and really listening to each other's feelings, and validating them. The person who has been cheated on must also accept what has happened and be fully committed to moving forward.'

Since I began researching this book, I've come across around ten women who've been cheated on by their husbands. In all cases, the affair was the catalyst that ultimately ended the marriage. Today, these women will tell you they are living their absolute best lives. They have profound insight into their unhelpful behavioural patterns, and know exactly what is needed – inside and outside of a relationship – to grant them true, wholehearted fulfilment. Every woman told me she was grateful to her partner for setting them free, despite the devastation that preceded it.

Now, nearly four years after she discovered her husband was sleeping with his colleague, Zoë is living in the Spanish countryside, having recently achieved a lifelong dream of renting a small house with farmland. She runs her boutique design studio from her picturesque, sun-drenched terrace, taking breaks to tend to her crops on quiet afternoons. She tells me she's recently met a man who runs a local bar and is 'lovely, very caring and thoughtful'.

'These days, I'm not too hung up on where it's gonna go, what it's going to be like. It feels good at this moment – and when it stops feeling good, I'll cross that bridge about what to do next. Right now though, I have a lot in my life to feel good about. I feel happy. I feel really, really good.'

Hannah's now ex-husband met another woman within a year of their divorce; she would later become his wife and mother to his three children. Hannah, meanwhile, had a slow and rather painful revival. After the aforementioned cruise, she decided on a plan to get her life in order – and put an offer on a house a stone's throw from her parents' village.

'It was a really lovely thing to concentrate on,' she says. 'It became my baby. I had friends and family around to help me with all the boring stuff, thankfully.' Of course it was scary doing it technically alone, having shared life admin with a partner for the past fifteen years. 'But it was also really free-ing. I didn't have to ask somebody else what they thought all the time, and I did begin to see the good bits of all of that.'

About three months after the break-up she embarked on a 'fling' with a local man which was 'quite fun but also quite weird', and regained some of her lost confidence. Then, six months later, she bumped into an old friend in the village shop. The friend was a forty-something man called James who she'd known in her early twenties. 'I used to fancy him loads but I remember thinking he'd never go for me because I was so much younger than him,' she says. 'But then when we met again, well, as he says, I just never let him go.' Hannah and James have now been married for the best part of a decade and have two children together – the first of which was born when she was thirty-six.

I was surprised she wasn't put off marriage for life. 'Not at all!' she says when I suggest as such. 'I knew I was going to marry James as soon as I met him. But we didn't really think about it at first, I guess because we'd both done it before and failed spectacularly. But then we had our first child and got a bit older and decided to do it.'

I asked Hannah if she planned to tell her children about her affair at some point. 'You know what, I would,' she says. 'I'd say Mummy did something that nobody should ever do. I think children should know that parents are only human, aren't they? I don't want them to make the same mistakes in life that I have.'

She says she often has to stop herself taking women who are 'ripe for affairs' aside to warn them off doing it. 'I've got a friend at the minute who is in an unhappy marriage and everything we do, everywhere we go, she's desperate for attention from men. And I want to say to her, it's not worth it. I've experienced doing something that horrible to another person and I beat myself up for it even years later. It's never the answer.'

Since Hannah and I spoke, I couldn't stop thinking of my own capacity to stay faithful – and the several occasions throughout my nine-year relationship when I was very tempted to cheat. There was that half-dressed Adonis who insisted on showering me with champagne in a Las Vegas nightclub. I could join him for an intimate after-party in his hotel room and no one would have to know about it, he told me. Or, there was the time that one of the handsome idiots on the picture desk cemented his hand to my arse at the office Christmas party – and I didn't exactly hate it. Arse touching was as far as I'd got. What had stopped me? Probably a mixture of having too much to lose, and the thought of Ben's kind smile greeting me at the front door, or the Tube station, or on a bright, sleepy morning just after I'd said goodbye to him in my dream.

A note on monogamy

Should we all be fucking people who aren't our partner? According to a 2019 YouGov poll, the prevalence of non-monogamous relationships in the UK has risen from 2 per cent to 7 per cent over the last decade.[5] However, some surveys suggest 'seeing other people' features in as many as one in ten relationships.[6] Meanwhile, around one in five British people admit they've had affairs,[7] and infidelity is cited as a contributing factor in around half of UK divorces, some analyses show. Are we fighting our natural disposition of forever horniness by pinning ourselves to one person for the rest of time?

Around a third of primates are monogamous, as are only 9 per cent of mammals.[8,9] The question of whether monogamy is in human make-up is one that's very much still up for debate among the anthropological and scientific community.

According to David Barash, an evolutionary biologist and professor of psychology emeritus at the University of Washington, having one mating partner is 'not natural' to humans. After all, 80 per cent of societies were polygynous (when a man has several wives) prior to the widespread colonialism of the 1500s.[10] Biology dictates: polygynous relationships, where a man can have multiple children concurrently with multiple women, means greater chances for a continuing gene pool, and hence the furtherment of humankind.

But other scientists take a different approach. They say

that delightfully termed 'pair-bonding' has proved crucial for spreading the seed of our species. According to anthropologist C. Owen Lovejoy, there is evidence of our monogamous nature dating back four million years.[11] He posits that soon after we began to transition from the great ape, our ancestors began engaging in three key adaptive behaviours: as well as forming pair-bonds, they carried food with two hands and females concealed signs of their ovulation. These behaviours worked together to help early male humans find food and bring it to potential female mates. There are other theories too. It has been said that, as women moved further away from each other, it became more difficult for a male to find multiple mates and increased the risk he'd get injured as he travelled to and from other territories.[12] Research also shows an alarming link between non-monogamous mating systems and increased violence against women.[13] A 2019 paper published in the journal *Frontiers* proposed the idea that offspring were more likely to survive with dedicated paternal protection, which was easier to achieve in a pair-bond.[14]

The *Frontiers* analysis, which examined the successes and failures of different mating systems, essentially concluded that there's a reason the vast majority of romantic partnerships are monogamous – and it's not just because of societal pressure. 'The pair-bond is a ubiquitous feature of human mating relationships,' the authors write. 'This may be expressed through polygyny and/or polyandry but is most commonly observed in the form of serial monogamy.'

In other words, we've tried lots of stuff, but monogamy has proven to be the most . . . convenient. And, more importantly, the most effective for keeping us alive. As summarised by

Dr Kit Opie, an anthropologist based at the University of Bristol: monogamy is likely 'how humans were able to push through a ceiling in terms of brain size'.[15]

I ask Deborah Hill of her thoughts on monogamy – does it keep couples trapped? 'Judging by the amount of people in my life in long-lasting monogamous relationships, I don't think so,' she says. 'Even with non-monogamous situations, there is almost always a desire for one person to be there for an individual no matter what. And I guess that's monogamy, at its heart. But quite apart from anything else, who has the time?'

Chapter 6

The Get

In the Ashkenazi Jewish language of Yiddish, the word 'besheret' translates directly as 'destiny'. The term derives from Old Testament scriptures that describe the marital match (or 'shidduch') made between Abraham's son Isaac and the Bible's second matriarch, Rebekah. It is written in the Jewish Bible that your life partner is predetermined, or besheret, forty days before you are born. In modern-day Judaism, particularly of Orthodox denominations, besheret has come to mean the person you are 'supposed' to be with – your soulmate.

Growing up in an Orthodox district somewhere between Florida and Ohio, before moving to religious Southern Brooklyn in 2008, Amber Adler – now a local politician – spent much of her childhood dreaming of her besheret. Roughly 70 per cent of people in her community are married before the age of twenty-four.

Amber is keen to disprove the widespread misconception that the Orthodox community, or Haredi Jews, to use the Hebrew word, marry off the young generation in their late teens and early twenties as a method of control and oppression that mostly disadvantages young women. Besheret is, she says, ultimately about love.

'The idea is that two people are supposed to be together, so they should find each other young and start building their life together,' says Amber, now forty, who is a former democratic nominee for the New York City Council.

But besheret has its downsides. As well as a positive force that breeds childhood hope and wonder, it is also a vehicle for fear. A fear so crippling that it leaves thousands of Jewish women trapped. To understand what I'm going on about, you need to grasp a critical detail of Jewish divorce: a contract drawn by the religious court, called a Get.

In both the UK and the US, a marriage between two Jews is legally binding – so long as it is performed in a registered location. But as well as a civil marriage, Orthodox Jews will also have their union recognised by the Jewish courts, or the Beit Din, which consists of a panel of older, 'learned' rabbis.

The Beit Din also deals with divorce. And it is the man who has to apply for the official paperwork, known as the Get. Without this, a couple can not be divorced according to Jewish law. They can, however, get legally divorced via the civil courts.

When I learned about this, my first question was: so what? If you're legally divorced, that's all that ultimately matters, right? Well, not for women, and the children who are born inside the broken marriage, according to Haredi tradition.

In ultra-Orthodox communities, a divorced woman without a Get is considered to be still married, and is not permitted to marry again. If she has children with another man, they will be known as mamzerim – born out of wedlock. They will only be permitted to marry other children born out of wedlock. But if a still-married man has children with another woman, those kids are not subject to the same rules.

It sounds a bit like a phenomenon that existed in another millennia. While the scriptures of the ancient Jewish Bible (Torah) haven't changed much in over a thousand years, Get refusal remains prevalent in the UK and US, campaigners say.[1]

Why? The only benefit for men who do this is the unwavering control it gives them over their ex-wife's potential to move on. According to Jewish divorce charity Get Your Get, male divorcees don't have the same incentive to give the Get that they used to.[2] The main reason to cooperate with an ex-wife was to protect your reputation, in order to avoid being seen as immoral by leaders within the community. Nowadays, however, the social fabric and power of the local Jewish community has disintegrated, and isn't as central to the average man's life. Globalisation has contributed too; it doesn't take much for men to escape a community that hates him for what he's done. In other words, there are fewer consequences to not agreeing to the Get.

This wildly archaic system has given rise to a phenomenon known as the 'Agunah crisis' – agunah being the term for this group of Jewish women, which literally translates from Hebrew as 'chained'. It means that in 2024, there are still thousands of women in Western countries who are denied fundamental freedoms – and in many cases are anchored to men who abuse and attack them.

Community insiders have told me some women have been forced to sell their homes and pay up to $420,000 to their ex-husbands, who charge their once-espoused eye-watering sums for this critical religious document. In 2021, reports surfaced of an uprising among Orthodox women in New York who were attending protests in their hundreds, chanting the phrase, 'Free Chava'.[3] The movement centred around a Brooklyn woman named Chava Herman Sharabani, who had been struggling for a decade to obtain a Get from her husband.

Chava's husband subsequently moved to Los Angeles and told her and their two children not to contact him. Four years later, she is still awaiting her Get. Amber Adler has been closely involved with the case, and is currently undertaking an ambitious attempt to introduce legislation that would make coercive control a class E felony in New York State, which, she tells me, would make Get refusal illegal.

'The Free Chava protests stopped eventually because men started issuing lawsuits against the women who took part for bringing their name into disrepute,' she explains. 'The lawsuits are obviously total garbage and there's no chance a man would ever win. But even so, a woman will have to pay an attorney to respond to the suit and, in some cases, pay court fees.'

Amber became involved in the Agunah crisis movement following the breakdown of her own marriage in 2016. She didn't receive a Get from her husband until 2018. 'Depending on where you live and the community, there's multiple ways a young person will meet the person they're going to marry,' she says, recalling the year that she and her ex-husband met. 'You or your parent might go to a rabbi, or you might go to a shadchan (professional matchmaker).

'In some cases it's friends of friends or family friends.' Amber's husband had been 'recommended' by a friend. 'I actually knew a few people who knew him and they all gave me great recommendations. No one wants to say that someone has bad qualities, and there is a general encouragement to just find a match.

'Now I recognise that what he did in the beginning was love bombing. He did everything for me; he was very nice, very caring. He knew that I liked volunteering and helping others, so he made some of our dates volunteering activities. I thought, wow, what a match.'

Within a few months Amber was married, aged twenty-seven, and a year later her eldest son was born, followed by her youngest the following year. She says it didn't take long before bright, full-mast red flags started to appear. He'd lie about odd, silly things. It wasn't long before he became more secretive, displaying strange behaviour and hiding credit cards.

In 2013, he was forced to return to his home nation, Canada, to complete his US Green Card application. He ended up staying for over a full year. Amber says the final straw came in 2016 after she'd been in a major car crash and was left with constant pain in her lower body. 'I went to Canada with the kids to see him and he refused to offer me any help whatsoever – despite the fact I could barely walk,' she says. She realised on that trip that the relationship was over.

Amber could apply for a civil divorce relatively easily (although her husband refused to cooperate with it until years down the line). Rather predictably, he also refused to give her a Get. 'I didn't know what to do, so I just started calling a lot of people who knew him to put pressure on him to do it. When that didn't work out, I tried rabbis. I found some in Canada and asked if they would speak to my husband, but they were all very hesitant to get involved. There was almost this surprise that anyone from that family could do what he did.'

Eventually, an older rabbi local to Amber's ex agreed to help. But even then, it took two years of constant badgering before he agreed. 'It was only after I started CCing everyone I could think of that knew him that I got somewhere. I had to list specifics so that the person reading it would cringe and think it bad enough to do something about. It was mortifying. I wrote those emails thinking, wow, you are so bad at picking someone.'

Amber's emails culminated in an intervention performed by the Canadian rabbi one Saturday evening after Shabbat (the Jewish sabbath that begins on Friday evening and ends at sundown on Saturday). 'He asked if my ex wanted to go for a drive and ended up talking to him for the whole night about the marriage. By 5 a.m., he'd got him to agree to give me the Get – he didn't let him out of the car until he promised.'

Today, neither Amber nor her children ever hear from her ex-husband – who still lives in Canada. He has refused to pay child support and requested Amber pay him alimony via the US family courts. His petition was rejected. 'Thankfully we didn't own a house together – he'd moved in with me. To the credit of my landlord, he wouldn't let me put my ex on the lease, and that was such a blessing.'

The experience has led Amber to discover the appalling

extent of this crisis infecting her community. She now devotes her life to speaking up for the Jewish women who have been robbed of their voice. 'These women are struggling with all types of marital problems. And a lot of the problem is that, at first, the couple will be sent to a rabbi who will help them reconcile. Unfortunately, this sometimes means that the woman's problems are shrugged off. They're told to just keep going. I've seen everything shrugged off, from small things to big ones. From differences in opinions on who does the daily chores, to suspected infidelity (on the man's side) – I've seen it all dismissed.'

During Amber's time as an agunah, she was running two major charities, supporting local democratic campaigns and raising her two children, as well as providing support through advice for the Orthodox women of Brooklyn. I ask if this was what I've noticed is somewhat of a pattern for many women: in times of immense trauma, do whatever you can to distract yourself.

'I keep going because there is no other choice,' she says. 'I have been forced to become stronger than I ever wanted to be. This is not the life I signed up for.'

I say I think it's more a case of her putting her unique knowledge about a topic to good use.

'I guess part of me being able to help people is reliant on me appreciating their pain. And I can because I've been through it. One of the biggest disappointments I have seen in politics is that, sometimes, people genuinely want to do good but they do not always understand what is needed. And there is so much opportunity for someone who understands what's needed in the Orthodox Jewish community. If I hadn't gone through what I have, I may have still been interested in these types of issues, but I wouldn't have understood what is needed.'

A change in civil law is what is needed, Amber says. The coercive control bill she put to the New York State Senate in 2023 would put men who refuse to grant their wives a religious divorce in prison. Keeping someone in a married union against their will is, by definition, coercive control, as is stated in the bill.

'The bill offers the potential of scaring men into doing the right thing,' Amber says. 'If a man believed he might go to jail, perhaps he'd issue the Get.' Unfortunately, the bill didn't get any further than the State Senate as some officials were concerned the definition of coercive control may be too far-reaching. Amber continues to work on the language of the legislation and is confident it will get through.

In the UK, Get refusal has technically been against the law since the Serious Crime Act of 2015 came into motion. But until 2021, men were able to get off on technicalities; the legislation was vague about whether a person could be guilty of coercive control if they didn't live with their partner. Thankfully, changes to the Domestic Abuse Bill in 2021 put this right and a number of men have since been successfully prosecuted in the criminal courts.

This includes Salford-based property executive Alan Moher, who charmingly responded to his ex-wife's admission that she'd tried to kill herself by asking what colour she wanted her gravestone.[4] The court heard that he'd met his former wife's multiple pleas for a divorce with responses such as, 'piss off' and 'curl up and die'.

Moher refused to give his wife a Get for several years after they were granted a divorce by the UK family court. He'd attempted to bribe her into accepting this by adding £80,000 to the divorce settlement, according to court documents. Thankfully he was prosecuted in April 2022, and ordered to pay £11,000 in court fees and sentenced to eighteen months in prison.[5]

In a statement, his ex-wife Caroline described marriage to her husband as 'put in a straightjacket, gagged, your hands and feet are tied'. She continued: 'You are blindfolded. You are in a cold, dark place. Your only weapon is that you are able to hear. You are dependent on your captor to set you free. That's how I feel still being married to Alan.'

What I haven't yet mentioned is that I am Jewish. Not religious, but I grew up in a 'we go to synagogue three times a year for holidays and don't have pork in the house unless Mum decides she fancies Parma ham' kind of household. I never had a bat mitzvah because it involved spending Sunday mornings at religion school where the other kids didn't want to sit next to me, and there was a superb TV schedule for twelve-year-olds between the hours of nine and twelve.

I can't help but feel ashamed that the religion to which I belong has allowed for this blatant abuse to flourish. It has disguised the entrapment of women under a cloak of 'tradition'. Arguably worse, some of the most well-respected leaders of the community have actively turned a blind eye.

I have always had a quiet sense of Orthodox Judaism's gender problem (as is the case with certain subsections of all major religions, it should be said). I remember synagogues with two-tier seating – men on the ground floor, close to the holy scriptures, and women on a mezzanine level, to stop them distracting the holy prayer with their womanly gifts, i.e. long hair and breasts.

Like many north London Jews, we'd often holiday on the Israeli coastline to hang out with my parents' friends who'd made aliyah (moved to Israel). Once, Mum and Dad took us to the Western Wall which, as an eight-year-old, I found quite shit. I have a vivid memory of clutching my mum's hand as we squeezed our bodies through the second, parallel wall of praying women, fighting for their own sliver of brick to touch. The men's side of the wall, however, was chill and sparse enough that my brother had space to drag a chair to the barrier, stand on it and shout, 'LOOK AT ME, EVE!' I later learned that this is because the women's section of the wall is about a third the size of the men's. I have no idea of the religious underpinning to this, but can only assume it is rooted in ancient sexist beliefs about which gender is most worthy of Messianic connection.

Then there's the whole thing about bar and bat mitzvahs. Boys have been having bar mitzvahs since the fourteenth century.* Girls, however, only got to do it for the first time in 1922. Most synagogues didn't allow it until the 1970s.[6] Still today, many Orthodox synagogues don't see the female ceremony as an essential and crucial rite of passage, as they do for boys.

---

* A right of passage when a boy turns thirteen in which he reads pertinent sections of the Torah (holy scriptures) in front of friends and family. This signifies the beginning of manhood. The synagogue service is usually followed by a party in which you dance to 'Grease' and hit all your friends round the head with inflatable guitars.

Having said all of this, I have always been proud of my Judaism. The Reform movement (sort of middle-level religious) has taken enormous strides in resetting the gender gap. Fifty years ago there was just one female rabbi in the UK. Now, more than half of all Reform synagogues employ at *least* one.[7]

(The rabbi who officiated my dad's funeral was a Canadian woman named Sheila Shulman who said the most insightful, beautiful things about my father before retiring to the garden to chain-smoke her roll-ups.)

I put my unease about all of this to Amber Adler, who tells me the problem isn't the religion itself or anything that is written in the scriptures, but the male interpretation of holy texts.

'People are very lazy when it comes to interpreting the actual laws. There's a big difference between Judaism and *applied* Judaism. There is actually a lot said [in the Torah] that could be used to further women's opportunities. But if the person reading it doesn't care about that, they won't prioritise it.'

I find it astonishing that, despite everything, Amber is still very much a woman of faith.

'There have been moments where I've thought, why do I have to go through this? I believe that Hashem [God] is putting us through everything for a reason, but sometimes it's like, surely there's got to be another way to teach me whatever lesson it is you want me to learn? But I do think that, in the end, I have benefitted. It has taught me not to be taken advantage of – which is something I was often guilty of. Another recurring theme in my life is that I've always tried to do everything meticulously and correctly. And I felt a failure for allowing my marriage to fail. But part of recovering from the experience has been accepting that it wasn't my fault, and sometimes you can try your best and it doesn't work out. Learning that lesson has taken some of the pressure off my life, I suppose.'

Learning about the Agunah crisis has reminded me of what I always knew to be true of Jewish women: they won't go down without a fight. And even more so when they come together in packs. In September last year, I stared at my laptop smiling as I read the latest on the case of Malky Gold Berkowitz – a thirty-year-old mother-of-two from New York, whose husband refused to give her a Get, allegedly after several years of trying.[8]

But I read that after six months, he'd finally caved. Why? A campaign spearheaded by Malky's friend Adina Sash, which encouraged other Orthodox women in the community to show solidarity with Berkowitz by refusing their husbands sex.

They pledged to opt out of 'mikvah night' – a day following a woman's period that is traditionally reserved for intercourse. Sash's Instagram campaign picked up seventy-four thousand followers, and images posted to various news websites showed groups of young women braving the New York winter to protest, calling for Berkowitz's husband to 'free Malky'.

Within six months, it worked. He granted her the divorce; she was free. Sash announced the news on her Instagram page, where she posts under the handle, @flatbushgirl. She wrote: 'Never give up! Mazel Tov to the Gold and Berkowitz family on this incredible simcha of freedom and new beginnings.'[9]

The post attracted hundreds of comments including one from a woman who wrote: 'Congratulations. May you continue . . . until the Agunah problem is solved for ever.'[10]

For advice about Jewish divorce, contact Jewish Women's Aid UK at jwa.org.uk. If you're in the US, go to Get Ora at getora.org.

Chapter 7

The Breadwinner . . . and an Escape

In September last year, a kingpin of Manhattan culture shut its doors for the very last time. Fotografiska – the New York branch of the Swedish-owned photography museum chain – closed its Flat Iron residence, citing problems with the size of the space, and its incapacity to deliver the 'artistic vision' the owners had planned. The museum – which has hosted exhibitions displaying some of the world's most gear-shifting artists (including David LaChapelle and zeitgeist-y contemporary artist Daniel Arsham) is soon to relocate to a new, more accommodating location that is yet to be confirmed. Virtuosos have been left bereft, as have the girlies who enjoyed posting selfies at the swanky fourth-floor bar and restaurant on their Instagram stories. Among those mourning this loss are former New Yorkers for whom Fotografiska signifies a moment in time that they will never get back – including me.

In the aftermath of a hideous break-up, some choose to embark on a journey of self-discovery, enlisting therapists and meditation coaches to help them adjust to their new life. Others retreat, evaporating from all social media platforms and only leaving the house for work or low-key dinners with one of three closest friends. Some, meanwhile, choose to run away.

Eleven months after Ben asked for a divorce, I packed up my life again, locked my belongings in a yellow storage box on the outskirts of north London, and moved to an apartment on the sixteenth floor of an intimidating building in the heart of the financial district of New York City. For months I'd struggled to sit peacefully in life as I knew it and, when the opportunity to take on a new role across the pond came up, I pounced. My best friend Emma had moved over two months prior with the company we both worked for, which was reason enough in itself. Best of all, I'd be three and a half thousand miles from the city with markings of Ben all over it. This was a fresh start – and I could be whoever I wanted to be.

I spent the first few weeks feeling like a lost toddler running around a playground looking for her parents. The freedom to be whoever you want is great if you have some semblance of an identity. But if you've no idea where to start, it's fucking terrifying. I latched on to the one friend I had, asking over and over if it was 'okay' to hang out with the group of colleagues she'd formed new bonds with. For the first time in my life, I felt socially anxious in big groups. My small contributions to discussions felt awkward and forced, and hung in the air for me to scrutinise and berate.

One evening in my Wall Street apartment, I decided my situation would only improve if I made at least one friend of my own. But I needed a place to start. I remembered a friend from London had sent me the numbers of at least three women in Manhattan who she thought I'd get on with.

I'd ignored the messages, thinking: Thanks, but no thanks; I won't need to connect with random strangers. And yet here I was asking 'Molly, Laura's Friend' (as she was saved in my phone) if she'd like to spend her weeknight immersed in small talk with a person she likely had nothing in common with. She replied within the hour, suggesting we grab dinner at an Italian restaurant near the Lower East Side called Little Frankie's.

That Wednesday night I was seated at the bar, examining the menu for a dish priced under $30 (there were none), when she walked in. I recognised her from her WhatsApp picture and smiled. She waved, and suddenly it felt like I was meeting up with an old friend I'd lost touch with. Molly and I hit it off instantly. What our mutual friend hadn't told me was that Molly was also recently divorced, and also in her early thirties. It was the first time in a year that I didn't feel somewhat freakish. I told my break-up story and waited for the familiar gasps and expletives, but no. Molly responded with a knowing, calm nod, instead focusing on her excitement for my new life stateside. She met my divorce with her own: a husband who had secretly gambled away their shared cash (and spent some of it on prostitutes). At the time we met, she was still waiting for him to repay thousands that he'd promised to return. I texted our mutual friend to thank her for the introduction seconds after I hugged Molly goodbye. Finally, I had a friend.

The following week Molly invited me to join her at an exhibition opening and impromptu gig at Fotografiska. Until that point, my New York consisted of a Williamsburg thrift store that sold $10 Carhartt sweatshirts, the Mexican food truck opposite my apartment, and the office. Every weekend I'd whip out the messenger bag, load it up with snacks and plan a day of exploring each of the five boroughs. But for reasons I still don't understand, I never managed to venture further than said Williamsburg thrift store, and maybe the brunch spot opposite. I wasn't afraid. I just didn't know where I felt like going.

Fotografiska on that Thursday evening felt like what you'd see if you sliced the best bits of Manhattan open and watched the insides spill out. There were the predictable artsy types in painter's trousers and thick-rimmed glasses, but among them was a wide range of folk, most of them alone, indulging a personal passion. It was the first time I realised that a partner was no requirement in this city. Afterwards, Molly and I sat in the foyer and yapped as the bodies emptied out of the building. I shouldn't worry about feeling lonely, she told me. She'd collected an army of friends since her divorce, and I was always welcome to join.

Within six months, I'd added about fifteen people to my very own collection. One was Alice, a thirty-two-year-old solicitor who was eighteen months out of a marriage with a man who was eerily similar to mine. I took her to Fotografiska on our first friend date (partly because, unlike 99 per cent of venues in Manhattan, the bar has enough space between tables for private conversations). At the time of writing, nine months on and in my new home back in London, I'm looking forward to our dinner plans next week.

There was a common theme underpinning the break-up stories told by Molly, Alice and myself, aside from us all being in our early thirties and spending fewer than two years as married women. We had earnt more money than our spouses. For most of our relationships, we had enjoyed more professional success. I found this fascinating.

Alice had been with her husband for six years and married for eighteen months when, out of nowhere, he announced he was 'too young' (aged thirty-three) to be settled down, and suggested they break up. He moved out of their London flat two days later, leaving Alice completely destroyed, not to mention baffled. She spoke of eerily similar thoughts to my own – the assumption he was having an unexpected mental health episode, and would soon snap out of it, for instance. Maybe it had been her fault for discussing her desire for children? But then again, she had been sure he wanted them too. It didn't make any sense. The absurdity of it all was the most torturous element, she says.

It goes without saying that falling victim to this behaviour is hellish, no matter who you are – and, from what I've seen so far, no one is immune. But the first time Alice told me the story of her break-up I sat gawking at her striking bone structure and perfectly tousled hair, aware that she had an early court hearing for one of the most high-profile cases in the city, thinking: is he mad?

Alice is, objectively, supremely impressive. At thirty-three she's worked her way up to a senior position in a world-beating law firm, and is regularly flown all over to represent high-profile clients. She could have had her pick of which global branch to base herself at, but landed on New York because – well, it's New York.

Her husband – let's call him Tony – had suffered a string of unfortunate career blows and consistently earned less than her. 'For the first few years of our relationship he worked for a sports marketing agency, which paid him a salary that wasn't great,' says Alice. 'It was frustrating for him because he was passionate about the work he did because he loved sports, while I'd moan about how boring my job was, yet I was getting paid way more money.'

He suffered a 'debilitating' competitive relationship with his older brother – a successful corporate executive with an 'impressive' salary. 'It was clear he felt that he had to go overboard to impress his brother about what he was doing at work – the celebrities he'd met and that kind of thing. I'd say it dominated most family dinner table discussions.'

But Tony didn't share the same competition with Alice. For the first half of their relationship he seemed to wear her success like a badge of honour. 'In social situations he was always quite boastful about his girlfriend being a lawyer, and would really big me up.'

It was clear money and status was important to Tony's sense of self, which has never been the case for Alice. 'He'd make comments about our combined income and talk about where we stood in comparison to other couples. He'd say stuff like, "Surely our combined salary is way higher than this or that friends'?"'

This is familiar. While my job hunts had always revolved around furthering my future as a well-respected editor and writer, as well as exciting challenges in areas I enjoyed, Ben was heavily swayed by cash. I admired his confidence in his financial worth, and gumption to demand a figure I'd always assumed was out of reach. I suppose I was the one guilty of under-selling myself.

About three weeks before the potential divorce discussion, Ben started a new job. It was a big step up – managing a large portfolio of brands for one of London's biggest creative agencies, overseeing a team of juniors for the first time. But whenever he was asked about what he was most looking forward to, I noticed he gave the same joking-but-not-really-joking answer: 'Well, I'm finally earning more than Eve.'

The gulf between our professional lives wasn't really about money. My passion and drive for what I do has never swayed. I am one of the few lucky people in this world with a vocation they love, who gets to fulfil a role they've had planned for themselves since the age of ten, every working day. But like many people, Ben hadn't been as lucky. Despite also training as a journalist, the career path had never carried the same weight for him. He went from job to job, frustrated and disappointed by his seniors, fed up with the lofty expectations, before eventually deciding he didn't want to write any longer, and pivoting into generating website traffic. He'd often tell me I should consider leaving an industry he saw as outdated, demanding and arrogant. He was right; journalism is all of those things. But he didn't get that I loved it.

When we first broke up, two details from his character assassination were stuck in the forefront of my brain. I cared 'too much' about work. And I didn't prioritise him. Maybe he had a point. There was no denying that my hectic newspaper job had sort of poured weed killer all over my social life. Greater responsibility at work had brought longer, more engrossing hours, which zapped me of energy I'd need to make conversation over mid-week dinners with friends. At points, I sacrificed weekend social plans to stay in and finish a blog post, prepare for an upcoming supper club or work on a new book proposal. I knew this irritated Ben, which irritated me. But was his exasperation with my work 'addiction' rooted in his desire to spend more time with me? It felt more like frustration at his inability to understand it.

In our final year of coupledom, I strove to dial it down. I'd ignore work emails on the weekend and try to leave the office as close to six as possible. I put a pin in the new book idea and stopped the supper clubs. Ben acknowledged his appreciation a couple of times, but never suggested an alternative way to fill our time together. Most weekends were spent pottering in between the supermarket and the tennis court, bookended by a kebab of some sort. I felt calm and well-rested on those weekends. But I wasn't particularly happy.

Now, nearly two years on, my extra-curricular professional activities have crept back into my spare time. I find myself waking up with the urge to write, so tap away at my laptop as the sun rises, before dozing off for another hour. I've dedicated a few evenings to crafting (fucking up) videos for social media while balancing a bowl of pasta on my lap. I've even, dare I say it, taken work home with me, and finished projects from the comfort of my own couch. I wake up feeling relaxed in the knowledge that my night-time efforts will make for a far less stressful day. I can work as much as I like, or as little as I like, and it is no one's business. I do not feel overworked, stressed or close to burnout. I am fulfilled and exhilarated by the work that I've always loved. Perhaps working 'too much' is part of who I am, and the only stress will come from fighting it.

Alice believes the professional imbalance between her and

Tony was ultimately the reason he left. 'I think that women like me are the type of person they [men like him] are attracted to at first. But because they are insecure, they need to be bringing more to the table to feel empowered,' she says.

Fourteen months after their wedding, Alice came off birth control. Just like Ben and I, they planned for a near future filled with nursery decorating and babymoons. A month after that, Tony got a new, dream job working as a marketing executive for a motorsport company, along with a hefty pay bump. And a little less than a month later, he came home from a work trip with messages from Instagram models popping up on his phone.

Alice confronted him one evening. He didn't bother denying, or backtracking. Instead, he said: 'I want a divorce.' Even two years down the line, Alice is still not entirely clear as to his reasoning. 'He didn't really explain, just saying he'd realised he was way too young to be settled and didn't want to be married. I kept asking questions and he just looked at me with this blank expression, unable to really say anything.'

Four months before I called Alice to do this interview, we met in a Williamsburg bar, where she told me a friend had recently seen revealing pictures of her ex on social media. He appeared to be partying at race tracks, his arms draped around glamorous, younger women. It cemented her suspicions that a romantic interest could have contributed to his change of heart.

'I think when there's an insecure, millennial man, as much as they are attracted to an independent, self-sufficient woman, their egos ultimately can't handle it,' she says. 'They thrive off feeling like they're worshipped, or that there is a girl who is super reliant on them.'

Alice says this was the immediate conclusion drawn by her ex's brother. 'I called him and the first thing he said was, "He's suddenly got this fancy promotion and he's earning more money and he's surrounded by these young girls who are stroking his ego."

'I genuinely think that's what happened. I would never have been able to give him the ego boost that those girls could.'

The flat Alice shared with her ex was owned exclusively by her, which meant a clean break was pretty easy, as he wasn't interested in fighting her for his 'share'. He did, however, text her two days after he dropped the bomb to ask if he could leave all his stuff in her flat for six weeks while he was away at motor races.

'When he was supposed to collect it he texted to say he'd been invited to stay with friends in Devon and could he re-schedule for another weekend,' she says. 'No consideration for the fact I'd been in hell for the past six weeks, sitting here staring at all his stuff and our shared life together. But thank goodness it was my flat and we hadn't bought anything together. It wasn't too difficult for me to turn it into my space again.'

A note on moving in together

My latest take on moving in with a romantic partner is considered, by many, to be controversial. Basically, if you plan to get married, I don't think it's particularly vital to move in together beforehand. Very war-time of me, I know. But hear me out. An overwhelming wealth of data suggests that those who live together before marriage (or cohabit, to use the grown-up term) are considerably more likely to divorce, compared to those who don't. One influential US study,[1] which followed more than a thousand couples in the decade after they got hitched, found 34 per cent of those who cohabited before engagement got divorced, compared to 23 per cent of those who didn't. Most fascinating is that, according to the study's authors, who've been researching this phenomenon for thirty years, the trend has remained stable. The researchers, Scott M. Stanley and Galena K. Rhoades from the University of Denver, have a theory as to why this is. Deciding to move in isn't always rooted in a long-term commitment to each other, but rather a decision of convenience. People 'slide' into living together, they say, creating 'inertia' towards the relationship and a shared future. 'Some are stuck in a place where they probably would have left,' Professor Stanley told local news site, *Deseret News*.[2] Once you're engaged or married, you've already made a commitment to be together, and are likely to be actively engaged in making it work. Another of the team's findings is telling: those who moved in together to 'test' the relationship were more likely to see their marriages end, compared to those who did it to spend more time with their partner.

There's some legal reasoning to my position on this, too. It is a widespread myth that living with someone gives you legal rights to their property or finances, due to your position as what is often referred to as a 'common law' wife or husband. This is total nonsense that divorce lawyers have long been fighting to squash. Unless you are married, your legal rights do not exist. It means if you end up 'testing' your relationship for several years and paying your home-owning partner thousands in rent, you could walk away with nothing, while they've built up a lump of equity in their mortgage. I'm not saying there's a right or wrong. It's just something to think about.

Alice asked her firm to transfer her to their Barcelona office a few months after her break-up. Most of London was embossed with memories of her ex. She didn't know how, or who, to be, if she wasn't a married person. But distracted by the novelty of a new city and extra professional challenges, her life began to take shape again quicker than expected. She threw herself into collecting enriching friendships – along with complex cases at work. She even met a man she liked. Eventually, though, she had to come home.

She describes a mild identity crisis that makes me repeat the word 'same' twenty times in the space of a minute. Your early thirties are somewhat of a polarising age, in which your relationship status is suddenly more defining than it ever has been before. If you're coupled up, your priorities likely revolve around some element of the future; be it putting down roots in a shared home, planning a wedding or starting a family. As single women adjust to a diminishing number of friends available for weekend mini-breaks and to help them carry boxes back from IKEA, they build a life that is filled with experiences and friendships far removed from those of their once-core group of pals that are in committed relationships. Maybe their free time now revolves around running half marathons with colleagues, or hanging out with friends of friends whose names you struggle to remember. Booking time to see your fellow single friends becomes more of a challenge, while those who've bought houses in the commuter belts or who care for young kids struggle to travel as far as they used to, happily confining themselves to a two-mile comfort zone.

Transitioning from single to relationship is pretty straightforward. But the same can't be said for the other way around. It is not as simple as slotting back into an independent life. Singledom in your thirties isn't the Friday and Saturday nights in bars followed by Sunday mornings at hungover brunch, that it was in your twenties. While you were picking out curtains and schlepping around Costco, your single friends were picking up new mates, moving to inner-city flats and discovering their true sexual identities. They built lives that were just as rammed with joy and fulfilment as your marital one, and, I'm afraid to say, you don't easily fit into it. You find yourself tagging along to a girls' night at a converted warehouse soundproofed with egg boxes, feeling prudish when the conversation veers towards the topic of pegging (google it). You keep drinking, thinking another vodka soda will give you enough confidence to at least pretend you belong. By 11.30 p.m., you're apathetically swaying to Wayne Wonder's 'No Letting Go', wishing you were safely in suburbia, sprawled out on your L-shaped sofa watching *Peep Show*.

The alternative is to hang out with the couples, continuing as if you were still one of them. You sit on sofas drinking cups of tea while they make tactless attempts to make you feel better by saying things like, 'I'll switch places with you!' when their partner refuses to turn off the football, and tell you having a baby is 'much more work than you realise' and 'thank God you didn't have one to cope with on your own'.

Your friend's well-meaning husband bangs on about how shocked he was to hear that your ex-husband is in fact a c**t and asks if you've had any contact with him. You watch them plan for birthday dinners at the same Greek restaurants you and your ex loved, and stop yourself declaring your long, romantic history with the place out loud. The last thing you want is pity. It's no wonder so many of us escape in an attempt to start from scratch.

After Barcelona, Alice set her sights on New York. We met in November 2023, a month after I moved to the States, while Alice was awaiting confirmation from her firm of a permanent role. My friend Claudia was visiting, and arranged a night at an East Village dive bar with some girls she knew through an old colleague. One of those girls was Alice.

The two of us drifted towards each other as the night progressed and spent most of it shouting 'OH MY GOD!' as the eerily similar elements of our stories came to light. Alice would go on to become a cherished friend. She was the only person who'd listen to me bang on about how my relationship had always been doomed and actually be interested. I leant on her during many of my identity crises. And I was the one she texted when her divorce came through.

Today, she is exploring a step up the career ladder that would involve her working in multiple US offices. She's still keen to be at a safe distance from her former marital home. Our discussions often lead us to the topic of regret: what we would have done differently? What have we learned not to do next time? Alice wishes she'd never got divorced. But she doesn't wish she was still married to her ex. We agree that our ex-partners have, unbeknown to everyone at the time, gifted us the greatest favour. Without their callousness, we would still be married to them – and, in all likelihood, be very fucking miserable.

'I am so much happier without him,' Alice says. 'The experiences I've had since the break-up have been some of the best of my life. If we'd stayed married, I would have been ignorantly living this unfulfilling relationship and would never have known there were genuinely amazing experiences to be had, or incredible people to connect with out there. I'm glad that he released me.'

Both Alice and I were in love with the safety of marriage. The control it gave you over a terrifying expanse of time stretched out in front of you. But were we in love with our husbands? Neither of us give a confident 'yes'.

'At first, I was desperate to stay with him because I thought happiness equalled continuing to be married,' says Alice. 'But if we'd stayed together, I would have ended up being so resentful. I am genuinely grateful for it happening when it did.'

When it comes to finding 'the one', professional heterosexual women are perhaps more damned than they ever were before. My research for this book has revealed a problematic phenomenon that is currently playing out in the dating sphere, driving thirty-something men and women further apart from each other.

To put it bluntly, many women are now out-achieving their male counterparts. And a vast number of said male counterparts suffer insecurity about this imbalance (likely due to shit male role models and the promotion of toxic masculinity by popular culture). This makes for an unsupportive environment for mutual respect and support of both individuals' hopes and dreams. It increases the risk the parties will grow in different directions and foster underlying resentment for one another.

It also means men have much more to gain, financially, from the women they marry than ever before, should it go horribly wrong.

About a quarter of married couples in the UK have a female breadwinner, compared to less than one in five two decades ago.[3] These women may be surprised to learn that, should they divorce, their gender would have no impact on a financial agreement. In fact, their spouse would be legally entitled to half of everything they'd earned.

Life coach and behavioural change expert Gemma Perlin says she's seeing this play out in an increasing number of her clients and thirty-something friends. 'Many of the women I work with have seen their finances very badly dented as a result of divorce,' she says. Solicitors tell me female clients are often shocked to learn women can end up worse off too, amid a cultural narrative that tells us the female counterpart generally does well out of divorce. 'The only surefire way to protect your finances is to not get married,' says David Brown, a divorce lawyer working in Leicestershire.

But judging by Perlin's experience of helping millennial women suffering (almost) midlife crises, increasing numbers of high-earning women are following this advice. She says expansive opportunities lead the women she sees to question the 'train tracks of life'. 'I've worked with multiple people cancelling weddings or getting divorced,' she says. 'It's a much more empowered generation who see models of people making decisions that aren't conventional and think, maybe this is better suited to me.

'People are very much aware that you only have one life, and they want to live it in an honest way. I appreciate this is a very privileged conversation to have, but a lot of women I see are concerned with whether or not they're living their best life, their truth.'

As ridiculous as it sounds, the onslaught of 'you do you'-themed clips on TikTok and Instagram explains some of the trend, says Perlin. 'You only have to go on Instagram for ten seconds and there's so much pop psychology about being your "authentic" self,' she says. 'There's lots of people on social media who do what I do – helping people to become the best version of themselves – their real self. I think some of that is actually really permeating.'

Many people in my life have described my relationship with work as dysfunctional. It's a distraction from uncomfortable feelings, and interferes with my capacity to relax. Writing is not a hobby if I get paid for it. Or so I've been told.

But I see it differently. Work, or at least my vocation, has been my saviour during multiple catastrophes in my relatively short life. It has offered a constant when everything else was in flux, and a reminder of my value when I felt worthless. Above all, it's been a routine, a reason to eat breakfast, wash myself and put on the skirt I love but hardly ever wear. At one time or another, the office has transported me from eating disorder thoughts, financial settlements and my biological clock, to the relative safety of medical scandals and menopause sex tips. I had no choice but to immerse myself in whichever story had to be reported that day. Often, when the tale at hand concerned terminal cancer patients campaigning for vital drugs, or disabled children denied basic care, it came with the gift of perspective.

In the days after my break-up, as my body fused with the sofa cushions, Mum's goal was to get me back to work as quickly as possible. She told me the same story she's been telling for as long as I can remember.

'When you were five, you'd pick up my work bag and march towards the door, announcing that you were off to work – just like Mummy.'

Chapter 8

The Gay Marriage

In November 2020, a number of male TikTok users were triggered by a statistic that hit the headlines, supposedly plucked from a set of 2019 data collected by the Office for National Statistics in the UK. It was this: 72 per cent of lesbian women who get married get divorced. The divorce rate for gay men was said to be around three times lower.[1]

An army of men's rights activists jumped to the sanctity of their Reddit forums to celebrate the validation: just like they'd said all along, men were not the problem when it came to maintaining healthy romantic relationships. If straight women thought men were bad, they should try dating women, was the general consensus.

The 72 per cent figure did come from the Office for National Statistics. But the widely circulated interpretation is not strictly true. What the research body actually found was, out of 822 same-sex divorces in 2019, 589 were lesbian marriages, while 233 were male couples. So around three quarters of the divorces in same-sex couples in one year were in lesbian unions, but that statistic might not necessarily hold true for other years. However, the higher chance of split in lesbian women has been evidenced in data from other nations – including Dutch studies which show 15 per cent of gay marriages ended between 2005 and 2015, compared to 30 per cent of lesbian ones.[2]

I am fascinated by this apparent trend, particularly because lesbian friends of mine have long attempted to convince me that fem romances are more unpredictable, combustible and emotionally fucked than the hetero kind. My own research tells me a) this is an offensive generalisation and b) these seemingly telling figures can be explained by a number of interesting factors which, together, show they are in no way a reflection of women's failure at relationships.

First it is important to highlight that gay marriage has only been legal – in the UK at least – since 2014. Some of the LGBTQIA+ couples I spoke with for this book described this moment as 'lighter fuel' for their relationship – including those that weren't really that great and were clearly destined for divorce. The communal elation about the momentous gear shift propelled many to sign up, simply because they could.

Depressing history of gay marriage and the law

Laws restricting gay and lesbian relationships remain in place in some sixty countries around the world, including six which sentence gay and lesbian people to death.[3] In the Maldives, homosexuality is punishable by torture; specifically whipping for 100 strokes.[4] Even in the UK and US, it wasn't until the early '00s that legislation that blatantly discriminated against LGBTQI+ couples began to be ditched.

For instance, in England, it wasn't until 2001 that the

age of consent was equalised to sixteen, regardless of sexual orientation (it used to be twenty-one for gay men). And up until 2003, schools were legally forbidden from 'promoting homosexuality', which translated as including any references to homosexuality in educational programmes, for instance in sex and relationship classes. In Scotland this appalling law only changed in 2013.

Civil partnerships were introduced across the UK in 2005, allowing, for the first time, for gay and lesbian couples' unions to be recognised by the state. In the US, the state of Hawaii was the first to introduce some form of civil union in 1997, with same sex-couples allowed to share medical insurance, state pensions, property rights and benefit from inheritance.[5] The killer question I am often asked by people who consider me (for reasons that remain a mystery) a divorce wizard is: what's the difference between a civil partnership and a marriage? In short – not much.

In the UK, civil partners have pretty much identical legal rights to those who get married, although it was felt the symbolism of marriage – including religious elements – was still being denied to them, as were certain pension inheritance rights. And so, after decades of campaigning, David Cameron's Conservative government pushed through the Marriage (Same Sex Couples) Act in July 2013, allowing same-sex couples to marry in England, Wales and eventually Scotland, followed by the Irish Republic in 2015, and Northern Ireland in 2020.

It wasn't until December 2023, however, that the Church of England agreed that clergy could conduct a same-sex marriage, although many priests won't carry out this blessing in a church. A Jewish lesbian or gay couple can get married in a non-Orthodox synagogue, provided both parties are Jewish. As there is no governing Muslim authority, it's unclear what the official rules are in Islam; however, some mosques and imams will perform gay and lesbian marriages depending on the circumstances. Some Hindu priests conduct gay marriages, with the Hindu community said to be 'overwhelmingly' welcoming of LGBTQI+ people.

Across the pond, the Supreme Court scrapped bans on same-sex marriage in all fifty states in June 2015, but some states were ahead of the curve. Massachusetts was the first, way back in 2003, followed by Connecticut in 2008 and three more – Iowa, New Hampshire and Vermont – in 2009, along with Washington DC. But recent political events mean the right to gay marriage may be under threat across the US following the clouded summer of 2022 – and the monumental overturning of critical abortion law, Roe v Wade. In the aftermath, several conservative senators and influential judges have suggested that the reversal of the right to fundamental women's healthcare cracks open the door for overturning of other legislations they deem to be irreligious. And first on the chopping block is Obergefell v Hodges – the landmark case that made gay marriage legal as per federal law.[6]

Anti-abortionist and Associate Justice of the Supreme Court Clarence Thomas said in July 2022 that the change in abortion law was an 'opportunity' to tear down half a century's worth of 'demonstrably erroneous' precedents including rights to contraception – and same-sex marriage.[7] More recently another influential Supreme Court Associate Justice, Samuel Alito, criticised the law following a case in which members of the jury were removed because of homophobic views. Alito said Obergefell has meant that anyone who doesn't approve of same-sex marriage is labelled a 'bigot'.[8] Quite rightly, you might say. According to some political journalists, overturning Obergefell is a 'bucket list' achievement for several of the most powerful justices who sit within the institution. Texas judge Dianne Hensley continues to refuse to perform gay marriages, despite receiving state warnings in 2019. She is currently awaiting a Supreme Court judgement on her stance – said to be based on 'religious grounds', and is confident Justices will rule in her favour.[9]

With such a long history of painful battles for this basic equalising act, it is hardly surprising that some gay and lesbian couples may have jumped at the chance to get married. Especially when, in the US at least, there is a very real threat that it may soon be taken away.

Some research suggests that lesbian couples are slightly quicker to move to marriage, compared with men, and are more likely to opt for marriage in the first place. One analysis of thirty countries by the Pew Research Center found that in all but four nations the marriage rate was higher among lesbian women than it was gay men.[10] There are key contributors to this phenomenon, brought to my attention by Lyndsey Marshall, now thirty-five, who married her university sweetheart in 2015, at twenty-six, and was divorced by early 2020, at thirty-one. The couple, who lived in Stoke-on-Trent throughout their relationship, got together aged nineteen, and were engaged within four years – before gay marriage was even legal.

The partnership was largely 'quite happy' – but they were

young and, as is often the case, teetered off on slightly different paths as they got older. I ask Lyndsey her thoughts about the suggestion that lesbian women are at higher risk of divorce than any other group. It wouldn't surprise her, she says, if same-sex female couples rushed into marriage before they were ready.

She describes a 'heteronormative peer pressure' that pushes along gay relationships in particular. Not only does she speak of 'a desire to fit in' among friends – most of whom for her, at the time, were heterosexual couples – but also a longing for validation of her identity from her family. No one ever had a problem with her sexuality, but there was a quiet voice telling her to prove conventionality to her parents. 'There was an element of trying to appeal to the heteronormativity in my parents and sort of say, I'm gay but it's okay because I am conventional with this relationship and this marriage.'

Also, Lyndsey had always known she wanted children, although her wife needed a little more convincing. And for gay couples, marriage comes with a specific advantage in this area. 'The birthing partner is the only one with rights to the child, unless you are married,' she says. It is an infuriating technicality; in both male and female same-sex couples, the partner who is not genetically related to the child must endure the legal adoption process in order to be considered their parent. But if you're married, this doesn't apply. This may spur women along more than it does men, given that studies show lesbian women are more likely to raise children than gay men.[11]

'It's helpful to be married if you want to have a family,' says Lyndsey, who married her second wife in October 2023, just under three years after meeting her. 'I was initially hesitant, and didn't know if I wanted to get married again. But it seemed like the right thing. I realised that the first time was the wrong decision at the wrong time with the wrong person, rather than a case of "marriage isn't for me".'

I tell Lyndsey that I find this decision phenomenally brave, explaining a little of the pangs of terror that flood my brain when I see one of those annoying 'she said yes' posts on Instagram. But, we agree, just as there's a 50 per cent chance your marriage will go down the shitter, there's the same odds that it'll last a lifetime.

So what was so wrong with her first marriage? And why did it take her almost a decade to see it?

'It wasn't a big dramatic thing,' she says, but more, 'slowly realising that, you know, the more sexual, romantic sides of the relationship were not what we'd hoped it would be. In the end it turned into a bit of a friendship.'

It seems there were two key elements to her matrimonial demise. One was a symptom of a patchy romantic connection, and the other a fundamental problem which I relate to.

Lyndsey says she fell victim to the destructive victim-rescuer dynamic which, in my experience, is like toxic waste for your sex life. Lyndsey's wife had long struggled with a range of complex mental health problems that left her unable to cope with a lot of daily tasks that most couples share equally. Lyndsey admits she was also to blame for the defined roles they fell into: 'I really wanted to be needed and wanted. I was more than happy to be in that kind of role,' she says.

In my relationship, I was the victim. Not that I ever truly felt like one. Somewhere between my discharge from hospital in 2015 and our engagement in 2019, Ben and I had settled into roles that were deeply unsuited to both of us. This only came to light when we broke up, of course. For a large part of our relationship, Ben was uneasy about me working late, or deciding to go out drinking straight after work and returning home with a packet of Doritos under my arm. It wasn't about keeping tabs on me, or jealousy, or the trail of crumbs I left on the stairs. He was worried I wouldn't eat. And so, around the six-year mark, he began cooking me dinners and leaving them in the fridge, ready to quickly warm up when I stumbled in at midnight after the pub, or was too stressed to think about cooking. I considered myself extraordinarily lucky to have a man at home that not only knew how to cook, but also sacrificed time doing what he loved (an early tennis game/*Football Manager*) to make sure I had a hot meal when I came home. I still think I was lucky to share a life with a partner who gave me so much thought.

But on the few occasions he was too busy, the mask slipped. His anxiety about my health transformed into blame worryingly quickly. Why hadn't I prepared a proper dinner for myself? He couldn't be expected to do everything. Perhaps unsurprisingly, his caretaking role made intimacy feel a little less natural than it had done before I became ill. I rarely felt sexy, even during the act.

I often found our splitting of monotonous house admin confusing. Ben had always taken it upon himself to handle just about everything: mortgage, bills, deworming the dog. It's not that I didn't want to. But our relationship had seen my working days become longer, more hectic and with less room for extracurricular activities like remembering to buy milk and finding a plumber to fix the non-flushing toilet. Ben offered to take care of the life stuff. Actually, he didn't offer – he just did it.

It wasn't until the last two months of our marriage that I learned Ben's true feelings about our accidental dynamic. He became increasingly annoyed when researching whether or not to fix our mortgage for another five years, or getting cash out for the dog walker. In hindsight, I am ashamed of the pitiful amount I did towards the upkeep of our shared life. Everyone has a job and everyone is busy. It is not an excuse to check out of adulthood. But Ben didn't choose his words carefully, instead choosing to splatter his angriest thoughts all over the kitchen one Sunday morning before my tennis lesson. He accused me of putting my job before his, and failing to make the same sacrifices he was. I pleaded with him to share the load, telling him I never asked him to be the designated bills organiser and, actually, I would quite like to be involved. I'd just assumed he was happy with our arrangement given that he'd never expressed otherwise. 'Let me help you,' I remember saying, with my hand clasping his. He nodded, hugged me and apologised for losing his temper. But the next week, he paid the bills, organised the plumber and took the dog for a haircut just like normal. I awaited his instructions to take over one mundane job or other, but they never came. Perhaps we were both victims of miscommunication, both of us expecting the other to step up to change the dynamic. Maybe he couldn't face burdening me with it, after all.

A day after Ben declared his 'second thoughts', I raked over my memories of these arguments with the girls. Maybe he'd felt used, taken for granted and unappreciated. I should have made more of an active effort just to 'do' things. My best friend responded: 'He was in control of the role he played in the relationship, not you. If he didn't like the role, he could have changed it.'

Speaking with Lyndsey offered me insight into the psyche of my rescuer. I realised his self-prescribed role wasn't at all what I thought it was: a genuine belief that I was incapable. It wasn't about me at all, actually. I now get that doing all the things were really for the benefit of the poisonous voice inside his head that told him he was worthless.

'I guess, early on, I didn't feel like I deserved to be loved or have a relationship. I thought that no one would want me,' says Lyndsey. Feeling needed quietened the voice for her, at least for a bit. Taking ownership of their life 'stuff' would 'get the latch on' the relationship, she thought. 'Lock it down, get it done. That was definitely part of it.' But things began to fall apart in 2019.

'Initially, it was her [Lyndsey's partner] who was unhappy, at least vocally. I was pushing her to talk about it with me so I could figure out what I could do to help. I wanted to fix it.' They had a few sessions of therapy and tried to reignite their fire with date nights, but, 'We were probably too far down the line at that point.'

I suspected a catalyst, and asked Lyndsey if there, by any chance, had been someone else on the scene, dangling the carrot of an alternative, more fulfilled life.

'There was this guy I knew she was talking to,' she says. 'He was sort of on the edge around that time. I know they were getting very close and messaging a lot. I mentioned it and said

I was uncomfortable about it, but we didn't ever explicitly discuss what was going on. I think after we broke up they did get together for a bit, but I don't know the details.'

Lyndsey was aware that this situation played into the hands of lazy stereotypes about bisexual women. 'There's this idea that bisexual women are always going to want to leave you for a man in the end, but I don't think our situation validates that theory at all.' The man was a symptom of their lack of sexual closeness she says. That summer they took their failing relationship to a friend's wedding and stumbled upon the conversation one night in the hotel room. 'She said she didn't feel attracted to me any more.'

'That was obviously . . . not nice,' says Lyndsey. 'And that's when I started thinking I needed to be more interesting, have more hobbies and maybe dress better to make it work.'

I have a flashback to the night I asked Ben if a drastic haircut might spice things up enough to make him want to be with me. He laughed, which made me cry. But looking back, I understand the hilarity.

'That was when we tried therapy – but it was clear quite early on that we weren't getting anywhere. Nothing could fix the things that we felt were missing.' The actual break-up came one evening in October, sparked by nothing else but a shared acknowledgement that they were both sick of feeling miserable.

'It ended up being quite loving, actually. It was a surprising outcome for both of us and we still had a lot of love for each other. We stayed up quite late and talked, had a drink, and reminisced on our good memories together. We both acknowledged that neither of us were in the right relationship.'

Another flashback to me hurling the word 'scumbag' at Ben's face as I stormed out of our house.

As far as divorces go, I think Lyndsey's is the one I am most jealous of. The ex-couple were able to exist pretty peacefully in the same house for several months, before Lyndsey was offered a new job in London, where she stayed for five days out of the week. Her ex happily returned the extra cash that Lyndsey had put into their shared home. They came up with a custody arrangement for their cat (Lyndsey would travel up from London so her ex could go on trips away) and there was absolutely no squabbling over vases they'd bought for one another's birthdays. They both filed for divorce citing irreconcilable differences, and stayed in amicable communication throughout.

'I was happy to keep on paying the mortgage while she was living there because I guess I wanted to kick the can down the road in terms of selling up and finalising everything,' Lyndsey says. 'But it was all very amicable and when we eventually did sell up, we'd agreed that I would get back more money because I'd put in more, and she stuck to it.'

At first, singledom felt like freedom to Lyndsey. A dream-like existence that was full of experiences that were novel enough to distract her from any emotional instincts. 'It all happened so quickly,' she says. 'I changed jobs, started commuting and was suddenly working in a big hospital, which was a massive change [Lyndsey works for the NHS]. I was really, really busy, and then Covid hit. So I didn't have a chance to take anything in.' This remained the case until October of 2020, about a year after the initial split and around the time the house was sold.

'And then it all hit me,' Lyndsey says. She slipped into an extended period of depression. 'Literally every bit of my life had changed without me really taking it in, and it suddenly made me very low. That's when I started having therapy and I took a couple of weeks off work to try and process it all. Well, really, I just got my head down and played computer games for two weeks.'

I wonder about a particular type of guilt that might impact divorced people who've married someone of the same sex. The overwhelming sense I'd let others down and catastrophically failed was crushing for me – but at least marriage hadn't felt like a luxury. I say I can't imagine the extra heaviness that comes with choosing to end something your community has spent decades fighting for.

Lyndsey's response tells me I'm overthinking it. 'I wouldn't say that the fact it was a queer marriage brought any extra sense of guilt or anything,' she says. 'But of course I felt embarrassed. We had this big wedding where we said all these lovely things about each other in front of our friends and family, and then we just went back on it all four years later.'

A couple of months before her 'depressive blip', Lyndsey met Suzie, a thirty-two-year-old sommelier from London, on a dating app.

'I wasn't looking for anything when I started dating,' she says. 'I was in London and single for the first time in my adult life so I thought, why not get stuck in?' Suzie had broken up with her partner two weeks before they met and, with Lyndsey not yet divorced and 'emotionally very close to my ex', they kept it casual. But then Covid happened.

'It sort of took the idea of seeing other people out of the

picture because we couldn't, and pushed things forward quickly.' They talked about marriage early on and, within a year of their relationship, Lyndsey had changed her mind about not wanting another wedding.

'We knew we wanted a family from the very beginning. I was thirty-four and she was thirty-three, so there was an understanding that we had to get a move on, which made marriage sort of inevitable. I proposed in June 2023, and we got married in October.'

By January, the couple had begun researching cost-effective ways to conceive, and came across the remarkable world of DIY insemination kits. For around £100, you can get a box featuring all the contraptions needed to make a baby: an extended pipette to distribute the . . . specimen, a pot to keep an excess of said specimen, and a silicone cup to trap the sperm in close proximity to the egg. Sperm donor not included.

Luckily, the couple had a genetically gifted friend who was willing to oblige. 'It led to some quite funny interactions involving us carrying various pots of semen around the house.' On the third go, it worked. But a few weeks into the pregnancy, Suzie miscarried. On the fourth go it worked again, and when we speak, Suzie is twenty weeks pregnant. And Lyndsey is dizzyingly happy.

Her ex is too, having recently given birth to a little boy. She met the father of the child – her new partner – a year or so after the split. They meet up for lunch occasionally. 'We spent most of our formative years together, including our entire university experience,' Lyndsey says. 'It was also the relationship that pushed me to come out. We did a lot of growing up together, so I'm glad we're still friends.'

She has no regrets about the past. Apart from maybe her desire to grow up too quickly. 'When I look back I think, wow, how was I making all these very grown-up decisions when I wasn't at all mature?' she says. 'But over the years – and thanks to a lot of therapy – I've learned to be a lot more compassionate to my younger self. I was just trying to figure it all out, and do the thing that I thought was best, even if ultimately those decisions weren't the right ones.'

We agree that everything doesn't happen for a reason. And, ideally, the first mammoth commitment would have been the only one. I tell her that, on dark days, my toxic perfectionism takes hold, and I struggle to shift the disappointment in myself. How could I have missed the iceberg ahead? Lyndsey says the trick is to see it not as a fault in your past, but a head start for the future.

'When you uproot your whole life and turn your back on everything you've built – a house, a person, a future – you feel as if, well, if it all goes to shit again, I'll probably be okay. I can back myself. If the happiness goes away for whatever reason, I know I can be happy again. Basically, life isn't always what you think it's gonna be. But it usually works out okay.'

Chapter 9

The Man

On Taylor Swift's bestselling 2008 album *Fearless* (famously re-released in 2021 featuring the subheading 'Taylor's version') there is a track entitled 'Mr Perfectly Fine'. In the immediate aftermath of my break-up, the girlies fired over endless cultural tools: copies of *Eat Pray Love*, links to 'Fuck That Bastard Break-Up Songs' Spotify playlists, niche feminist poetry and, of course, a special curation of Taylor Swift's most appropriate bangers.

I found most of the said bangers to be not quite right. There was too much hand-holding and pavements and seasons and salty air. Also I don't own a blue dress and he doesn't have dimples. But I played Mr Perfectly Fine somewhere in the region of two hundred times in a two-week period. The song highlights a peculiar disparity between men and women who end a long-term relationship. She experiences a hiatus in her ability to speak, move and clothe herself. He, meanwhile, has a little cry, maybe smokes some weed, and is basically back to normal by the end of the week. I admit this is an enormous generalisation. But it is my experience, and that of my friends.

One girl I know learned that her ex-boyfriend of eight years was flat-hunting with his new girlfriend just six months after they broke up.

On the third meeting after our break-up, I asked Ben what I guess was an indulgent question. The answer, I expected, would confirm my assumption that he was also suffering the chronic, existential turmoil that haunted me every minute of every day.

'Has it been weird without me . . . like, in the house? Have you missed having me around?' We had lived together for six years and spent no longer than two weeks apart in that time. And we weren't one of these couples who did different things on the weekends but reunited at dinner time. Our Saturdays were an embarrassingly stereotypical schedule of middle-class suburban activities. During the Covid lockdowns, we coordinated our lunch hours so we could walk to the Italian deli round the corner; he'd insist I keep him company even if I didn't fancy mortadella in my sandwich that day. It must have been odd without me, at the very least.

'Erm, a bit, not really,' he responded. 'I think it's probably been more odd for you because you're the one who hasn't been living here.' Ouch.

When I visibly winced, clearly holding back tears, I thought perhaps seeing my heart crack and rot in real time might trigger a little cry. But nothing. He stood in the hallway looking on with a half-smile as I wiped tears from my chin and hyperventilated. He walked forwards with his arms held out and pressed me into a non-consensual hug. He muttered something about 'we'll both be all right', but I couldn't really hear him.

Within two months of delivering his final decision, he'd found a divorce lawyer, organised our shared possessions (which we'd sell and which we'd split), and begun the process of buying his own flat. His packing up of our house was painfully efficient. I'd walk in on one of my visits while he was out and see his pile of boxes neatly sealed, stacked and labelled in the living room. I, on the other hand, couldn't bear to face the finality of cardboard boxes, so shoved my crap in various holdalls and tote bags, as if I was packing for a mini-break.

I guess you could say Ben was simply being practical. And, given that I was living at my mum's, who else was going to divvy up our stuff? Still, I was just about mustering the strength to get through a week at work. It would have taken me several months to make any sizeable dent in the burial of our shared life.

Side note: statistics show that men move on faster, and in greater numbers, than women. Some 64 per cent of men remarry post-divorce, compared to about 52 per cent of women, according to US studies.[1] It takes an average of three years for these men to move on to another relationship, compared to five for women.[2] My mum once told me about a support group for bereaved partners that she'd entertained one evening about a year after my dad died. Only one man attended; the rest were women. The widows, most of whom had been alone for several years, spent most of the evening discussing the difficulties of moving on; both practically and emotionally. The only attendee to have met someone new was the man – who had found a new girlfriend six months after his wife died.

So what is it? Do men have another, testosterone-fuelled

empty space in their brain, primed and ready to store emotional trauma for another day? Do they feel all the same things we do, but are masters of disguise? Or is there just something about the Y chromosome that programmes them to give less of a fuck?

Psychoanalytic psychotherapist and relationship counsellor Susanna Abse has a fascinating theory. Many of us assume that a man's strained relationship with his father is the reason he never quite knows what he wants – or how to communicate it. But Abse says the mother has more to answer for than we might realise.

'The reason why more men end up in situations they're dissatisfied with and pull away from a long-term commitment is likely rooted in childhood,' she explains. 'Men are usually brought up, in the main, by their mothers. And if things go well, they can form a very strong bond. But they also need to separate from their mothers and form a sense of self-identification with their own masculinity.'

She says this presents a challenge that's unique to men, as they can't 'mirror' their mothers in the same way they would their fathers, with whom their bond is often less emotionally intense.

'It means it becomes more tricky for men to manage that process of close intimacy and separateness,' she says. 'This makes it tough for men to form a sense of self they are comfortable with, and leads to feelings of confusion about what level of emotional connection is appropriate for a man. This of course relies on very traditional and stereotypical gender roles, however, which doesn't always apply to both parents.'

Simon Yantoff is twenty-nine years old and lives in

Portland, Oregon. He got married at the age of twenty-two. And in a few months, he will be divorced. When we speak, he's been separated for about eight months and is settling into his first home as a single man.

In a nutshell: he met his former partner when they were both in the military in their early twenties and, within a couple of years, decided to get married. They eventually left the forces and started college, renting a house together. But about three years in, the relationship got hard. She (let's call her Lisa) had residual anxieties about intimacy stemming from past relationships, which made her 'difficult to reach' and caused an 'aura of heaviness'. This, coupled with a general sense of missing out on fun in their twenties, resulted in a build-up of quiet misery.

The couple tried counselling twice, which proved effective in stopping their arguments – but their sex life remained virtually non-existent. Things came to somewhat of a head the summer before last. The month before their break-up, the couples' therapist suggested the pair spend some time apart, to give them some breathing space. Neither of them expected it to be the end.

'It was hard to think about the challenges and the negatives of our relationship because we never stopped being really good friends,' Simon says. 'I was willing to overlook the true challenges because I cared about her so much.' But the break proved far more conclusive than either of them thought it would be.

'We sort of realised that a lot of things about the relationship had been holding us back. And by the time the break was over, it felt clear to me that we couldn't continue on. I got a sense of how it felt to be on my own, and it made me aware of all the things I've missed out on in my twenties because I was in this married life. It became clearer how little I prioritised myself because I was always thinking of her and doing things for the relationship. It was sort of a mindset shift. I was thinking about my wants and needs and that was an eye-opener for me. I guess I needed the break to know that, if this really is over, it's okay.'

The night of the break-up wasn't long after the hiatus finished. 'We were catching up about the break and what it meant for us. We talked a lot and ended up doing a bit of prancing about, like we were on the edge of the cliff. In the end I was the one who said we should break up – and she agreed. We sat, cried and talked for six hours. It was a very meditative and informative break-up. There were no big arguments or anything like that. We still both loved each other very much as humans. But maybe we just weren't in love with each other any more.'

Simon stayed in the house for a few weeks, sleeping in a separate bedroom, and it was agreed that the divorce papers could wait; 'we wanted to get our head around the separation first.'

When Simon and I begin our chat, it's . . . a struggle. He is nonchalant, reserved – aloof, even. I probe his feelings, the details of the hurtful things they said to one another, and why it took him so long to end it. He skirts around my questions, giving a few words of vague explanation – wildly unlike the conversations I've had with the women in this book.

There is a definite reluctance on his part to appear emotionally vulnerable, or unable to pick himself back up again.

He says he 'felt pretty good' about finding an apartment alone for the first time, and didn't worry about missing her choice of furniture or scatter cushions. 'We actually used to get a lot of compliments on the decor that I picked for our shared place,' he said. 'I made it very homely almost immediately. That was very important to me.' He says the break-up pushed him to restart hobbies he'd let slide, like running and writing a book. But there were clues to something bubbling under the surface.

'The night I got into my new place, I drank a few bottles of wine and stayed up all night,' he told me. 'The place was covered in boxes and I decided, there and then, to just unpack and decorate it all that night. It could have been very overwhelming, looking at all the boxes and thinking, "This is everything I own in the world right now, here in this room by myself" . . . but instead I just started chipping away at it.'

On the same night, he decided to delete any trace of his marriage from Instagram. 'Maybe it was dramatic after I drank all of that wine. It felt weird to have all those pictures there. It was best to get rid of them.'

A note on social media break-up etiquette

On matters of Instagram picture erasure: prevention is better than cure. I am not in the business of telling anyone what to do with their social media profiles. But my experience taught me the value of a varied Insta grid, peppered with your friend Ali eating a giant pickle and that night you met Gemma Collins – as well as the odd selfie with your significant other. Basically, if your entire social media persona is your partner, it will feel even more shitty to deal with, should the unimaginable happen. A varied profile gives you more choice – you don't have to erase giant sections of your life after a break-up. That's my two cents, anyway.

I ask Simon a few times how friends and family felt about the break-up, hoping I'll get a better idea of how he was feeling via his parents' behaviour. No luck. They were 'shocked', he says. He does, however, reveal that his three best friends came to stay for his first weekend alone for support. 'That was really nice,' he says.

About an hour into our conversation, I think I've cracked him. It seems there are specific parts of the break-up that hit hard, and maybe these are the bits that most women usually find relatively easy.

We start talking about going out with friends, living the supposed bachelor life Simon missed out on throughout his coupled-up twenties. It hasn't been as frivolous and exciting as he'd hoped. 'I've felt really out of place on my own, like, around a group of people. I'm used to going to social things with someone I feel super confident around and who I could lean on. It was a bit like a crutch. But now I've lost my social foundation, and being single has felt a little awkward. I've struggled to fit into the world, basically.'

One of the many wonderful things about female friendship is that, wherever you are in the world, you are always in the best company for a good cry. Or a freak-out, or an unhinged rant about how he tried to steal your toaster. Although I often experienced slight identity crises with my single girlfriends, I always gained something from being around them. Perhaps because I was able to wear two hats: party girl Eve who thinks rubbing up against that man will cure her divorce trauma, and sad Eve who really just wants to spend all night talking about her divorce trauma. While none of my girlfriends had been through divorces (although this changed after I moved to New York), their collection of horrific break-ups meant they got it. The same has applied to friends of friends that I didn't know very well. It's as if we're all part of the same secret, miserable club. Perhaps it's more black and white with men; you either have to be on or off.

The millennial favourite writer Dolly Alderton spoke extensively about the nature of male heartbreak while writing her 2024 fiction release, *Good Material* – which tells the story of the aftermath of one man's break-up.

In one interview, with *IMAGE* magazine,[3] Alderton spoke about her reluctance to tar every man with the same brush, and how her interviews with scores of men about heartbreak debunked a lot of the traditional stereotypes we might believe. But one, she said, held true.

'Every single man I spoke to, no matter what their age or background or personality type was, said that in the wake of the break-up, they didn't feel that they had the space to process those feelings with friends. They felt that opening up about their heartbreak would either bore their friends or make them uncomfortable, that their dignity would be compromised, or that they would feel pitied. They felt they had to go through the emotional understanding of events on their own.'

This would certainly speak to my experience of my partner of nine years consulting zero people before he announced he wasn't sure he wanted to be married any longer. Psychologists

tell me this is relatively typical of men, mostly due to two factors. It's a combination of discussing emotions being viewed as
unmasculine and men, on average, having fewer close friends
than women.[4] One 2021 survey found one in five men said
they'd called on a friend for emotional support in the past
week, compared to nearly half of women.[5]

Simon has recently started dating again (he's on the apps
and is not looking for anything serious just yet). With this
part at least, it seems we share a lot of the same neuroses. He
doesn't have the wasting of child-bearing years to worry about
('I'm undecided about kids, but I lean towards no'), but he is
concerned about finding someone new.

'I feel like everyone is hitting the next stage in their life –
getting engaged, getting married – and I've just hit this big
reset button. There's a part of me that worries about my
baggage. I was married so young and that makes me self-
conscious. Will people think I'm weird? Is it a red flag? I am
optimistic that I will find someone one day. I guess I am just
worried about the logistics.'

About three weeks after I moved back to my mum's, my
friend Jack popped over one Sunday afternoon. We somehow
got on to the subject of dating apps, and how the general consensus was that they are full of nutters. I said I'd downloaded
a couple out of interest (distraction from lonely evenings), but
couldn't even fathom the idea of being remotely romantically
interested in anyone for at least a year. 'No offence, Eve,' he
said, 'but I'm not sure anyone would want to get involved with
you right now either.' He was joking. And he didn't trigger a
complex – my brain had been stewing on that one for several
weeks at that point.

A couple of nights later I was swiping before bed (I found it to be an effective insomnia aid) and got a match. He seemed uniquely normal and pretty harmless. I could do one of two things: ignore and forget it by the morning. Or send a message to further the distraction from my shit life (it was Bumble, the app where the woman writes first).

I sent a stupid message and a week later we went on a date. And all I'll say is that my friend Jack could not have been more wrong (but more on this in the final chapter).

Men: just what is their problem?

Research for this book has taken me to many curious places including, as mentioned in Chapter 2, various corners of the social media forum Reddit. The AskMen forum includes a subreddit entitled: 'Men: Why did you break up with your ex-girlfriend or wife?'[6] Some 667 people have joined in the conversation.

The chat is a treasure trove of male absurdities that made me very much regret that this is the species I choose to date. Reasons ranged from comical: 'Because she tried to "nest" too soon/clear out drawer/closet space/leave toothbrush or whatever behind', to the noble: 'I have mental illnesses [and] I wanted her to choose her career/education over me', to the straight to the point: 'because I like my women like I like my coffee . . . without another dude's dick in them'.

There are definite common themes. These include:

◆ Women failing to take culpability for their mistakes: never apologising, always blaming the man for disputes, etc.

- Women suffering mental health problems that prove too challenging for the men to support.
- Women feeling so insecure that they provoke arguments and 'manipulate' their partner.

Another source of information came from a popular podcaster and Instagram star who I discovered on my travels called Preston Smiles. The self-professed 'transformational leader' attracts around four hundred thousand social media followers to his 'motivational' videos that claim to teach young men how to be better at work, life, money, business and relationships. There's also a podcast, *The Preston Smiles Show*,[7] which features episodes such as: 'Babies and Breakups – Relationship Issues After Having a Baby' and, 'Thinking About DIVORCE/BREAKING UP? Listen To This'. According to Smiles, the rationale behind a man's ending of a heterosexual relationship can usually be boiled down to one of three reasons.

First, what he calls 'lack of ownership' – similar to our Reddit friends' problem with too few apologies, which essentially means making the guy feel like he's always in the wrong. Second is what Smiles calls speaking 'globally'. His explanation does very little to outline what exactly he means by this, but I think it's something about making broad, catastrophic and blame-attributing statements about the relationship rather than addressing one event or feeling. You see problems as his character fault, rather than one behaviour you don't like. Finally, men leave if they feel unloved, Smiles says.

I don't know how true any of this is but I'd be lying if I said it didn't resonate at all. In arguments, Ben would often accuse me of failing to recognise my faults; he was always the one who got the blame. That's because he was always the one in the wrong, I'd say. I know there were times I could have been more forgiving, but seething anger does preposterous things to you. But also, maybe he was always wrong because he was wrong for me. I'd often cry out of frustration that he'd fail to see the blindingly obvious reason for my bad mood. I like to think that, thanks to a decade of on-and-off therapy, I'm pretty stellar at communicating my feelings. But more often than not, he just couldn't get it. We'd go round and round until the problem was no longer the problem, it was my raised voice or cold shoulder. It's only now I see that it wasn't that he didn't want to deliver what I was asking of him; he simply couldn't.

Major studies looking at why couples file for divorce offer a duller and perhaps more expected picture. One 2017 analysis of around two thousand men and women, published in the journal *PLoS One*, found no significant gender differences in the common reasons cited for relationship breakdown. 'Growing apart' and 'arguments' were referred to the most – in around 30–40 per cent of cases.[8] The next most cited reason was adultery – interestingly by just 18 per cent of men, compared to a quarter of women. Slightly more women said feeling unappreciated was the clincher, compared to men, which would perhaps contradict point three of Preston Smiles' theory. Some 4 per cent of men said they broke up due to domestic violence, compared to 16 per cent of women.

A 2018 South African study homed in specifically on young couples, aged eighteen to thirty-five, referring to data that suggests twenty-five-to-twenty-nine-year-olds are more than twice as likely to divorce compared to older age groups.[9] Unresolved identity issues came up on top, or 'character problems'. In other words, the person you marry morphs into someone else that you don't like as much. Poor communication and infidelity were also heavily referenced – again, with little difference between men and women. Most interesting to me was the researchers' observations about the unique characteristics of those in this age group: they're not the best communicators.

'I worry about healthy relationships in young people because a lot of their connections are formed online,' says psychotherapist and relationship counsellor Deborah Hill. 'It means they're missing out on a lot of the important challenges at the very beginning that help us really get to know someone and potentially spot red flags.'

For instance, she says, seeing how a potential spouse acts around other people can indicate problems with jealousy. But if the first three months have been virtual, you might be too far in before you find that stuff out.

I spent several months hunting for men who would be honest about their relationships (including their failures) for this book. I had just about every friend's boyfriend and colleagues hunting for my perfect case study that would speak to the male experience. Or at least that of one or two men. It likely says something about the circles I run in, but compared to the hundred-odd women who volunteered, I found just two dudes.

I was particularly grateful for Martin – a thirty-four-year-old journalist and young divorcee who admitted to cheating on both his long-term partners (including his wife) and offered insight as to his reasons for doing it. 'If you're being cold about it, it was about me feeling as though I had unfinished business from being single,' he says. 'I needed validation outside of the relationship. I wanted to be wanted and a quick fix from another woman would do that for me. So I kept doing it.'

He admits that his marriage – which lasted three years, between the ages of twenty-five and twenty-eight – wasn't a union of two people promising their lives to one another, but a couple of love birds who got 'carried away'. 'We changed our relationship status on Facebook to engaged as a sort of joke and then a few hours later I asked her, do you actually want to get married? She said yes, and that was that.'

I'm intrigued by the fundamental role he says social media played in the progression of his relationship – perhaps speeding ahead of its natural course. 'We really, really enjoyed putting everything on Instagram and Facebook. Back then, showing off the milestones in our relationship was a really big thing for us. In some ways, diving into a marriage was an extension of that. I guess we thought it would make us look good.'

Within a couple of months of the engagement, he knew his heart wasn't in it. I ask, on behalf of blindsided women everywhere, why the fuck didn't he tell her? Martin is honest about a problematic characteristic he thinks is held by many men. They don't want to make a fuss. 'I think we just want a simple and quiet life,' he says. 'Once the wedding plans were made, there was this feeling that it was in the schedule and so it had to happen.'

He recognises that the confrontational skills it would take

to call off the wedding were not in his 'arsenal' at the time. 'As horrible as it sounds, the only option I had was to make our lives miserable by cheating and hope that she'd get sick of me and end it herself.' Ultimately, that's what happened.

After a make-or-break holiday in Croatia failed to magically fix their catalogue of issues (as well as broken trust from multiple affairs by both parties, a four-year age gap meant a defining difference in stage of life), the couple decided to call it quits. 'We were exhausted by the cycle of our relationship and both said we didn't want to keep it going any longer.'

Luckily, Martin and his wife shared a rental flat and, apart from a few hundred pounds in credit card debt, not much else. It meant he could move out – and back in with his parents down the road – pretty seamlessly. 'There was no great zeal on either of our parts because we both knew that we'd tried to make it work for so long.'

They kept in touch for another two years after the split and even slept together once again. 'I stayed with her for a few nights when I first moved to London,' he says. 'I think it goes to show that, when it comes to someone you've shared parts of your life with, there is always going to be a connection that you never quite lose. You're always going to have history.'

There was some back-and-forth texting at the height of the Covid pandemic, but communication died a death when Martin's ex met someone else in the summer of 2020.

Divorced at thirty and back into the wild, living alone in London: how did it feel?

It's fair to say that the men I've heard from are less affected by young divorcee anxiety, compared to women. In general, Martin felt 'okay' about existing in the world as a thirty-year-old divorcee. 'I didn't feel like I'd lost that much time,' he says. 'I felt as though I'd learned a fair bit about myself – it was a good training ground for the future.' Martin accepts his privilege. 'I'm a bloke, so obviously I don't have the pressure of a time limit that a woman my age might be thinking about. It's very easy for me to get back into the swing of things.'

That said, at first, dating came with some anxiety. 'I was worried that I'd never find a connection that was as strong as the one I had with my ex-wife. I went on a lot of dates and met a lot of people in the period afterwards – cracking people, really funny, but none that I liked as much as I liked my ex. There was a bit of a thing in the back of my mind where I thought, have I massively screwed up something that was really good and special?'

Within a year Martin had met Ellie, a student seven years his junior who he 'barely ever' argued with. At the time, he thought their calm waters were blissful. But it wasn't enough to stop him cheating. 'It was different from the last time, be-cause I didn't want her to find out, because I knew it would break her. I wasn't doing it to get out of the relationship; I was doing it because I wanted validation.' Roughly a year in, the couple agreed to open up their relationship so they each could see other people. 'At that point our sex life had virtually fallen off a cliff,' he says, explaining that Ellie developed illnesses that caused dramatic changes to her body, destroying her libido. 'She said it wasn't fair that I couldn't have sex because she didn't want to, so we agreed to open up the relationship.'

But after two years of dating – and over a year of living together – Martin called it off. He wanted to be single again.

For Ellie, the news came totally out of the blue. I tell him this is the golden chalice I've been looking for: inside the mind of the blindsider. He says he did it for a few reasons. Firstly, their silent agreement to ban any kind of confrontation. 'We didn't really talk about things we weren't happy with in the relationship, we just sort of kept going,' he says. He was also reluctant to throw in the towel in case 'this really is as good as it gets'. 'Very selfishly, I thought, what if I don't find anybody as good as this? So I kept it going to see what happened. It was the only plan I had for a while.'

Martin says it was ultimately a fear of confrontation and upset that led him to keep schtum, before finally exploding when he couldn't pretend any longer. 'As men, we generally want a quiet life for everyone involved, with no complaints and no issues. But that attitude typically ends up causing far more hurt in the long run. We want to try and please everybody, but this usually results in the opposite happening. Because obviously telling someone you want out when they don't expect it will cause a lot of hurt too.'

Martin says he's getting better at sharing his honest feelings. 'A big part of growth for me has been learning how to share in a relationship and raise concerns much earlier.' I suggest that perhaps his communication problem stems from poor modelling from the men in his life, and maybe the male friendship thing of conversations that don't venture too far from the sphere of new-season football shirts and taxation policies (admittedly a generalisation, but one informed by conversations about conversations with a handful of millennial men).

'My dad and my grandad on my mum's side were the two biggest male influences in my life growing up and they are great, great men,' Martin says. 'Their vibe is very much, you work hard and you provide for your family, you get stuck in and do the jobs that need doing. Very practical and pragmatic in terms of their advice. But I don't think I've ever had a conversation about any one of my relationships with my dad and, to be honest with you, I don't think I would want to. It would be cringe for us both. I guess it shouldn't be that way and I would like to do better with any son that I might have in the future.'

Martin then offers some fascinating insight into the mysterious dynamics of male friendship groups. Last week, he tells me, he went for dinner with two friends – one of whom, of his own accord, broached the topic of sex. Specifically, how often you should be having it. Having been with his partner for seven years, he was concerned that intimacy had lost its spice – and that it wasn't happening often enough. The other friend, who, on paper, appears to 'have his shit together' – high-paying job, married with a kid, typically macho – gave his two cents, commenting that once a week is 'probably okay'. 'And suddenly, the way my other friend spoke about the issue completely changed. He just nodded and said, "Oh well, if you think that's okay then that's fine," and we moved on to a different subject. That was as far as it went. We spent the rest of the night speaking about immigration policy.'

The main barrier to deep and personal conversations between some men is competition, Martin says. Concerns about perception of their manliness act as a blockade against emotional vulnerability. In the last year, Martin has had a taste of another life experience. He has taken on a stepfather role, having entered a relationship with a mother to a toddler.

It must have been unnerving at first, particularly for some-one who said they were never sure they even wanted children. 'Actually, of all the things that could give you grief in a re-lationship, this one has been pretty insignificant,' he says. If anything, it's brought him extra joy that has 'broadened' the enrichment you get from falling in love with someone.

'I saw it as something a bit unusual rather than a compli-cation,' he says. 'It's been a really informative and interesting way of getting to know somebody.' I tell him his enthusiasm for step-parenting will no doubt be welcome news to single parents who've convinced themselves a loving relationship is no longer possible.

'Most people, unless they are psychopathic, are just look-ing for someone they really, really like. I don't think there's a checklist of things a person needs to have – like kids or no kids. I'm in a relationship with my girlfriend because she's a fantastic, world-class person who is brilliant to be with. Everything else is sort of by the by.'

Who knows if this partnership will be the one that ends Martin's days of infidelity? As I've learned over the past two years, everyone has the capacity to change – for better or worse. But as our phone call ends, I can't help but feel hope-ful for us unfortunate women who have a habit of falling in love with men.

Chapter 10

The Woman Who Walked Out

I left Ben about five times over the course of our nine-year relationship. And by left, I mean escaped to my mother's house,
cried into cups of tea and eventually trudged back to him
after a night or two, having missed him too much to bear. The
comfort of my return was overpowering, causing any residual
anger to immediately evaporate. We'd hug, apologise, order
a curry and pretty much carry on as normal. The first time it
happened was on the day we moved in together.

It was the first time I'd left home since coming back from
university two years earlier, while Ben was no stranger to
roaming about – having moved out aged fifteen for board-
ing school and then to Liverpool for university, followed by
London.

We'd dreamt of our first place together for the best part of
a year. Our plans for an ex-council red brick with floor-to-
ceiling bookshelves had been shelved while I recovered from
anorexia both in and out of hospital. The minute I got a semi-
stable job, we booked in a handful of viewings. We went with
the second: a hideously inconvenient one-bedroom box on the

fourth floor of a converted Victorian house, with no space for a wardrobe or kitchen table – and in a part of London where we had no mates. Still, it was five minutes from the Tube station and the taps looked shiny. We were twenty-four.

Moving day was unexpectedly stressful. While I packed my life (clothes) into my Fiat 500 – and by this, I mean, left the bigger half of my worldly belongings all over the floor of my childhood bedroom – Ben hired a man with a van he found on Facebook to cart the furniture he'd accrued halfway across London.

When we pulled up at the new place, I was hopping around like a kid on blue M&Ms, running to Ben with an armful of knickers to kiss his face in celebration of our enmeshment.

He didn't seem so thrilled. His moving in 'help' wasn't helpful at all, leaving most of the heavy belongings at the entrance of the building for us (me, Ben and my sixty-year-old mother) to lug up four flights of stairs. The mattress was left on the pavement, balancing against the front gate, making it an easy target for our upstairs neighbour's English bulldog, who promptly pissed all over it. Mum and I were in the way. An annoyance and a burden, in Ben's eyes. My attempts to lug boxes of his records up the stairs were met with irritation. 'Just give it to me,' he said. I couldn't tell if he was annoyed I was walking too slowly, or if his anger was in fact a mask for guilt that I was doing what he saw as his job.

Either way, it was painful. Somewhere between the piss-covered mattress and the box with the Nespresso machine ('BE CAREFUL!'), Ben snapped at my mum. Admittedly, she has a tendency to stand in doorways, but she darts out and apologises profusely the minute you point it out. Plus, I could see she felt like a spare part, reminded that days like this would be far easier if my dad were still around.

I can't remember what he said to her exactly. But it wasn't kind. She was suddenly like a terrified cat sidestepping a fire. 'Sorry, sorry, I'll get out of your way,' she babbled.

I looked at his furious red face and froze. This was the man I wanted to live with? I told him I was driving Mum home and ran to the car as fast as I could, Mum following behind.

I cried for the duration of the drive. And when we got to Mum's, I told her I wasn't going back. I'd pay the first month's rent and then I'd suggest we call the landlady and tell her we'd broken up and she'd have to find other tenants. I'd go back when he was out, to get all my things and bring them back to Mum's.

It took about an hour before I realised I was being dramatic. It had been a particularly stressful day and I probably could have carried a few more of the heavier boxes rather than admiring my new towel sets and arranging condiments in the kitchen cupboards. Plus, I knew Ben. He was the type of man who'd run across a road to stroke a dog and walk five miles across London to get me the macarons I liked. He'd do anything for the people he loved. He was not a hot-head. I went back to the flat a few hours later, he apologised, and we cuddled on one corner of the pissy mattress while he told me of storage hacks that would ensure all my clothes were housed where I could see them.

The next time was more significant. About eighteen months after we moved in, I started a new venture arranging supper clubs for people with eating disorders. Having built a social media community to support others in recovery, I'd come to feel relatively useless – the need for some sort of effective service was mounting as access to medical treatment became more and more scarce. The only thing I could think of was to set a good example by cooking dinner for people who were struggling, and eating it with them. It really worked. And I loved it.

Ben was happy to help for the first two – although I'd never asked him – but by the third, he'd had enough. And the following day, he made his grievances known: I'd neglected him, I was working myself into the ground, he was never the priority. Halfway through the blazing row he revealed he'd taken to smoking out the window every night and hiding the smell with air freshener for the last six months. My dad had died of cancer that had spread to his lungs. Ben knew how much I hated smoking and, as far as I knew, he'd long given up.

The smoking I could deal with. But why had he lied? Through hysterical tears, I told him he'd ruined everything, packed a bag and went to my mum's. I stayed for just over a week, and was pretty sure that this was it. We were over. Ben's explosion had laid bare the gulf between our characters. My professional endeavours would always be crucial to my identity, and there might well be times when work was the priority. I knew Ben didn't quite get this. We were also on different pages with our coping strategies. I internalised my anxieties and distracted myself with passion projects and brunches with pals. I also had a small army of women to dump on and to shower me with love and acceptance every minute of the day. Ben wore his moods on his sleeve. And with his extremely small social circle lacking a sensible person to confide in, I was his only support. It meant when the outpourings of anger and frustration came, I got soaked.

I'm not saying either of us won in the game of how best to handle your emotions. Our approaches were just different.

Five years later, and on the day after the initial 'I want a divorce day', my best friend said: 'You should have broken up after the secret smoking thing. At least, we were all hoping that you would.' Apparently, they had also had concerns about our polarising approaches to work. I don't know why I decided to go back to the flat and the relationship a week later. It was probably a lot to do with a dearth of faith in my ability to cope as a single woman. But also, in the words of *Sex and the City*'s Steve Brady: there was 'good stuff' there. I wasn't ready to pack it in.

Sometimes, on particularly sad weeks, I lay awake wishing I'd ended it for good that day. I'd have had the hottest part of my twenties to fuck about and spend my savings on girls' trips to Greece and handbags from TK Maxx. Instead, I emerged from our dead relationship as a thirty-one-year-old who hadn't been single in a decade, while the women around me welcomed new baby bumps. The dregs of my fertility were edging dangerously close, and instead of retreating to my own place, I'd been forced to move back in with my mum. If I had time to win back my independence and, after a couple of years, inevitably met the one, I'd be roughly in line with everyone else. But then the sun rose and I laughed, thinking, if only life actually worked like that.

Just about every available dataset will tell you that women are a lot more likely to ask for divorce than men. The latest statistics from the US and UK show that, in roughly 60–70 per cent of cases, it's the woman who files for divorce.[1] The most recent UK data shows that, while roughly twenty-seven thousand divorces every year are granted to men, around forty-nine thousand are for women.[2] A plethora of online commentary attempts to explain this, suggesting women get pissed off with doing the lion's share of childcare, or rush into bad marriages so they can get pregnant before time runs out.

Actually, I've come to learn that this is kind of bullshit. Divorce lawyers and relationship counsellors I've spoken to over the past year have told me the same thing. It is not the case that women are more likely to want out than men. The truth is, men often light the match, but they don't quite get round to sorting out the necessary paperwork – or perhaps, in the interest of clinging on to stability, they avoid it. Eventually, women get fed up and think, F this, I'm filing for divorce.

Harry Benson, research director for Marriage Foundation UK and researcher in marriage and union dissolution at the University of Bristol, says that 'disrespectful' and 'indifferent' men are often the reason a woman will file for divorce. In a recent blog post about the intriguing trend of falling women-led divorces in straight couples, Benson theorises a pattern of behaviour among men who married in the '70s, '80s and '90s, who were victims of societal pressure to make relationships 'official'.[3] He writes:

> Over time, and perhaps with the arrival of a baby, inevitable little conflicts emerge between him and his wife. Instead of dealing with them responsibly, he feels less constrained in the way he behaves because he knows he never really bought into a long-term plan in the first place. But just as he was sucked into

marriage without making the decision for himself, inertia and indecision keep him in the marriage. Quite
soon his behaviour appears increasingly indifferent
and disrespectful to his wife.

Benson goes on to note that it only took a few years before
wives became aware of their partners' indifference towards
them, and, unhappy with tiptoeing around their relationships, they ended them.

Admittedly this is a wholly generalised view of a complex
and often nuanced phenomenon. But it is the story that's
echoed by divorce lawyers as an explanation for male affairs
and other destructive behaviours. Interestingly, Benson
says marriages that took place after the millennium are less
likely to fall victim to this dynamic, as men were 'under no
such family or social pressure' and committed because they
wanted to do so. My wedding was twenty-four years after
the new millennium. Perhaps I just got really, really unlucky.

But there are a significant minority of couples that buck
this trend. What happens when it's the woman who develops
'disrespectful' and 'indifferent' tendencies, before eventually
deciding she wants out?

I met Rebecca about six months after my break-up, when
she approached me after hearing about my experience. Since
her own break-up a decade ago, she'd established herself as a
divorce coach, helping the heartbroken in her north London
community to avoid getting financially screwed. We bonded
over our partners' sudden metamorphoses into cold, tight aliens.

Unlike in my case, much of Rebecca's husband's unpleasant
moves post break-up were a form of revenge. He was pissed

off that, after seven years of marriage and three children –
then six, three and two – she'd asked for a divorce.

'I was really, really scared. I'd tried to confide in my parents about feeling unhappy but it always ended in feeling
pressured to stick it out for the kids. It just led to this feeling
that when I did leave, I wouldn't cope. And to top it all off I'd
probably ruin my kids' lives too. But the alternative, staying
in the marriage, was more unbearable.'

Once the couple had separated, bailiffs knocking at the door
before the school run was a regular occurrence for Rebecca.
She borrowed whatever she could to pay the mortgage: payday
loans, credit cards, friends' savings. Notably, it took her husband eighteen months before he paid any child support. It
took him just a week, however, to announce he planned to
fight her for the house that her parents helped pay for.

'He made a spreadsheet of everything that was in the house
and how much it cost and what I had to pay him for it. I remember reading it and responding, fine, with pleasure, take
what you want. I just wanted him gone.'

Rebecca met her husband when they were sixteen through
a mutual friend she met at a youth group gathering. He lived
in Manchester – two hundred miles from her north London
home – not that it phased her; she spent pretty much every
weekend of her adolescence traipsing back and forth on seven-
hour coaches to see him. Now, twenty years later, she sees the
relationship for what it was.

'He wasn't particularly good-looking or even particularly
nice to me. We weren't even friends. But we got on and, in
my child brain, I knew I could get him. He was attainable.

'I was a chubby teenager who was achingly insecure and

always craving attention. I cleared out the loft the other day and found the cards I sent to him from around that time, and it made me so angry. There were about sixty, and only three from him. Reading them made me cry. I'd write things like, I love you so much, I think you're amazing, but then I'd couch it by writing, I know you think I'm so cringe, or, you think I'm crazy, because that's what he would say to me. I was just this sweet, innocent girl who desperately wanted to feel loved.'

At nineteen they decided to get married. He would move down from Manchester and into a new marital home that Rebecca's parents helped the couple buy. She didn't have a good relationship with her parents and was 'desperate' to move out of home. She and her husband had their first child within eighteen months; a symptom of Rebecca's intent on keeping up with the women around her, who all seemed to be having babies in their early twenties.

Was she in love with him? 'Yes, I guess. But I was a baby. Like a real, actual baby. People always tell themselves they were always unhappy, but of course that's not true. There must have been happy times.'

But, for the most part, she felt overlooked and unloved for the majority of their relationship. 'He made me feel unattractive and unwanted, which just made me crave attention even more from elsewhere. But he always wanted to have sex, even when he wasn't speaking to me. Intimacy wasn't ever about us connecting, it was about him getting what he wanted.'

There were plenty of occasions when he decided not to speak to her. 'When he was upset, he'd just go cold and stop talking to me for like, two weeks at a time. I mean, literally not say a word. I'd go and sleep on the sofa for weeks because

I couldn't stand him ignoring me, and he wouldn't even react. It killed me.'

She said he didn't 'really know me', not even in the way a colleague you're friendly with would.

'He couldn't even tell you what I'd like to order from a restaurant, or what snack I choose, or what music I like, or films I watch. I could tell you everything there was to know about him, but he couldn't do the same for me. The truth is he wasn't interested.'

Rebecca admits she wasn't easy. At twenty-two, she had no idea what to expect of her husband, so assumed she could ask for pretty much anything.

'I told him I expected us to go on a big family holiday at least once a year, which he had to pay for [Rebecca gave up her job in a nursery after her first child was born], and I wouldn't take no for an answer. I nagged him endlessly about studying for his accountancy qualifications, telling him he wasn't working enough in the evenings.

'I had absolutely zero clue about financial hardships and commitments. I didn't know what it took to pay the bills and all of that stuff. But what I would say is that I was a real trier. I wanted to learn, I always wanted to improve.'

Something happened between her first two children that she now recognises as the event that destroyed any faith she had in her husband's capacity to have her back. Rebecca gave birth to a stillborn baby in a toilet cubicle within the hospital.

'As soon as I came out of the toilet, my sister-in-law rushed over to comfort me, while he just stood there, looking gormless, and couldn't talk to me about it.' She got pregnant again a few months later and was 'terrified' for the duration of the pregnancy in case it happened again. She wouldn't leave the house for weeks on end.

'He was completely emotionally unavailable,' she says. Thankfully, she had a healthy baby and, fourteen months later, another.

'I'd convinced myself that I couldn't get pregnant again or that we'd miscarry because it had happened a few times before,' she says. 'So I decided to use this sperm-killing lube thing instead of birth control which, lo and behold, didn't work.'

The children made her stick around. 'He was, and still is, a brilliant father, very hands on and great with them. I think it made me think I was lucky and should feel grateful, like ultimately my children are the most important thing.'

One summer, a friend and her two children had come to visit from Hong Kong, and the families went out for lunch.

'We were walking back to the car and my husband and I were in a huge fight, screaming at each other,' she says. 'I looked over at my friends' kids' faces and saw they were totally horrified, scared even.

'Then I looked at my kids and noticed they didn't even flinch. They were walking along happily as if nothing was happening. That's how accustomed to our bullshit they were. And I thought, wow, this is really fucking up our children.'

After much persuasion, Rebecca eventually got her husband to agree to separate for a short period, on the assumption they'd eventually come back together for the kids.

She went to her mother for advice, who insisted she do whatever it took to make it work, telling her, 'You think you're unhappy? Darling, no one is happy.'

'That's just what she's told herself all her life to get through the miserable relationship she has with my dad,' she says.

After a couple of weeks, Rebecca moved back into the family home. This dance continued for the best part of a year.

'There was a lot of pressure from families around us and our friends and even the wider community to be together for the kids. Everyone saw how great he was with them, but no one saw how he treated me.'

One night, after the second separation ended in a reluctant reunion, Rebecca lay on the sofa alone with one thought wafting through her mind:

'You're allowed to leave. It's okay.'

She waited until the following morning to tell him this was it. It was officially over. For good.

She was surprised by his surprise. 'I don't really get why. It's not like I was silent.' He insisted on going ahead with plans they had to attend a friend's party that evening. 'He got really drunk and told loads of people that we were divorcing, but it was his decision, he had called it. If I'd only listened to my gut and hadn't kept going back to him, it wouldn't have been so messy.' He moved out six months later, cancelling all the bills and other financial commitments that kept their shared life afloat. Rebecca was suddenly alone with three children aged twenty-seven, and not a clue how to stand on her own two feet.

It was the life admin stuff that frightened her, rather than being single for the first time ever.

'I was really, really scared. I didn't know how I would cope. And I guess I didn't.'

Within six weeks, she'd got a job working part-time in events for a local charity, which she could do between school runs. Still, 'There were days when the kids would have just left to go to school, and the bailiffs would show up to collect council tax that I hadn't paid for months. I'd be so terrified I'd collapse into a ball on the floor and just sit there crying.'

And then things got worse. Her ex came after half of everything she had, including the house. He refused to return half of the £30,000 her parents had loaned them for a house deposit a few years earlier.

Unlike my situation, this didn't come as a surprise to Rebecca.

'He'd always been tight with money and kept spreadsheets of everything that we'd ever spent.

'When we were married, he'd call me at work and say things like, I've been looking at these bills, what did you spend fifty quid on in the deli last Monday? And I'd say, oh, I don't know, fucking cocaine?!'

It took a four-hour mediation session, in which her ex battled for her parents' money, for Rebecca to give up fighting.

He could have half the sale proceeds of the house, including the deposit money from her parents, but she got to hang on to it until the kids turned eighteen.

'I thought, fuck this shit. I don't want to be sitting in a room with this man for hours. It's just money.'

A note on letting go

I never even wanted a pizza oven. The £300 outdoor cooking device was one of about five items that Ben added to our wedding registry. He promised he'd be the one to operate it, clean it up and host pizza parties for all our (my) friends.

And there it was, eight months later, sandwiched between

the new cutlery set and the Japanese knives on the list of our shared belongings soon to be carved down the middle. Ben instructed me to put my initials beside the items I wanted; he'd already chosen his. Including the pizza oven.

My immediate thought was, who cares? Seeing as I now had no chic patio dining space on which to feed my loved ones artisanal pizza, I had little use for culinary gadgets. But then I remembered who'd bought it.

It was a gift from my mum's best friend of fifty years, our honourable auntie and regular attendee of the Simmons' birthdays, bar mitzvahs and funerals. I knew money didn't come easy for her.

When I saw she'd pledged the pizza oven, I was wracked with guilt. I suggested to Mum we told her we didn't want it any more to nudge her towards buying us something cheaper. Mum told me I should accept it with love; she wanted us to have it.

Except now he had it. The man who promised for ever but actually delivered just shy of two seasons.

Over a period of a few months, I grew furious about the fucking pizza oven. I spent evenings trawling through the back catalogue of our shared belongings to come up with a reasonable trade, until I reached the conclusion that this wasn't a bargaining situation. Why should I have to give up anything for this break-up that I didn't even want?

The next evening I stayed at our house while he was away visiting his parents. I'd been out with some old colleagues after work and had sunk somewhere between three and four glasses of Prosecco. As I closed the front door behind me, I felt the fury leach out of my body like expandable foam. I was seething.

I caught my reflection in the mirror in the hall and noticed I'd put my cardigan on inside out. You're drunk, Eve, I thought, have something to eat. What had I stuck in the freezer a month earlier? All I could picture was the remnants of our wedding cake that we had been saving for the one-year anniversary we never quite got to. And maybe a packet of pitta bread.

I grabbed a pitta and went to place it in the toaster on the counter to the immediate left of the freezer. The frozen bread slammed on the granite countertop. He'd taken the toaster.

It had definitely been on my list. A fancy toaster brand had sent it to me for a feature we'd been running on efficient household appliances a few years back, when I helped out with the lifestyle section. My boss had suggested I take it home – he got the expensive hoover. My rage was suddenly revived and I found myself ferociously opening and slamming every cupboard door as if it were the part in the movie where the wife discovers her wayward husband has reignited his smack habit.

I was a woman possessed, ripping open every cardboard box with his name on it (he was irritatingly good at packing) and launching his various cables around the room. I rifled through every drawer in his desk, occasionally stealing packets of gum and Post-it notes (that'd show him), as if my toaster had somehow squeezed itself into a pencil case.

I stood back from my cardboard apocalypse and realised I'd gone mental. As I resealed the boxes, I thought about how relatively fortunate I was to have an ex-husband who was packed and ready to go. The priority was to get this man out of my life pronto. With or without my toaster. The toaster was just stuff.

Once I'd had this epiphany, the rest of the break-up was a lot easier. Not easy. But easier. Sure, I lost that art deco vase that was the perfect height for supermarket bunches, and the Japanese knife I'd bought for Ben's birthday that had cost me £200, but it was a small price to pay for peace.

In divorce, you must consider the long-term benefit and cost of each mini battle. If giving up the fight will allow you to get to your next chapter quicker, and with less distracting anger, perhaps it's worth doing. Unless you really, really like toast.

So what did Rebecca do next? Well, she worked, mostly. 'Really, really fucking hard at about a million different jobs for about four years,' she says. 'It helped, but it wasn't enough to get rid of all my debt. I was managing to just about keep on top of it.'

When Covid hit in 2020, and the family were confined to the house, she saw it as an opportunity to save like she never had done before. 'I was like, fuck it, I am going to pay off every single debt by the end of this year,' she said. 'And I did it. Every single penny. Every payday loan, every credit card.'

Now, she's in a much better financial place. 'I am still kind of living hand to mouth, but at least I am dealing with my finances, without racking up loads of debt.'

A couple of years back she saved up enough to buy two brand-new sofas for the first time ever. 'It was a huge moment for me,' she says. 'I sat down on them and felt so proud of myself. I thought, I fucking paid for these outright. I did it, no one else.'

Today, some ten years after their split, she and her

ex-husband have landed on a relatively fair custody arrangement: she has them during the week, and they go to him three weekends out of the month.

'He is very territorial over his time,' she says. 'Like, if my daughter wants me to take her to swimming class on Sunday morning, he'll be difficult about it – not only with me but with her, too. Whereas I am happy with whatever they want to do. I don't own my children's time.'

The idea of finding yourself divorced with three kids at twenty-seven might sound like the definition of hell for many women who don't have buckets of cash to cushion them from disaster.

But Rebecca says it made her feel 'like Teflon'.

'When it's all over, you feel fucking invincible. I remember there was one point where it was literally like being hit in the face with a brick wall over and over again, and each time having to get up and try again. And this was true despite the fact I was the one who made the decision.'

But with the living nightmare came 'liberation' from the hopes and dreams that she says, in hindsight, had kept her trapped. 'We all buy into the fallacy of what a future "should" look like – two parents, two children, laughter at the dinner table – but it's bullshit. Even if you're in a solid relationship you truly have no idea what is going to happen. And bursting that bubble for me has been massively liberating. It forces you to think that whatever situation you're in might not be for ever, and that's okay. Instead, I am much more focused on what things look like today, at this moment. I enjoy what it is right now because who knows what's going to come tomorrow.'

It just so happens that Rebecca's today looks pretty close to what many of us are looking for. She is a mother to three healthy, beautiful young women, with whom she is uniquely close – and who know never to settle for less than happiness.

She has an army of new friends with similar experiences, who she's collected in the last decade.

At the time of writing, she is celebrating her one-month wedding anniversary.

Five years ago, she fell in love – and decided to do it all again. Slightly differently this time, of course.

His name is Jack and they met through friends. He is also divorced and has two children, similar in age to Rebecca's three.

'At first it was really bad. He was fresh out of his divorce and I found that difficult. Every time she was on his mind I felt like I was sharing him with her, and that caused a lot of fights.' He was hurt by her subconscious need to hammer home the fact she 'didn't need' him. Over and over again. 'I'd say, I am choosing to have you in my life. I don't need you. I was so bruised by a person who made me feel like I couldn't exist without him, I overcompensated. But he was very patient with me and spent a long time knocking down that barrier.'

She describes her new husband as a 'lover lover'. 'He is so full of love and good feeling, it has made me softer,' she says. 'He tells me he can't always get everything right, but he promises he'll never stop trying to do better. And I think that's all you can ask of someone.'

Rebecca's youngest daughter celebrated her twelfth birth-day last year with a party for all the family. 'I do this thing where I invite everyone: my ex's new wife, his sister, the sister's family, his mother, Jack's mum and his siblings. I stood back and watched everyone dancing together and thought, look at the love I have brought into my children's lives. Everyone told me divorce would destroy them. I laughed and thought, what bullshit.'

Rebecca has recently taken up cold-water swimming. 'Every time I get in the water, I think what the fuck am I doing – I can't do this. But then I think, of course I fucking can. I can do anything, I just have to put my mind to it. And divorce, if you think about it, is no different.'

I met Natalie Thompson on Twitter last year. She responded to my call-out for women who'd left their husbands at a relatively young age, and felt comfortable to speak openly about it.

She was infectiously enthusiastic – contacting me to arrange a time to speak within minutes of connecting, with words of her excitement and thanks for my interest. Now thirty-seven, she's been divorced for a decade, having rushed into marriage for religious reasons. I assumed her story would be much the same as Rebecca's – married young due to cultural pressures, only to realise they weren't at all suited.

But about halfway through our conversation it became clear that Natalie's ex wasn't just the wrong fit. He was patently abusive. I was unsure if Natalie was completely aware of the severity of the situation she had found herself in, and I was conscious of sounding patronising, or picking at a scab that needed to be left alone.

Either way, I was struck by how easy it could be to

sleepwalk into a poisonous environment, and get stuck, simply for fear of your life alone. She did get out eventually and, in what proved to be a monumental feat, is now living her absolute best ever life as a freelance photographer in north London, living in her own flat, relying on nothing else but her own power and tenacity. By the end of the phone call I was teary, amazed by the superhuman resilience possessed by some women – and their ability to achieve utmost happiness despite a history of horrors. If Natalie was all right, then I would be too.

Natalie's story begins aged twenty-three, shortly after she finished her law degree, and just before she started law school, where she planned to train to become a barrister. She describes a 'premature identity crisis' which, for reasons she now doesn't quite understand, led her to become involved with her local church.

'I became like a sort of a devout born-again Christian, which was odd as my family weren't religious at all,' she says. 'And that sort of separated me from everyone in my life.' She met her ex-husband in church. He was nine years older and worked as an art director (although times spent actually earning were 'few and far between').

They dated for a year before he proposed. 'I thought he a genuine, decent human being. Looking back now I guess probably that was because he was religious, which I deemed a mark of decency. I saw getting married as the next step and honourable thing to do. But it was my first proper relationship so I didn't know any better. I didn't grow up with my dad around so I wanted to have a family and be stable. I was very young and thought, why not?'

The veil lifted when Natalie had to move in with her husband's family, as they couldn't afford a place of their own.

'I'm from north-east London and their house was in Surrey, so I was forced to move away from my family and friends. I ended up never seeing them because he'd refuse to come with me to family gatherings. And when I did go and see them I couldn't be honest and say he didn't want to be there, because I felt ashamed, so I made up things to protect him. That was a constant battle.'

He didn't insist she pause her legal training. But he didn't encourage her either. 'I didn't have any money to go and do my training at the time, so it was very much a case of: no, you work for me, you'll help me do what I do. He didn't pay me enough for me to finish my training, and it also meant I was completely financially dependent on him.'

And then, a few months after the wedding, her laptop broke and he refused to help her buy a new one. He also refused to fund her phone contract, forcing her to switch to a pay-as-you-go plan, which made her reliant on his cash to speak with friends and family.

'I remember trying to log on to my Facebook on his laptop once, and he'd changed the password.'

Natalie's days became 'very depressing'.

'I felt compelled to pay my way because I wasn't contributing financially. So I'd go and walk around my local park for hours and then I'd feel I had to come home and cook and clean. He'd tell me I should be "monitoring" stuff like that.'

Natalie was given cash as and when she needed it. 'Say, if I had to do a food shop or something, I'd ask for money that morning. But I couldn't buy things that I personally wanted to eat like, say, a particular packet of biscuits. I had to get food for everyone in the house.' This arrangement, she said, meant that she started to lose weight. 'I was eating, like, bare minimum. I didn't want to keep justifying the cash that I needed, so I just went without.'

His behaviour grew increasingly controlling. 'I couldn't go to friends' birthdays – even if they were female, he'd say, well, men might be there. He didn't like me going on social media in case I was "talking to people I shouldn't be talking to". I was just like, you're crazy.'

Natalie recalls pacing the circumference of her local park, rehearsing her 'I'm not happy' speech in her head, for most of the second year of marriage. 'I'd be thinking, if I say it like this, he'll say this, or if I say it differently he'll respond like this. But in the end I didn't say anything.'

He'd often 'use God' against her; suggesting he'd blessed her with the sanctity that is marriage, and she'd better not fuck it up. 'I'd convinced myself that the situation must be a sign that I'm a really bad person and God is punishing me. Marriage felt like one of the pillars of Christianity and so, if I wanted to be a good Christian, I had to make it work.' Here is a line of thinking that is blatantly mentally destructive.

Within a year, she was suicidal. 'The way I saw it, the only way out was either a divorce, or die. I used to think about how I'd do it, planning the details. I'd have this vision of myself lying on the floor, motionless. Sometimes I'd walk the streets of Brixton late at night and hope someone would pick me up and hurt me so I didn't have to do it myself.'

After one particularly bleak day, she decided to give her

husband an insight into the black hole in her head. 'I said, I've got to tell you something really serious, I'm really struggling. All he asked was whether I'd cut myself – and he checked for cut marks – and when he didn't see anything, he didn't take it seriously.'

With contact with those who knew her well vastly limited, Natalie looked to her only nearby beacon of morality: the church. The first time she asked for advice – from an older woman and big dog in the congregation – her husband found out, and insisted they move to a different church.

'He was like, why are you talking to other people about my business? I just thought, what else am I supposed to do to improve this situation?'

She entrusted a new pastor, who told her, 'Whatever you do, don't get divorced.'

'It became very clear to me that I was stuck,' she says.

'I thought, right, what's holding me back from breaking free from this situation? He'd told me whoever makes the money makes the decisions, so I thought, fine, I'll get a job. I got three – doing just about everything, and eventually made enough to put a deposit on a flat to rent. I guess it was naive, but in my mind, I thought if we had our own space, the relationship might get better.'

A few days after moving in, Natalie's in-laws came over to inspect the place while she popped out to visit her mother on the other side of London.

'The one thing I said before I left the flat was, please don't move my stuff. I'd been collecting lovely crockery and cutlery and everything, which I loved because I hadn't had the chance to do it when I was living with his family,' she said.

She came back to find her belongings dotted around the place, as if a judgemental inspection had taken place.

'It was a last straw type of thing,' she says. 'When they finally left, I picked up this box of old mugs on the counter and just started throwing them on the floor, one by one. It was as if everything over the last two years had built up to this point. It was my outlet.'

Natalie's ex flinched when a ceramic shard rolled towards his direction. He started shouting, accusing her of a physical attack. Furious, he grabbed a wooden dining chair and threw it at her. The abuse had now become physical.

A note on coercive control

Over the last twenty years, regions across the globe have gradually criminalised psychological and emotional abuse by romantic partners, which is often referred to as 'coercive control'.

According to the European Institute for Gender Inequality, a staggering 44 per cent of women have experienced some form of psychological abuse at the hands of a partner over the course of a lifetime.[4] The figures for men are less clear, but some studies suggest that around five per cent of coercive control victims are male.

Most recently, Queensland, Australia and several US states like New Jersey, Vermont and Massachusetts have acted to make behaviour that is threatening, intimidating, controlling or compelling compliance in a household member illegal. France was the first, in 2010, while the United Kingdom followed in 2015. But only a handful of US states have so far enshrined punishment for this particularly pernicious type of abuse in law, and according to the European Institute for Gender Inequality, it has only been criminalised to a 'limited extent' in all EU member states.[5] For instance, some states outlaw a small and specific number of behaviours, while others exclude abuse committed online or against someone who isn't their intimate partner. Basically, we've still got a long way to go.

Natalie tells me the chair-throwing incident was just one of many similar acts of aggression that she'd rather not go into. Sex with her ex-husband, for example, she describes as, 'horrific'.

'I was so desperate and scared and I didn't have anyone to speak to.' Then she thought of the wife of her husband's friend, who had always been kind to her and told her to come to her with any problems she had. 'I reached out to her and told her, I need to speak to you, and she invited me over to their house. I explained the whole scenario to them, including that I was feeling suicidal, and they were so kind to me, but said that I should do what I can to make the marriage work.'

The couple offered to support her through a trial separation, and followed Natalie back to the flat so she could pick up her belongings and move in with her mum for a while.

'It was the first time someone outside of the relationship had witnessed the reality of him,' she says. 'They both asked him if he loved me, and he said, of course I do, and then they said, well how come she left, and said, she's feeling scared of you, and he didn't know what to say.

'The wife told me she'd realised how manipulative he is. Apparently when I was out of the room and they were helping me get my stuff together, he was humming the song "Gold Digger", by Kanye West, really loudly as if to make some sort of a point.'

After five months of recuperation at her mother's north London home, Natalie called her ex to tell him it was over – she wanted a divorce. She'd be back to collect her things the next day. She arrived to find a suitcase of her stuff in an abandoned church hall next to the flat.

'The worst part was the thought of him touching all of my things and going through everything,' she says. With her mum and brother for support, she walked into the flat to search for the £700 in cash she'd stored in various drawers.

'It was my way of saving money at the end of the month. I'd stash £100 here and there in envelopes to make sure I didn't touch it, but it was there if I absolutely needed it.' The cash was gone. When she asked, her ex told her it was 'the least he was owed', given the 'allowances' he gave her when they were together.

'But it doesn't quite work like that, does it?' she says. 'In the end I thought, if that's what I have to pay to get rid of this man, so be it. Leave it alone.'

She filed for divorce on grounds of unreasonable behaviour, which he contested, hiring a legal team to support his battle which ultimately landed them both in court.

'We were both told it would be a waste of public funds to take our case to court, but he wanted his day in the spotlight so he could accuse me of being a liar.'

The very simple form on the HM Courts & Tribunals Service website left me paralysed with fear. Didn't she find the thought of solicitors and court hearings fucking terrifying?

'I was very, very lucky, because I worked for the legal department of a charity at the time and there were a couple of women there who had recently gone through a divorce. Also, someone in the legal department had way more experience and knew exactly what to do. They all helped me so much and it meant that, in the end, I didn't need to pay much more than around £500.'

Natalie prepared a letter to read out in court, detailing examples of the abuse she'd experienced during the three-year marriage.

'The judge said just two of my examples were enough to convince him that I should not be married to this man,' she says. 'He [the ex] tried to say I was a liar and had daddy issues and all this crap. The judge said his claims were not helping his case and granted me the divorce.'

What next? 'I had therapy. Really, really good therapy. I didn't have any money and I was living at my mum's for the best part of two years. I told myself that I'd take it one step at a time and try not to rush into any big decisions.

'I realised that I'd become a shadow of who I actually am. I'd morphed into this quiet, meek version of myself who would internalise my feelings so as not to upset other people. That was how I survived the marriage, I suppose.'

Within five months, Natalie had started dating someone else. They quickly moved in together. The new relationship lasted five years which, at the time, she thought were filled with happiness and adoration for one another. It's only now she realises that wasn't the case at all.

'I remember just thinking, at some point, that I was fucking done. I asked myself, what am I doing with him? What am I getting from him? But I stayed for so long because of the fear of being alone. I hadn't really done it since I was twenty-three. I didn't know how.'

This particular terror is one I know well, as do most women featured in this book. Having said that, some studies show this is not confined to women: polls suggest roughly the same proportion of men fear singledom as women.[6] The fear of an untethered future that converges from that of your friendship group trumps the reality of deep unhappiness and even abuse. What's this all about?

Some of it is our panic about loneliness. One US poll found that a third of women are more afraid of being lonely than they are a cancer diagnosis.[7] Objectively speaking, it is a pretty unfounded terror, given the well-established phenomenon that women tend to have more close friends than men. One UK poll found 88 per cent of women have at least one close friend.[8] I know it's not the same as a romantic partner. But still.

Research seems to suggest that it's basically all the fault of Walt Disney. Well, sort of. Studies carried out in the 1990s found that entrenched beliefs that singledom equates to misery and failure are rooted in pernicious messaging from popular culture: films, TV, books. And the single person suffers a particularly bleak fate if they happen to be a woman. The happy ending *is* the life partner; imagine if Sleeping Beauty went without her prince, or Mark Darcy didn't buy Bridget Jones a new diary and chivalrously cover her knicker-clad arse with his coat while they kissed in the snow?

A concurrent theory is that the fear stems from the stories we tell ourselves about what it says about our personality, should we remain single. We internalise heteronormative ideas that to be sans partner is to be unlovable, undesirable and unattractive, because you haven't been 'picked'. A shitty relationship feels safer than facing the elements of our character we are most ashamed of.

But, dear reader: science shits on your bleak inner narrative. Data from 2019, collected as part of the American Time Use Survey – a representative sample of around eight thousand people – showed the happiest demographic of women are those who are single and child-free.[9] Other studies have highlighted that satisfaction with singlehood dramatically increases once you hit forty, although twenty-five-to-thirty-five-year-old single women are still happier than their married counterparts, a 2018 survey published in *Advances in Social Science, Education and Humanities Research* found.[10]

Even better; there's some evidence that single women are happier than single men. In 2017, research by consumer analyst firm Mintel found two thirds of unattached women said they were happy with their relationship status, compared to half of unattached men.[11]

Experts put this down to the added stress that relationships often bring for women thanks to the burden of domestic duties, as well as the fact that friendship groups bring us girls deeper support and kinship than they do for men.

Natalie speaks to a phenomenon I wish I'd had faith in in my mid-twenties when I had doubts about my relationship – having confidence in your ability to create a happiness on your own that is both safer and more exciting than any relationship you have ever been in. It might take a year or two, but knowing you'll be fine – more than fine, in fact – without a romantic partner, will feed your soul in ways you never expected. It means you won't settle for a sub-par choice in the future. You'll be free of the fear of asking for what you deserve.

After her relationship broke down, Natalie decided to make some other major life changes. 'It felt like I was an ele-phant chained to a tree, running round and round the same small bit of grass. It was like, I could either carry on doing this for the rest of my life, or I could cut the chain and do what I've always wanted to do.'

Natalie had always been a talented photographer, and had perfected her skills in her free time. When Covid hit, and the world started working from home, she quit her job at the law firm she'd been at for the past few years, and tried her luck as a full-time freelance photographer.

Within a few months she'd pinned down a couple of loyal clients. Within eighteen months she'd made enough money to put down a deposit to buy a flat.

'I've been self-employed for four years now and I am hon-oured to be able to say that I am actually living my dream,' she says. 'I work for myself, I do what I want and I work with whoever I want.'

Natalie reels off a list of 'big' clients she's shot for over the past few years – the NHS, Amazon Music and the UN are just a few. 'I've become successful – and without help from anybody. I've travelled the world and met so many amazing people through work, and we've bonded over the most insig-nificant things. Now these people are my genuine friends for life. I can honestly say my life is richer than it ever has been before, and I never imagined it could be.' She gets particularly enthused about taking her mum on an African safari – a trip she's planning in the next year or so.

Natalie has been single for around a year now – the last, short-lived romance ended because he cheated on her. 'It was much easier for me to confront things in that relationship and articulate it well, than I was [doing] before,' she says. 'I've dated a few people and I guess I am still trying to figure all of that out.

'I'm now in a place in my life where I've got enough self-worth to know how to spot a person who loves me and treats me the way I want to be treated.' And if things don't work out? 'There is life afterwards. Like, the world doesn't end. Sometimes things just don't work out. I know that now.'

Natalie and I agree to have cocktails as soon as I'm back in London. We'll have to stay north of the river, though.

'That's my home,' Natalie says. 'I spent far too long away from it, I guess I'm making up for lost time. At the end of the day, it's where I feel safe.'

Chapter 11

The Nikah

I am ashamed to say that I only learned about the work of London-based solicitor Aina Khan OBE last year, while researching for this book.

As it turns out, she is the one-woman force behind the biggest disrupting influence of UK marriage and divorce law in recent history. For context, here is a disturbing fact about divorce in the UK and the US that you might not be aware of: a Muslim marriage, a Nikah, is not legally binding. This is also true for Jewish weddings in the instance that one member of the couple isn't Jewish, as well as Catholic and Hindu weddings. In all these cases, couples must have a legal ceremony (which can be literally signing a piece of paper with a licensed registrar) in order for the marriage to be recognised by the state.

The only three religious groups this doesn't apply to are Jews (when both individuals share the same faith), Church of England Christians and, oddly, Quakers. So long as there's a registrar present and at least two witnesses, you can legally marry pretty much anywhere, and however you like, as long as the premises are approved.

While Hindu and Sikh marriages are also not automatically legally recognised, they often take place at a temple or religious building which has its own in-house registrar to take care of the legal bit, or a registrar will attend a ceremony held elsewhere. This, some experts have told me, is partly because families are careful to ensure the dowry – which must be paid by the bride's family – is legally protected, in case of divorce. Muslim weddings traditionally take place at a mosque, the family's home or at an independent venue. Unless the mosque or venue has a registrar present – which campaigners say is uncommon – there will be no official legal oversight.

In 2014, Khan launched a pioneering campaign named Register Our Marriage that aimed to change the law in order to require all religious ceremonies to be legally registered. In 2018, she was awarded an OBE for 'services to the protection of women and children in unregistered marriages' and in 2020, the Law Commission of England launched a consultation paper on unregistered marriages and consulted with Khan. It was hoped this would mark the first step in the process of adapting the 1949 Marriage Act for the multicultural, modern Britain that exists today. But then Covid hit. Despite the distractions, the Commission issued a response in 2021, urging the Government to reform wedding procedures, Khan tells me. But the aftermath of the pandemic, coupled with a new Labour government, has stalled progress, and a verdict is still awaited.

Khan's campaign is rooted in the overarching theme of many of the cases she's dealt with over the duration of her career: Muslim women who separate from their spouses and find themselves entitled to absolutely nothing. 'I started getting calls from women telling me their husband had left and, when they'd started enquiring into a divorce settlement, they realised they weren't even legally married,' Khan tells me over afternoon tea at Whitehall's National Liberal Club. She is among the most impressive women I have ever met; fiercely bright and spirited, while exuding a motherly warmth that makes me want to confide my deepest traumas.

'Some of these women had been with their partners for thirty years and had two or three kids with them. A few of them gave him money for a deposit on a house. Then, one day, he kicks her out and there's not much she can do about it.' Khan tells me about one woman, a friend, who'd climbed the career ladder in the technology industry, accumulating £400,000 in life savings. The vast majority went to her husband, who invested it in their shared home. But when she discovered his affair and kicked him out, he revealed she couldn't; the house was in his name only. Worse, there was nothing she could do about it – they weren't legally married.

Research shows more than 60 per cent of Muslim women in the UK who've had a religious wedding are legally unmarried, and therefore unprotected.[1] 'Some thirty years ago Muslim women started saying to me, "You should know how to sort this out; you're Muslim",' Khan says. 'I quickly had to learn. Not just about English law, but also Islamic law, and how to unpack the cultural baggage.'

She says it's not the religion that's the problem. 'If you study the Qur'an, you realise there are many passages in which it states women and men are equal. But the men at the helm of the community don't like that, so they don't publicise it. You have the Muslim community saying, oh don't worry about an English marriage, just do a Muslim one, that's more important. And then you have the English law which essentially tells them, you're an intelligent woman, it's your job to know whether or not your marriage is legal. The onus is on you. But very few religious women will do their research into what's legal and what isn't. They just listen to what the people in their community are telling them.'

According to Islamic law, there's two ways to go about divorcing your husband. The most common is a tafriq, which involves a woman obtaining cooperation for the split from a council of local sharia arbitrators. This is also sometimes called a faskh, although technically that's equivalent to an annulment. The other is what's known as a khula, where a panel of arbitrators approve the divorce on the condition that the woman will return a chunk of cash/property (otherwise known as a dowry) that the groom gave the bride when they got married.

It is easier if you're a man who wants to divorce your wife. Called a talaq, the process involves the man telling his wife he is divorcing her. He then has to wait for three of his wife's menstruation cycles, during which he is permitted to change his mind. But if three cycles pass and he does not withdraw the divorce notice, the religious split is official. A talaq can be delivered verbally or in writing, and does not require any input from the wife. All scenarios, the talaq, khula and the tafriq, require a certificate of divorce from the sharia council.

However, these days, most Muslim communities have found ways to adapt the ancient laws to speed along the process. 'Many scholars would see a civil divorce as a legitimate religious one too,' Shaykh Ibrahim Mogra, an imam and former Assistant Secretary General of the Muslim Council of Britain, tells me. And of course that's only if the civil wedding happens in the first place. The Qur'an lays down very firm instructions about talaq, he says, pointing to specific religious passages.

'The Qur'an states: "And the divorced women must wait for three menstrual cycles . . . and their husbands can take them back during the waiting period (iddah), if they desire reconciliation." It continues: "Divorce may be pronounced twice; then the wife may either be kept back with fairness or allowed to separate with fairness. So, if a husband divorces his wife three times, then it is not lawful for him to remarry her until after she has married another man and then is divorced."' Elsewhere in the text, he adds, are instructions that divorce ought to be 'utilised only as a last resort after all efforts of arbitration and reconciliation have been exhausted'.

'That is because the Prophet Muhammad said that of all things made permissible by God, divorce is the most hateful in his eyes.'

While this fosters a respect for marriage that acts as a cultural disincentive for infidelity and betrayal, it may also lead unhappy couples to stay together, Shaykh Mogra says. 'There may also be times when the wife may be in physical danger or is suffering domestic abuse; in such serious situations divorce must be pursued without hesitation and without delay.'

When researching for this chapter, I came across a number of different sources that suggested, according to Islamic law, women are unable to seek a religious divorce without the consent of their husband; that doing so would prove near impossible. I later learned that this is nonsense. According to the Qur'an, a khula can absolutely be obtained without a woman's husband's permission.

The idea that it can't is a harmful myth that many campaigners say is reinforced by some local heads of community, who use it to keep women stuck and under the impression that they cannot leave.

'Islam dictates that marriage is a contract and, to that contract, both the husband and wife can add stipulations before they enter into it,' says Aina Khan. 'This includes that the woman can divorce whenever she wants, for whatever reason she wants, known as a tafweed.'

But, she adds, few women know this can be done and, of those that do, only a handful act on it. 'It's seen as unfeminine and unseemly,' she says. 'If a lot of women had done this, there'd be far, far fewer in this dreadful situation.' It's the interpretation of the Qur'an by male community leaders that's the problem. 'The majority of the people in positions of power are men, and they use their warped reading of religious law to exert control over women. It's nothing to do with the faith itself.'

Shaykh Mogra agrees that widespread misunderstanding can keep couples stuck.

'Islam permits couples to separate rather than be miserable for the rest of their lives. I know of divorces that have not been messy at all. It's important for couples who are thinking of divorce to consult Islamic scholars and seek guidance. A large number of Muslims believe divorce only works with three talaqs. Yet we know from the Qur'an that a single talaq will suffice.'

*

I want to begin the following section with a warning of sorts. Some of the detail you're about to read is disturbing, featuring themes of domestic violence, coercion and rape. As important as this story is to air, your mental health is a priority, so please skip ahead to Chapter 12 if you think you might need to.

Late last year, Aina introduced me to fifty-two-year-old Ameera, who lives in London, having escaped Iraq during the first Gulf War in her early twenties. She had a religious wedding ceremony in 2012 and, like a lot of Muslim women in the UK, didn't bother with a civil one. The marriage was short-lived. In summary: he abandoned her after subjecting her to a year of tormenting sexual and physical abuse. Despite this, it took eighteen months to find a shaykh who would give her permission to divorce her husband.

'Do you want to know what a friend of mine was told when she asked a shaykh for a divorce on the grounds her husband was hitting her?' she asks when we speak on the phone. 'He said, "It was good you took a beating. Perhaps you didn't cook for him enough."'

Ameera has forged an impressive career in her line of work. She spent the majority of her twenties and thirties defying preconceptions about Arab women; living a fulfilled, independent lifestyle as a single working woman – supported by a reliable pack of female friends. On meeting Ameera though, you might assume she needs more assistance in life than the average person.

In 1993, an operation to fix a slipped disc in her back went disastrously wrong, leaving her disabled for life, and reliant on a wheelchair to get around.

'I refused men for most of my life,' says Ameera, who

moved back home after the accident. 'I thought, I have health problems and men won't tolerate them. I didn't want to rely on anyone or be a burden. I told my mother this over and over when she'd try and convince me to find a partner. I was happy on my own.'

But at forty-two, she decided she didn't want to give up on becoming a mother. And fertility tests proved there was no reason why she couldn't have a child. If she wanted a partner, she'd have to move quickly.

While living in Germany to undergo an experimental spinal treatment, Ameera met a man. He was also Iraqi, and a widower in his forties, who seemed very interested in her work.

'I wasn't even very attracted to him to be honest,' she says. 'But he was very pushy, and he made lots of effort with my mum, and came across as very caring and devoted to me. I guess when you meet someone in later life you feel you are mature enough to make the right decision. Everyone was trying to convince me. So I thought, well, okay.'

As is traditional in the Arab world, Ameera's brother went to meet her would-be partner to check he was a suitable match for his sister. He was a 'good guy' who would look after her, was her brother's testimony. He seemed 'accepting' of her health problems.

The plan was this: they'd have an Islamic ceremony in Germany, followed by a civil one in London, where they eventually planned to settle. He'd fly back and forth from his home country of France in the meantime.

Within a few months they'd found a German mosque that agreed to marry them. Immediately after the ceremony, the newly-weds travelled to a hotel a few miles down the road, where they'd spend their first night as husband and wife.

'As soon as he shut the door behind him, his attitude changed,' Ameera says. 'It was like something switched in his eyes.'

As she slowly manoeuvred herself on to the bed, he jumped up, pulled down his trousers and pants and forced himself inside her. She begged him to stop, telling him she was in pain, but he carried on.

Eventually, he pulled himself off her, throwing a tissue in her direction as he shouted, 'Virgin.'

'He told me I'd become a woman and demanded I get up and wash myself,' she said, without taking a breath. For the following three days she could barely move from the bed due to extensive bleeding from vaginal injuries.

It has taken Ameera the best part of a decade to be able to talk about the details of that night, as well as the years that followed it.

'He made me too scared to tell anyone. I was so embarrassed because he'd mock me over and over again. I went to the GP and I couldn't even talk. I just sat there crying and crying and, eventually, she got it out of me. She said, this isn't a marriage, this is rape.'

For reasons Ameera doesn't quite understand, the doctor didn't pass on safeguarding concerns to the police or social services. She was told to consider talking therapy. Going to the authorities wasn't an option; she was too terrified.

Meanwhile, the abuse continued in their home, in between Ameera's husband's prolonged trips to France – the reason for which Ameera was never really sure of.

She tells me that the treatment for her spinal injury was discontinued as a result of ongoing gynaecological problems, which she now recognises were caused by internal damage related to the sexual abuse she suffered.

In 2013, she moved back to London to live with her mother, with her husband to follow in the coming weeks. Within days of his arrival, the pair had visited Marylebone Town Hall to give notice for their intent to be legally married in the UK. A week later, Ameera's husband flew back to France to finalise some paperwork, for what she believed would be the last time before settling into their new British life.

'He called me from there to tell me it was over. He wanted a divorce,' Ameera says. This brought about, as you might imagine, a wildly complex range of emotions. She felt simultaneously unchained and safe, while also terrified about disappointing her mother, and losing her vanishingly small chance of becoming one herself. And then it dawned on her: they weren't legally married. She was entitled to nothing.

'So he'd raped me, abused me, left me and then was able to run away without taking any liability or giving me a penny? It was terrible.'

It wasn't that she was desperate for his money. Ameera had retained her financial independence throughout the short marriage. But the fact he could put her through hell and escape scot-free felt agonising. Not to mention the cash she said he'd taken from her pot of disability benefits while they were together.

She withstood the unimaginable pain of telling her mother the truth about what had happened to her. 'She said I should have left him,' she says. 'But I told her he is a very scary man and, the truth was, I was scared of what he would do if I told him I was going to leave.'

And so began the year-long pursuit for an Islamic divorce; a task that would prove far more gut-wrenching than Ameera had ever realised. If there was one favour Ameera's husband did for her, it was giving his unreserved agreement for divorce. According to Islam, providing the man demands divorce three times – be it over the phone, in person, or in writing – obtaining a talaq or khula should be relatively straightforward. Note the term, *should* be.

'I started calling everyone, all the local imams and shaykhs, asking if they would issue my divorce,' Ameera says. 'I was told to contact the person who married us in Germany, or to ask if my husband could fly to London. It was obstacle after obstacle.'

In the end, Ameera thought it easier to fight for a khula – where the divorce is approved by a panel of local religious leaders without the man's written consent, providing she returns assets given to her before the wedding.

This would be simpler, she thought, given that her betrothed had given her nothing at all. But she was wrong. 'I went to the local Muslim council to meet with the director. He said that he'd approve a khula so long as I gave my husband everything I had. I picked up a copy of the Qur'an and shouted at him: "Show me where it says that here – show me!" He didn't know what to say, so he got up and walked away.'

Exasperated, she began obsessively googling in hope of a solution she'd not yet discovered. That was when she found Aina Khan.

'Aina told me there was a shaykh at an Acton mosque who

might do it as he's helped other women before,' she says. 'My brother had to be there as the man acting on my behalf, and my ex had to tell the shaykh three times, over the phone, that he wanted to divorce me. But that was it. He gave me the divorce papers.'

It's important to say that there are plenty of shaykhs who are not using Islam to enforce sexist ideals; quite the opposite, in fact.

Zara's religious divorce was relatively straightforward (despite the fact her ex refused to sign anything). It was the four-year battle with the British courts that sent her spiralling into a state of despair.

One of the biggest misconceptions about unregistered Muslim marriages is that the problem is reserved for 'foreigners' – women who are born abroad and are blighted by another nation's laws, says Aina Khan.

'It's utter nonsense,' says Khan. 'I've spoken to members of the House of Lords who will say patronising things like, "Oh, those poor women who come here from other countries." It's not the case. These are British women who are born and bred in this country. Many of them are bright and professional, and have spent years contributing to this economy. They should be protected.'

Zara, now fifty-one, owned her own London house by the time she was thirty. She'd spent the best part of her late twenties clambering up the career ladder in the male-dominated world of IT consultancy. And it paid off; by thirty-seven she'd made enough to quit her full-time job and start her own firm, which saw her squirrel away savings totalling around half a million in cash.

By thirty-nine she had no money and was living in her parents' spare room, which she shared with her two children, aged seven and three. They spent eight years taking it in turn to sleep on the mattress on the floor.

Despite being the mother of her husband's two children and the co-owner of the family home, Zara exited her marriage with no legal entitlements whatsoever – because her wedding wasn't legally binding in the UK.

She found herself in this difficult situation due to the misconception, often reinforced by families, that Muslim marriages are legally binding in the UK, so a civil wedding isn't necessary. She remembers a previous conversation with her ex-husband, who seemed ambivalent about having their marriage registered. Looking back, she suspects that he knew that an unregistered religious marriage would offer her no protection.

Zara thinks much of the misunderstanding in the Pakistani community can be explained by the fact many older couples who had religious marriages didn't need to register – because their weddings took place abroad. They assume that a religious wedding in the UK would be automatically legally binding, as it would be, for example, for those who married in Pakistan and then moved to the UK. Unfortunately, this isn't the case.

Zara got married relatively late compared to her peers and parents. She was over thirty, under pressure and feeling short on time. She went on Islamic dating websites out of amusement and curiosity, and it wasn't long before she came across a man, six years her senior, who seemed like they could be a decent prospect. After a few weeks of chatting online they eventually met at a mutual friend's wedding. The pair weren't allowed to live together or have a sexual relationship due to cultural norms, so they went on dates at coffee shops and restaurants. She reflects on the difficulty of truly knowing a person from these kind of surface-level encounters.

Within a year and a half they agreed to get married, even if, on reflection, Zara found parts of his personality unappealing: he was a show-off and held some very conservative beliefs, and was also very focused on money. He was insistent on the pair moving to live near his parents, and wouldn't compromise. He also expected her to stop working as soon as they had children, even though Zara had always been financially independent. Still, she went ahead with the marriage, fearful that her age meant she had no other choice.

They got along relatively well until about three years down the line, when Zara was pregnant with her second child and the couple were preparing to buy their own house down the road from his parents in Cheltenham. In the run-up to completing on their house purchase, Zara noticed that her name was not listed on the paperwork, despite the fact that she had contributed the majority of the deposit from a previous sale and that they'd agreed to buy the property together. Incidentally, the property her husband owned on his own was registered in his sister's name, which Zara always found odd.

This just so happened to be around the same time she'd overheard her newly divorced brother-in-law brag about the fact his ex-wife had received no settlement, because they weren't legally married. She started to do her own research, realising with a shock that with the paperwork as it stood, she would have no rights to their property.

Zara sought advice from a solicitor in Manchester who told her she must register the marriage to protect herself from financial ruin. Her husband refused.

It got worse. About six months before the house disagreement Zara had left her full-time job to set up her own consultancy company, which would give her the flexibility to look after her two young kids. Her husband already had a (dormant) limited company in his name and promised to change the directorship to her if she transferred her funds into his company. He never did, and when she chased him, he accused her of being greedy.

After two years of persistent badgering, Zara got her name added to the house deeds. But by that point, her faith in the relationship had evaporated. She went back to London, moving in with her mother to build up her life again.

Zara knew she had virtually no leg to stand on when it came to asking for cash from a man who, in the eyes of the state, was not her husband. Friends and family advised her to leave quietly, but Zara decided to go through the courts, hoping to prevent him from getting away with treating her so badly.

Only, he did get away with it. It took nearly four years of battling the court system – and at least £200,000 – to get a judge to order him to sell their house, and return some of Zara's share of the cash. Because the pair weren't legally married, she was unable to argue that, as the sole carer of their children, she should be able to keep the house that the children are living in until the youngest turns eighteen. Instead, she was entitled to only 50 per cent of the deposit after the property was sold, rather than the 80 per cent she contributed. The house sold at a loss, meaning she didn't even make back what she'd put in.

The court eventually concluded that, technically, Zara's ex-husband owed her a total of £250,000 – accounting for some of the cash he took from her business, child benefit and extra funds tied up in the property. But, because the pair weren't legally married, there was no route to enforce that decision, and her ex-husband paid her a fraction of that amount. Zara reckons she lost a total of half a million pounds, including the endless court fees. She looks back on it as a waste of time and money, paying expensive solicitors who were unable to do much to help her case.

As for her religious severing, her ex's refusal to sign the paperwork means there's still a chance she's not officially divorced in the eyes of Islam. Zara applied with the local sharia council for a divorce but her ex-husband refused to sign the documentation. To her, however, she is divorced.

Zara says her Muslim divorce was unusually seamless – apart from the part where her husband wouldn't play ball. For tens of thousands of women, like Ameera, it is a secondary hell.

'They [shaykhs] are using Islam as an excuse for terrible behaviour,' says Ameera. 'I now know this is a trend because I've heard of many Arab men following the same pattern. They "marry" a woman, get what they can out of her, then discard her for another woman. And they know there won't be any repercussions, financially or legally, because the religious "rules" allow them to get away with it. But nowhere in the Qur'an does it say this is an acceptable way to treat a wife.'

Ameera and Zara faced different challenges when it came to slotting back the pieces of their fragmented lives.

It took Zara seven years before she had enough cash to move her and her two children – then ten and fourteen – into their own home, with their own rooms. She rented it out while she lived at her mother's to save up money, and, in 2020, she renovated the property so the family could move in.

It's only recently – twelve years from the split – that Zara's started to feel like the heaviness from the trauma has begun to lift. She's pleased that her ex has a relationship with the children, and offers to pay for some of their 'big cost' needs (but only very occasionally, she says).

She's hopeful for the next generation, with cultural mindsets changing. However, she still has friends stuck in difficult relationships who know that, as they're not legally married, their options are extremely limited if they do decide to leave.

Ameera didn't share financial assets with her husband, which doesn't offer any solace from the horrors she went through. But it did mean she could cut the cord with him instantly, with virtually no back and forth.

But he still walked away better off. 'He'd disappear when we had to pay a bill, for instance at a hotel, so I would be forced to pay every time. I received disability benefits and he'd insist some of it was his, and use it to pay for things he wanted.'

'It was clear this man had about ten different faces. He was presentable, and said all the right things. But no. Now I feel like we have to expect the worst of every man until he proves he is a good one.'

As you might imagine, Ameera's attitude to life has never quite recovered from what happened to her. An extract from a short story she wrote about the days before meeting her abuser tells of a woman who is one of life's optimists, blessed with the tendency to blur the grisly edges and absorb all that she finds beautiful:

A sunny but breezy day this autumn. My physiotherapist gives me a day off from the treatment. There is still a very long road ahead with treating my spinal problem and the spasms. It would be nice to explore the town in fresh air away from the hydrotherapy pool. Mom decides to stay indoors, advising me not to lose myself in nature, especially if it's going to rain. Going brick by brick, I wheel myself, slowly, swallowing pain with a hopeful smile. I reach Lichtentaler Allee, the beautiful stream of the Black Forest. I enjoy the drizzle but soon I take refuge in the Frieder Burda Museum, just across the Allee: a very modern building integrated in this historic town on the hill. Wonderful, and suitable to my electric wheelchair with its wide and smooth ramps. I explore the three floors with less pain and more time to enjoy art.

Some days are brighter than others. But the crack in Ameera's voice tells me the last decade has broken her spirit. She still finds comfort in writing and has recently completed a diploma in creative writing at Cambridge University. She continues to contribute to a number of Arabic magazines. Shortly before we connected, she penned a short story detailing the rape in an attempt to start the healing process. It was the first time she'd faced what happened to her in black and white. It stung, but with it came a sense of relief.

'It was good timing when you got in touch, because I feel ready to start talking about it,' she said. 'Mostly I am trying to concentrate on writing about what happened to me.'

Ameera's published words were, for the majority of her career, in Arabic. But her priority has now switched to English. 'I can't write about the rape in my mother tongue. The words hit deeply. I find it too painful.'

Aina Khan is facing an uphill challenge. At the time of writing, she is preparing to relaunch her campaign with the hope of renewed support from a sprightly Labour government. But it's no small task.

'Before Covid, the Conservative government gave my Register Your Marriage campaign a budget to hire people on the ground to help me and set up steering groups in three locations, who could immerse themselves in communities and spread awareness of the problem and the need for upcoming change in the law,' she says. 'There was a grant, a good website and a social media presence. After a series of roadshows around the country, and appearing at many Muslim conferences and events, I had everything ready for an updated marriage law, including registrars from all faiths ready to get couples legally married.'

But four years of stagnation since the pandemic has killed the momentum and the small pot of money is now empty.

'The Conservative government was supportive because they are supposedly the "party of marriage",' she says, although she felt Tory MPs lacked a grasp of the injustice of the issue, and blamed Brexit for a lack of legislative time.

I ask Aina what the justification is for not implementing her recommendations. The short answer is, there isn't one.

'Basically, they think it will upset the Muslim community, to which I reply, well, have you asked them? Some officials have said to me, "The Muslims won't like it because they want polygamy and we don't want to interfere." Not only is this view completely ignorant and offensive, it's not true. In every religious group you'll get men who want lots of women, but it's in no way representative of everyone. It's just an excuse.'

Aina plans to lobby the new Labour cabinet, including the Muslim Lord Chancellor, Shabana Mahmood, who she thinks will 'better understand the importance of this for communities across the country'.

'Practically speaking, it's pretty easy to get done,' she says. 'It's just a case of making a very small change to the legislation. It's simple: people of all faiths must be legally married before they have a religious ceremony. Once they are protected by UK law, they can do whatever they want. This is not a small issue; it affects hundreds of thousands of people.'

As the evening draws to a close, Aina tops up my tea and invites me to finish off my half-eaten scone. 'Make sure you've got cream and jam on there.'

She asks how long it's been since my marriage ended, and enquires about the progress of my 'healing'. I'm slightly overwhelmed at the realisation it's been almost two years. I tell her I worry about running out of time, having wasted nearly a decade.

'Nonsense, you've got plenty,' she says. 'Your first marriage was what I like to call your starter marriage; you've still got the main meal to come. Can I offer you a tip?' she asks. 'When you come to choose your next partner, make sure it's someone who loves women. They're not threatened by them and are celebratory of us. Perhaps they have sisters or female cousins, or lots of good female friends. A general appreciation and respect for women and how amazing we are. That's always a good start.'

For support for concerns about domestic violence there are several charities that you can contact. A selection includes: womensaid. org.uk, refuge.org.uk or, if you're in the UK, you can contact the Freephone National Domestic Abuse Helpline, run by Refuge, on 0808 2000 247. Scotland's Domestic Abuse and Forced Marriage Helpline is 0800 027 1234. If you're interested in domestic violence support for Muslim women, contact the Muslim Women's Network at mwnuk.co.uk or the Sakeenah Foundation at sakeenahfoundation.co.uk.

Chapter 12

How Not To Get Totally F**ked In Divorce

On 27 January 2023, two months after we separated, my (now ex) husband sent me an email with an attached Word document. It appeared to serve as a notice of everything I stood to lose, should I fight him for my mother's money.

He was 'disappointed' that I'd rejected his proposal to pay me just a quarter of the cash my mum had gifted (even if, as ended up happening, our house sold at a profit). The next step, should I choose to fight him, would be mediation, he rather patronisingly informed me. And he'd like to caveat that if we did go to mediation the following pieces of information will be taken into account:

'Yearly salary and bonuses and savings, current assets such as pension schemes, and stocks and shares, forecasts for future expenditure.' The court, he explained, would take a 'starting position' of a 50/50 split of marital property accrued during our time together – including the six or so years we spent living together. 'This includes any money that has gone into pension schemes, stocks and shares, and savings over the last six years. This will also include the £25,000 gift to both of us from your mum, given this was "mingled" with marital property and has gone into the family home.'

Some important context for the following section: when requesting my mother's money back, I'd added that the cash would be particularly useful as, due to differences in our earnings, I'd have less money than Ben would to buy a new property after the sale. I said this was particularly gut-punching given that I didn't ask for the break-up in the first place.

His letter continued: 'In terms of property there is no legal obligation for us to both buy a property at the end of this for the same price, or to the same standard; the main issue the court will be concerned about is whether both of us will be able to rehouse.' Then came a stomach-churning suggestion that perhaps I'd like to pay off my student loan in order to borrow more, or lower my budget if I wasn't happy with the funds I had to purchase a new property. He ended by informing me of a number for a divorce mediator (an independent, non-legal party who offers a 'safe space' for ex-partners to reach difficult agreements) that he'd found, in case I'd forgotten how to use Google.

This letter clearly wasn't written by him. But the most infuriating element of it was that everything he said about our legal entitlements was true.

And this, my friends, is the absolute financial fuckery that is marriage. I remember reading the letter over and over again in disbelief, shouting, 'WHY DOES NO ONE TELL YOU THIS?'

In summary: the minute you get hitched, at least some

of your money technically becomes the property of your husband or wife. This is especially true if you 'mingle' your money in any sort of joint account or investment, if you make a significant amount of cash during the marriage, and if you stand to inherit a significant amount of family wealth. In fact, these financial rights even apply to money earned in the time *before* you got married (as long as you've been living together). While it's rare for an ex to be granted a slice of your personal pension, it's not impossible, particularly if the court deems the other party or children to be financially worse off.

Oh and, while rare, it is also possible for an ex-wife or husband to come after you for newly acquired income years after your divorce is final (I'll reveal how to avoid this in a minute).

Most couples like to think that, if a divorce was on the cards, they'd divvy up their bits and pieces between them, eliminating the need for extortionate solicitors and traumatic court appearances. 'The truth is there is always something to argue about,' says Sandra Davis. 'You can't rely on a verbal agreement that you arrived at when things were good. You never know how someone will behave when push comes to shove.' Having said that, Davis explains that court can be avoided if said negotiations can be dealt with at mediation – which is a hell of a lot cheaper.

That is the first – of very many details – you MUST know about divorce before you get married.

How to get divorced

When it clicked that I was about to go through a divorce, all I could think of were the press releases that landed in my inbox roughly once a month entitled something along the lines of:

'UK POLL REVEALS TOP THREE MOST STRESSFUL LIFE EVENTS'. Divorce is usually number two, below death of a close relative and above moving house.

I was terrified. I had no clue where to start, and found the UK Government's 'Get a divorce' web page brought up more questions than it did answers, such as, why the fuck do I have to pay £593 for this shit?

The truth is if you don't have children and you aren't interested in taking one another's money, divorce in the UK today is relatively straightforward. A new 'no-fault' divorce was introduced in April 2022 (which, rather poetically, was the month I got married), aiming to stop the 'blame game' that has long muddied otherwise non-acrimonious splits. In its simplest terms, the legislation means you no longer need to prove anything to get divorced. Previously, fault-based divorces were only applied if you satisfied one of five criteria: adultery, desertion of at least two years, unreasonable behaviour, two years of separation with consent of both parties, five years of separation without. Now, the only prerequisite for divorce is that you've been legally married for at least a year which, in the case of my six-month marriage, was very fucking annoying.

A note on annulment

Despite what you might have seen on *Friends*, in the UK, an annulment isn't really a thing. It basically means the marriage was invalid and can only be applied for in very specific circumstances, like, say you didn't know your partner was in fact an illegal immigrant, had an STD, was pregnant by someone else, in the process of transitioning to a different gender, under eighteen or . . . related to you. The law technically allows for an annulment if the marriage wasn't consummated, but lawyers tell me this rarely gets approved because it is virtually impossible to prove. In the US there are a few more circumstances in which an annulment is possible, such as if a woman claims she's pregnant to 'entice' someone to get married and (most interestingly, I think) if one party has claimed to want children when in fact they don't.

So, no-fault divorce goes like this: one party fills out a simple online application, pays £593 (!), and waits for the other party to respond to an email from the UK family courts informing them that their partner is out. You basically have to tick a box; either you agree that you should be divorced, or you don't. That is pretty much it. The rest requires waiting for the family courts to approve the application and email you updates a bit like the ones you get about the status of your Uber Eats order. 'Dear Eve, the divorce your husband applied for is in the works!'

It wasn't exactly like this, but you get what I mean. The case will be presented to a judge in a family court somewhere in the country, who will decide if you can get divorced (it's very rare that they rule no). You can, if you so wish, attend the court in question to experience the pomp of hearing your heartbreak announced in a small municipal building in north Birmingham. I decided not to. Around five to eight months after the application was lodged, and providing the courts agree, you can apply for something called a conditional order – this is the paperwork that essentially says you will be divorced. Like a pre-divorce, if you will. A few months after that you can apply for a final order confirming that you are now divorced. Congrats!

Another irritating detail about the UK divorce system: it is only the person who applied for the divorce initially who can seek the conditional and final orders. This leaves the other party subjected to a cruel waiting game (they also have to wait around at least five months before chasing).

You technically don't need a lawyer . . . But it will make your life a lot easier

There is no doubt that the new no-fault divorce will change hundreds of thousands of lives for the better. Most importantly, it allows for discreet and swift legal separation, which is crucial, and possibly even lifesaving, for those in abusive or controlling relationships. But there are downsides. The first is that it removes all accountancy for bad behaviour. When I ticked my boxes, I was asked if I agreed or disagreed with my husband's decision that we should be granted a faultless divorce. I agreed, of course, despite the agonising truth that there was a party to blame, and it wasn't me. Where was the box for, 'he told me he wanted to fuck someone at work' or 'he didn't want to try therapy'? I felt as if he'd got off on a technicality.

This seems insignificant, but, for me, official acknowledgement of his apathy about our marriage would have soothed the burns somewhat. To me, it reinforced his skewed narrative: that 'sometimes these things just don't work out'.

Practically speaking, a no-fault divorce does away with the need for a lawyer as there is no imperative to prove anything. While this will save you thousands, it means you're not privy to very important information about how to protect your finances. Thankfully, you're reading this book.

After the conditional order is granted, you can file a legal document with the courts known as a consent order – and it is very important that you do this. A consent order is essentially a contract you both sign that states neither of you will go after each other's money in the future. Divorce lawyers have told me about a case of an estranged ex-wife who took her former husband to court to fight for half the profits of his new business venture twenty years after the divorce was finalised. And she won. A consent order should be drawn up by a divorce lawyer, although it is a pretty basic contract and you might be able to find a template online. If you're only asking a solicitor to check the document, it could cost you just a couple of hundred pounds.

I initially attempted to draft my own, determined that I would not part with a penny for this mess of his making. But after a few weeks of bugging my planning lawyer friend (I guessed a contract was a contract, right?) I caved and hired a divorce solicitor. I was extremely lucky to have the savings to spare: my outgoings were virtually nothing, given that I lived with my mother and spent most weekends watching *Girls* reruns in the dressing-gown Mum had bought me for my sixteenth birthday. It was one of the most sensible decisions I have ever made. The lawyer, not the weekend plans. For about £1,300, I was relieved of the daily reminder of my life's chaos. I didn't have to make contact with my ex to ask for his financials. I could be fully distracted by my working day and focus on rebuilding my life. It's easy for me to say, I know, but the freedom of passing your personal hell over to someone else and saying, 'Call me when it's done', is priceless. But shop around. I was initially quoted somewhere in the realm of £3,000–5,000 from London-based solicitors. I had to venture a little further afield to find someone I trusted who didn't charge a small fortune.

It must be said that some divorce lawyers have told me it is perfectly possible to do the legwork without a professional. However, divorce lawyer Sandra Davis describes failing to enlist a solicitor as a 'fool's paradise'.

'It's a bit like if your washing machine breaks. You can attempt to fix it yourself, but you probably wouldn't do a very good job. Most people would sooner get a professional in to be on the safe side.'

A note on prenups

If you have the means to pay a lawyer to draw up a contract – and have a significant amount to protect – get one. Each solicitor you speak to will tell you something different about their value. It is possible to fight the terms of a prenup in court (for instance, if it was drawn up less than a month before the wedding or if some assets weren't disclosed) which is why some will tell you they are pointless. But said legal battle would be costly, and the opposing partner would probably end up spending more on court fees than the amount they stood to win – which is why most people won't bother fighting it. One sensible divorce lawyer told me that whether or not you should get a prenup is a numbers game. Is the amount you want to protect – both before and after you get married – significantly more than the £5–8k it could cost you to get a prenup drawn up? If so, a prenup could be worthwhile.

Sandra Davis tells me she wishes more engaged couples

would consider it. 'You don't have to have huge amounts of money for it to be helpful, but it can be about future-proofing – for instance, if you have disparity between the number of assets you and your partner have. It is very common for families to want to protect inherited wealth. It's also not unusual for those entering second marriages to want to protect their wealth for the benefit of children that came from the first marriage. Why not protect your money? It might not be an easy conversation to have, but it is one worth having. It is better to have some form of security than none. It's about negotiating at the best of times for the worst of times.'

Divorce as we know it has only been around since 1973

The history of British divorce law is, like many elements of our country's institutional past, mired in depressing patri-archy. Before the late 1850s, divorce was only achievable via a private act of Parliament – afforded to only the upper echelons of society.

But following campaigns by social reformer Caroline Norton (the wife of George Chapple Norton MP, who she wished to split from), a revolution was triggered.[1] From 1858 came a series of acts that massively increased the accessibility of divorce and did away with archaic rules like children being the property of their fathers.

However, the conditions for divorce were deliberately sexist. A husband could apply based on adultery, but for a woman to apply, their husband had to have cheated on them as well as have committed incest, bigamy or another criminal offence. Also, no financial support was provided to women (only roughly a third were working at that time), which led many to abandon their petitions halfway through.

(Quick depressing fact: in the UK, rape within a marriage was only made illegal in 1992. In the US it was 1993, although some states had legal loopholes that weren't closed until 2023.)

In 1937 the Matrimonial Causes Act remedied many of the unfair conditions for divorce, along with laws introduced in 1882 that gave women the right to property. However, a woman still had to prove adultery, cruelty or desertion, and it was rare that they would be entitled to more than a third of their husband's assets. Divorce still screwed us pretty bad.

Finally in 1973 came the new Matrimonial Causes Act – game-changing legislation that determined the divorce law that still stands today. Conditions for divorce were amended to incorporate 'behaviour which makes it unreasonable to expect the petitioner to live with the respondent'. Both parties were absolved of the burden of proof, with a focus on meeting all of the couple's financial needs as individuals.[2]

The next development came in 2010 following the historic case of a French husband and his millionaire German wife. While the pair had a prenup drawn out before they married, the court all but ignored it, ruling that the husband was to be paid five million pounds and two properties – all funded by the wife's inheritance. The wife appealed the ruling and, in a landmark decision made by the Supreme Court, it was decided that he was in fact entitled to far less on account of the prenuptial agreement.[3] Since then, prenups have held far more weight in court. A 2021 report by the think tank

Marriage Foundation revealed that around 20 per cent of couples marrying now have some sort of prenup, compared to 8 per cent in the '90s.[4]

The curse of state law

Thankfully, the misogynistic state of Britain's divorce laws is consigned to history. But the same can't be said for the US. Or at least, in some of the fifty states.

One of the most shocking restrictions is the ban on divorce for pregnant women in four US states: Missouri, Texas, Arizona and Arkansas. Analyses have concluded that, technically, the legislation does not forbid divorce during pregnancy, but it does state that paternity must be proven in order to agree a custody plan – which is a requirement for divorce. Judges in these states therefore apply the legislation by refusing to grant a divorce during pregnancy. It means women in abusive relationships have to remain tied to their partners, and denies those in need of financial support any resources that may be ordered by the court.

Also appalling: in forty of the fifty states, child marriage remains legal. Worth noting that it was only in 2023 that marriage for sixteen- to eighteen-year-olds was made illegal. There is no minimum age of marriage in five of the US states. In the remainder, it's fifteen, sixteen or seventeen, according to the non-profit organisation Unchained At Last.[5] The charity says around three hundred thousand children – some as young as ten – have been married since 2000 in the US. Worse still, federal law prohibits minors from enacting legal action – so a divorce is impossible before the age of eighteen.[6]

Some eight in ten females in child marriages report experiencing physical, sexual or emotional abuse by their husbands, according to a 2020 report by the International Center for Research on Women.[7] Around half of respondents to the survey said they 'weren't allowed' to use contraception during their marriage.

Also, it wasn't until 2023 that rape within marriage was criminalised in all US states. Until then, legal loopholes had existed that meant a perpetrator could get off scot-free in certain absurd circumstances, such as if the victim was intoxicated at the time of the attack.

Less extreme, but sneakily harmful, are the widely varying rules about how long you have to wait before both filing for divorce and finalising it.[8] In seven states, couples must be able to prove they've lived in separate households for between six months to a year before filing for a divorce. Until recently this was up to two years in some states, although most have introduced reforms that shorten the cooling-off period to two or three months. It appears to be part of the chronic, statutory effort to keep Americans married and having babies. And needless to say, it's a nightmare for those who need to get out of their marriage quickly (most of whom are women).

It also means finding the resources to live separately and co-parent; a challenge that usually lands at the feet of women. Around 70 per cent of primary caregivers in the US are women, according to careers advice website Zippia.[9] Only 16 per cent of heterosexual marriages in the States involve a working woman earning more than her husband, according to data from Pew Research Center.[10] And with no legally binding agreement for splitting funds or accommodation while separated but still married, there is little to stop the financially worse-off partner getting royally screwed.

Now let's look at the rest of the world for a minute.

The majority of countries have divorce laws that are relatively similar to those in the UK and the US. But there are some very extreme exceptions.

Most notably, a campaign that frames divorce as a human right is gaining traction in the Philippines – the only country in the world where divorce is illegal for 99 per cent of its population.[11]

Oddly, those who are Muslim (the country is 80 per cent Catholic) are able to divorce, due to legislation signed in 1977 by the then president. Annulments are technically available, but few are granted, and those that are have a price tag that's unaffordable for most women.

Mercifully, there is hope. Polls suggest that around half of the Filipino population are in favour of divorce, which has piled pressure on politicians to make tangible change.[12] Recently, the House of Representatives approved a bill that aims to legalise divorce for the first time in thirty years. Said bill is now awaiting approval from the Philippine Senate.[13]

The only other international region where divorce is not permitted is the minuscule Vatican City near Rome, ruled by the Pope, which measures 121 acres and has a population of roughly 764.

In Saudi, whether or not a woman is entitled to a divorce depends on a judge's decision. If a woman is being abused by her husband, she must prove mistreatment in order for the law to grant the separation, and this adjudication process often lasts up to two years, according to Amnesty International.[14] Saudi men used to be able to divorce their wives without their knowledge, until a new law was introduced in 2019 that triggered notifications via text message.[15]

The sad truth is, in most parts of the world, divorce has always been more shit for women.

Lawyers have told me there's long been a misconception that women 'do well' out of divorce. Sandra Davis says that, technically speaking, the UK is the 'divorce capital of the world' for women divorcing wealthy men, because there is 'no upper limit' to how much she might be entitled to, depending on her needs. But for couples of average income, women often end up with a greater struggle.

'That's not necessarily because of the divorce legislation in this country,' she says. 'But because of societal problems. For instance, women, on the whole, earn less than men and they usually bear the brunt of the childcare responsibilities – the cost of which is obscene.'

And then there are women who earn more than men. 'People are often shocked when I tell them divorce settlements have nothing to do with gender,' says David Brown, divorce lawyer. 'Judges will be looking to split assets as close to 50/50 as possible, while taking account of the needs of any children and the parties themselves.'

Experts tell me that in most divorces involving children, women hold on to the marital home until the youngest child reaches eighteen. This is because, in the majority of heterosexual relationships, it's the woman who is responsible for the lion's share of caregiving responsibilities, so it often makes sense for the man to move out. According to UK divorce law, the parent living in the home where the children also live the majority of the time can keep it until the kids are adults.

While this may seem like an unfairly large asset, it also lumbers women with excess financial burden – childcare, upkeep, clothing and feeding little people, etc. It also means women may have to limit working hours, reducing the amount they have coming in. American studies have found that divorced men, on average, hold twice the amount of wealth that women do, and a woman's household income falls 41 per cent after divorce, compared to men's 23 per cent.[16]

David Brown says women today have more to lose than ever before – because we've never been more successful. 'The only reason people thought women did well out of divorce was because men traditionally earned a lot more money and assets,' he explains. 'But now that's no longer the case.' As noted earlier, a quarter of married households in the UK have a female breadwinner, according to 2020 research.

The truth is that the law is on the side of neither party when it comes to divorce.

What about children?

Matt O'Connor from the dads' campaign group Fathers 4 Justice has spent the best part of twenty years fighting to change UK divorce law to reflect modern families today.

'At the moment, the law is sexist,' he tells me. 'It assumes women are always the ones who look after the children, and the father is always the one who earns more. I have dads on the phone every day telling me they can't see the children without a court order because of this stupid law.'

Matt's talking about the legal protocol of custody agreements, officially known as 'child arrangement orders'. To some extent, he's right, but it's not because of any legislative power. As it is usually the case that the father moves out, he automatically relinquishes his status as primary carer – albeit unofficially. It means if Mum decides she doesn't want the children to see their dad, there's little he can do about it.

'They [the dads he supports] call me up telling me they're gonna take her through the courts and fight her until they get what they want and I think, good luck, you're not going to get anywhere,' says O'Connor.

Obviously anything involving the family court will be hideously expensive. But it's not the case, as men's rights activists have long maintained, that men have 'no rights' to their children.

'No one has "rights" to children,' says solicitor David Brown. 'That's not how it works. Although it's true that parents have responsibilities for their children. It is true, however, that if the parent with whom the child lives is objecting to contact, the other parent has no automatic legal right to see a child unless there is a court order to say so.'

So what happens with kids, practically speaking?

British law doesn't require you to have anything in writing that instructs that your ex will have the kids every second Tuesday and Sunday afternoons. If the situation allowed it, you could agree a plan between the two of you alone without a single legal professional knowing.

Sandra Davis says it's a good idea to make it official. This involves getting a solicitor to document the details of the arrangements in another legal document known as a shared care arrangement. A lot of couples come to these decisions with the help of a mediator.

Things get complicated when couples disagree about where the children live, how often they see both parents, if there are safeguarding issues and if one parent wants to take their shared offspring out of the country. Some couples may also engage in legal disputes over who pays for what.

While court is usually reserved for the most 'contentious' of divorces, in the UK, proceedings are usually relatively civilised, I'm told – at least compared to the US.

'In the US the trials are much longer and they seem to engage in forensic examination of people's characters, whereas we try to avoid doing that,' says Sandra Davis. 'Retribution should have no place in legal proceedings. Children should not be used as pawns in the battle between parents behaving selfishly, or not in the interest of children. It creates a big legal bill and helps no one in the end. Especially not the children.'

When I first found myself thrust into the uncoupled space, I was insufferably passionate about men being, in the main, total and complete scumbags when it came to separation. I read every article going about elaborate male affairs, watched Netflix's back catalogue of 'she gets her revenge' type films, and inhaled anything ever written by Nora Ephron. As far as I was concerned, you couldn't blame some women for wanting to keep their kids away from the man who had incinerated their heart and taken a giant dump over their shared life together.

Sandra Davis says my view doesn't reflect reality. Women can behave just as badly as men, she tells me.

For instance, she tells me that the husband of one

high-profile woman she knows never sees his children. Not because he doesn't want to; he's spent the best part of thirty years attempting to have a relationship with his kids, but they want nothing to do with him.

I'm aware of the circumstances of the break-up (he had an affair and left her) and instantly respond with: 'Yeah but, fair enough, isn't he a scumbag?'

Sandra stops me. 'Why do you assume that, just because he made a mistake in his romantic relationship, he'd be a bad father, and shouldn't be involved in his children's lives?'

Mine is a popular conclusion, she says – but an unhelpful one that only serves to destroy relationships between children and their fathers who, in most cases, are perfectly capable of looking after their kids.

'She made a decision that, because of how their marriage ended, the children wouldn't see him. As the kids grew up they were fiercely loyal to their mother. He has tried for years and years, sent cards, made phone calls – he even tried to go through the courts – but they don't want to know. He wasn't invited to the children's weddings and he hasn't met his grandchildren. It's tragic, really. And for what? So that the mother could get her revenge. But it's the child that will inevitably suffer.'

Much has been written about the 'right' way to help children cope with divorce, and grow up to be well-adjusted, emotionally literate adults. I'd recommend that those interested in this seek out the kind of literature that's written by world-leading child psychologists who have been studying this stuff for decades. This is not the book to read for parenting advice. However, my dalliance with the scientific research on this subject flagged one major 'don't' that I think is worth mentioning. A wealth of psychological data shows that the riskiest element of divorce, when it comes to a child's future mental health, is parental conflict. One 2019 study in the US followed 240 children of divorce over a period of eight years, and found that 39 per cent of those exposed to frequent fights between parents went on to develop serious mental health problems.[17] A 2017 blog post by family relationships expert Professor Tamara Afifi summed this phenomenon up well.[18]

Professor Afifi, who is based at the University of California, Santa Barbara, writes that the negative effects of adult conflict 'transcends' divorce, with children exposed to it having 'the most difficulty psychologically'. She explains that this is because adult fighting fuels a child's sense of cognitive dissonance – when two things appear contradictory, in this case, that the loving, doting father they idolise is also a useless husband, according to their mother. The psychological conundrum of dissonance is known to trigger anxiety, especially in children.

'This often causes them to align with one parent over another to ease their discomfort,' Afifi writes. 'As a result, their relationship with the other parent diminishes ... the bond may be difficult to re-establish.' She says warring parents are commonly unaware that their 'seemingly benign' comments about each other can sound barbed to their kids.

'For example, Dad might say, "Can you remind your mother that you have a dentist appointment on Tuesday?" The child passes along the message. Mom responds, "Why didn't your father tell me that? Why doesn't he ever talk to me? You tell him he needs to talk to me more." The result? The child feels caught between them.'

Professor Afifi outlines the disturbing results of a study performed by her research team, involving children of divorced and non-divorced parents. The researchers found that discussing their parents' arguments led to a significant spike in levels of the stress hormone cortisol in the children of divorce, which lasted for up to forty-five minutes after the discussion ended. The anxiety caused by fighting parents usually pushes children to one of three different behaviours, Afifi says. Two are dysfunctional: avoiding their emotions and thus storing up problems for a later date, or mimicking the conflict they see, resulting in aggression. The most protective is confrontation – talking to their parents about what's going on, and how they feel about it. 'Since most children have been raised not to talk back, this response tends to come only with age and maturity.'

So it would appear the best evidence-based advice would be this: try, as hard as you possibly can, to remain civil. And encourage children to talk. The studies appear unanimous in the healing effect of honest communication with kids every step of the way – which is hardly surprising. Professor Afifi tells of a parenting tip that I've also heard recommended by a GP friend of mine. When it comes to talking to children about serious stuff, try and veer away from the intimidating family meetings that summon everyone to the living room and conjure feelings of dread. Research shows children are much better communicators when they're partly distracted by mixing a cake batter or browsing a shoe department. 'If your child is young, you can play Lego with them on the floor and talk,' Afifi says. 'My daughters used to tell me everything about their days while I was washing their hair in the bathtub.'

I am aware of the naivety I bring to this table given the obvious fact that my divorce was child-free. But I couldn't help but be surprised that so many divorcing couples are un-aware of the harm their infighting will do to their children. Or worse, they are well aware, but fail to put their child's interests above their anger towards their ex. Divorce lawyers tell me parents spouting vitriol towards each other remains common, regardless of the presence of minors.

Both Brown and Davis say it's not as difficult to understand as you might think. 'Think about it,' says Brown. 'Often someone's ex-partner becomes the person they hate most in the world. They think that person has caused them the most damaging heartache they've ever experienced. Now think about how any parent considers a child – their most precious thing in their life. So, they want to protect their most precious thing from the thing they think is the most evil. They both think they are doing their duty for the child, which makes financial and emotional costs of litigation pale into insignificance. I'm not saying it's right, but that's often the way it is.'

In Davis's experience, said fights are rarely really and truly about the children. 'There's no forum in which couples can release their anger about things that went on in the marriage,' she says. 'Sadly, often if there's no money issues to squabble over, the children become the vehicle with which to express this discontent. All too often, they're used as leverage.'

Chapter 13

The Woman Who Did Everything Differently

In 1971, Jo Robinson, then in her early twenties, was at the helm of the roaring Women's Liberation Movement electro-cuting the spirits of mothers, daughters and wives across the country.[1] The year before that, she'd sprayed a bouncer with a water pistol filled with blue ink as part of a protest at the Miss World competition at London's Royal Albert Hall.

By 1979, she was pregnant. Her situation wasn't ideal for child-rearing; living in a flatshare with friends, in Islington, north London. The father was present, but they weren't together.

She wasn't the only woman in her friendship group to find herself in such a predicament and so, after some discussion, she and a close friend decided perhaps it would be sensible if the two mums and two babies moved in together.

The foursome moved into a three-storey townhouse in Islington. Soon, more friends joined. And then some more. It was the beginnings of one of the UK's first ever women's communes, a revolutionary movement that eventually spread its tentacles across the country, with similar set-ups arriving in Oxford, Leeds and Sheffield by the mid-'80s. The adults were mostly women, although men were permitted if they agreed to pay their way in housework. Everything was shared between the tribe: cooking, cleaning, taking kids to school. The groups mostly lived off a combination of savings and benefits, although some members worked in public service jobs like nursing.

Jo Robinson, the pioneer, invented a shared surname for the children of the commune: Wild. She and her son, Sam, lived in the Wild household until he was five, when they continued their commune in another property in Hackney, east London. The children in both houses were 'akin to brothers and sisters', Sam said in a 2009 interview with the *Guardian*.[2]

Sam went on to study politics at Belfast University. Jo eventually left the commune and trained to be both a midwife and a teacher, before packing it in at sixty-five and becoming a part-time gardener. By the late '80s, the Wild movement had mostly disintegrated. But the children remain the legacy.

'I feel most proud of the way we challenged the way houses are formed, partnerships are formed and the way children are brought up,' Jo told the *Guardian*.

Sometimes, you read about stories that feel important because of their subject matter alone. Other times, new information strikes you with an odd sense of gravity, as if it had been written especially for you to stumble across. As though you almost had a personal connection with it in a previous life.

When I first learned about the Wild communes, I was captivated. I had to tell someone of my discovery and couldn't think of anyone better than the most ardent feminist in my life: my mother.

When I stopped talking she paused and said, 'Yes, I lived there for a brief time.' Wait – what?! Subsequent discussion would conclude that she didn't live in that particular commune, but one based in London – probably south, she couldn't be sure – and it definitely had roots in second-wave feminism.

When Mum was twenty-one she moved from my grandparents' home in Finchley, north London, to Peckham, south-east London, to be closer to university. In the mid-'70s, Peckham was not the gentrified hub of natural wine bars and new-build tower blocks it is today. It was notoriously crime-ridden, especially in the eyes of middle-class girls who'd grown up within five minutes' walk of a Waitrose.

Anyway, within twenty-four hours of living in her Peckham flat, Mum got robbed. She came back to her flat late one evening to find the place completely upturned, with expensive items (including a prized sound system) missing.

Panic-stricken, she didn't know what to do. She couldn't call her parents – it was almost midnight and my grandmother could win awards for her irrational anger should someone dare disturb her sleep. Plus, she didn't feel like trekking back to north London.

She remembered a friend of a friend who was local (they'd bonded over their shared involvement in Women's Lib), so gave her a call.

'She came and picked me up and said she'd take me to the house where she lived nearby, which was essentially a female commune. I seem to remember there were a couple of kids,' Mum told me.

She can't remember much of the trip to the house, due to her state of shock and terror, but can recall waking up the following morning. 'It was this bright, large bedroom with a huge window looking out on to a beautiful garden with lots of trees. It must have been in the suburbs somewhere, or near the countryside.

'One of the women came to my bedside and brought me a cup of tea and asked if I wanted anything to eat, and what else I needed. It was odd; they were strangers, but I felt totally at ease. Like these women would really look after me.'

Mum says she can't remember staying more than a couple of nights. 'I don't know why I didn't stay. I think I wanted to get back to north London, in the end.'

I spent a good ten minutes trying to jog Mum's memory: did she come downstairs to a round table of the most fascinating characters she'd ever met? What did they do for jobs? Were any of them Julie Burchill? Sadly, she didn't have much detail to add. Some forty years had passed since.

I picture old, rickety kitchens filled with the howling laughter of six best friends who sit around a teak table decorated with empty bottles of wine. Someone offers to make their speciality lasagne for dinner tomorrow night, while another is happy to take on the school run if it gets her out of pick-up (she has a networking event). One of the kids appears at the kitchen door with a request for water which is subsequently fulfilled by her three mothers; one picks her favourite cup from the dishwasher and fills it up, while the other two chaperone her back to bed and take turns doing the voices of various characters in whichever bedtime story she picks.

'It really was like that,' Al Garthwaite, the former Lord

Mayor of Leeds and co-founder of the Oxford and Leeds Wild households, tells me when we speak on the phone. 'It worked in the same way that an extended family does. We all made a commitment to each other. It allowed us women to do what we wanted in our careers and go to meetings that spanned into the evening, because there was always someone who would rather stay in and was happy to look after the kids.'

It was undoubtedly an 'invaluable' experience for the children of the household – of which there were three at one point.

'They always had the company of others,' says Al, now seventy-six, whose biological daughter Shelley Wild was born into the household when Al was in her early thirties.

But the key benefit, she says, is that the children were surrounded by adults who wanted to spend time with them.

'The adults chose to look after them and would plan great activities. It wasn't treat, treat, treat all the time – we didn't have the money for that – but we did arrange days that both the adult and child would enjoy. The kids got to spend time with people who very much wanted to be with them.'

Within a year of setting up in Oxford, the 'non-biological family' ('which sounds like a brand of washing powder', Al says) moved up to Leeds where they could afford to rent a multi-storey house big enough for the two men, two women and newborn that made up their household at the time. The house acquired another woman and baby in 1973, after a pregnant friend asked to join to escape her abusive partner.

Some of the men and women were 'loosely' couples, but every aspect of running the household – including childcare – was split equally.

'There were a lot of rotas,' says Al. 'Who was doing the shopping, who was going to the market, who would do the cooking. We kept a pool of money with which food and other items for the house could be bought. We all ended up having a pretty good diet, actually.'

Some had jobs and some didn't. 'I was working for the Department for Employment at the time, but I started a teaching course soon afterwards. Eventually I went to work as a researcher for Channel 4.' One of the men worked at the passport office, while the other women lived off state benefits. The house was a hotbed for activism, with all adults contributing towards communications for the local Women's Liberation group and attending various feminist meetings.

'At the time, if you were an unmarried woman with a child, you were almost expected to live on social security until your child was sixteen. But we were all heavily involved in Women's Liberation,' says Al.

In 1978, Al had her own daughter, Shelley, whose father was an 'old friend'. It was around the same time Al had come out as a lesbian. It was also around this time that the men moved out, and the Leeds Wild contingent became an all-female household.

Al says watching Shelley grow up taught her that the idea that every child needs a man around the house is 'a load of rubbish'.

'It's a fairly good idea to have some sort of contact with both [genders] so children can see how decent men behave: they aren't all macho and controlling, and they cook and clean too. But do I think you need to have *a* man and *a* woman to bring up children? Absolutely not.'

As far as Shelley was concerned, she was raised by four mothers, Al says.

'She really was. One of them moved to the US when she was nine and she'd fly out to see her, or the mother would come here and stay with us. They felt a real sense of obligation to each other.

'I know a lot of lesbian women who have brought up their child without the man being involved, and the child isn't at all interested in meeting their father. Or, they get older and express an interest, meet them once and then decide, actually, that's enough thank you. But I also know of children who have wanted to reconnect with their father in adulthood and end up igniting a relationship with them. Children vary, don't they?'

Crucially, none of the Wild children she knows feel they've missed out on anything, she says.

But the set-up isn't without its challenges. For instance, to what extent does a biological mother have overarching say over their child's best interests?

'One of the other women couldn't have children of her own – and she was desperate for one,' says Al. 'So she really wanted Shelley to be her child, and to live with her, and be around her. But I was clear that, when we disband, Shelley is coming with me. There was a clear power imbalance there, and I could have handled the situation better, I think.'

Depressingly, it was a plague of misogyny that led to the collapse of the Leeds-based Wilds.

'Being an all-women household, there was a barrage of abuse from men,' she says. 'Men would throw stones at the house, shout things at us. Once we had a Polaroid picture of a man exposing himself posted through our letterbox. It was dreadful.'

At the time though, sexual harassment was 'accepted'. 'There was no such thing as a hate crime or anything like that. There was nothing you could do. We felt very much on our own.'

In the end Al and Shelley went to live in a different part of Leeds. But in traditional Wild fashion, their house became home to various lodgers, old friends and visiting Wild children.

In 2015, a Wild mother died, leaving her biological son 'desperately marred' by grief. He couldn't cope with the death admin, which was made especially complex by the fact his mother had not left a will.

So, his second mother and adopted father stepped in. 'Myself and Roger – one of the original men from the Oxford house – took over and said, "Right, we'll sort this out." We spent morning after morning going through everything: various bills, council tax, what have you. Some people couldn't understand it. But we are committed to each other. We are a family. And that's just what you do.'

It's a kind of home life that may, for some, feel too extreme an abandonment of everything we know to be 'normal'. But is it really? If the last two years have taught me anything, it's that Nickelodeon was lying. The two parents, two kids, doer-upper in the suburbs isn't always the emblem of success and contentment. It might be a road to misery. And you can still have everything you want; it just might not look exactly how you imagined. My research for this book has taken me to women who personify a plethora of options that now await us – and that very much didn't fifty years ago. I'm not saying the answer to a marathon of shit dates is to reproduce with a stranger and move to an all-women's commune with your best mates. But I'm not saying it isn't.

I suggest to Al Garthwaite that she was ahead of her time. Does she think the life she led in her late twenties and early thirties is the straight woman's solution to today's dating-app-ridden climate of commitment-phobes?

'I guess it depends on age,' she says. 'We started living together when we were in our twenties and had little to lose. We didn't think about anything in much depth. And as people get older, some crave more of their own space. They might want to be in a living room that's their own, rather than a place that's always filled with people.'

Given all that, it's a good option. 'There's a lot to be gained from it,' she says, 'and it's certainly much better than isolation' – or worse – 'being stuck with some man who you don't have a lot in common with . . . or even like.'

I've learned that this rejection of nuclear set-ups is undergoing a bit of a resurgence. A year ago, my mum emailed me a link to a report in the *Guardian* about a new cohousing initiative especially for older women – mostly professionals, aged between fifty-eight and ninety-four.[3] Mum had recently moved to a three-bedroom flat in a vibeless part of north London, where her neighbours were either elderly couples or young families. I could tell she felt unmatched. And lonely.

It just so happened that this new feminist utopia was just up the road – a stone's throw away from my old school. Called New Ground, the community comprises twenty-five flats and twenty-six residents. Seventeen 'units' are owned and eight are rented at a discounted rate for those with financial difficulty. While the women live separately, life is very much shared: there are common meeting rooms for weekly dinners, and an in-house cinema for film nights. Residents have access to regular exercise classes at the on-site studio, as well as a flourishing garden complete with its own orchard. Men can visit for a night or two, but they can't live there.

'The first question I get asked when I tell anyone about New Ground is: why is it only for women?' says Maria Brenton, researcher in social policy and one of the founders of the development. 'I say because men of that age are all too often unreconstructed.' By this she means they still believe life is simpler when they rule the roost. 'One of the founders of New Ground summed this up rather pithily, I seem to remember,' says Maria. 'She said: "All our lives we've been told what to do by men. I don't want to live my old age that way too." A lot of men in their seventies, eighties and nineties are used to being in charge and think, why change the habit of a lifetime?

'The statistics also show that women are far more likely to be living alone well into old age than men are, for a whole host of reasons, including that we tend to live longer.'

I ask Maria why she thinks today's boomer women have adopted modern attitudes, unlike their male contemporaries. One word, she says. Feminism. 'Most of the women who first came together to campaign for New Ground were the feminists of the 1970s. The movement taught them a new set of dynamics and relationships between the genders.'

It's not necessarily feminism that binds all of today's twenty-six residents together, but rather a set of core values and beliefs. 'There's an emphasis on neighbourliness, shared responsibility and supportive community,' says Maria, who tells me the women arranged socially distanced lawn parties and Zoom memoir writing sessions during the Covid lockdowns.

'We also have a health buddy system whereby each person will be assigned another resident to "check in" on. Taking note of the last time someone emerged from their flat, looking to see if their curtains are open, that sort of thing.'

It's difficult to go unnoticed at New Ground, she says, given that the sunny common room (which boasts a large panel of floor-to-ceiling windows) is the first on your right as you walk into the building. 'It provides a perfect opportunity to pop in and say hello to everyone on your way back from doing your shopping.

'When we researched what women wanted in old age, they told us two things: they didn't want to be told what to do, and they didn't want to be somewhere where no one would notice if something happened to them, like a fall for instance. New Ground is designed to tend to both of these needs, and it does it pretty well.'

With women in the UK roughly twice as likely to live to ninety than men, I am baffled that such an obvious solution to old-age isolation hasn't been executed before.

Maria says it's difficult to get politicians, housing developers and local authorities interested in the plight of older women – which explains why it took eighteen years to get New Ground up and running.

There were concerns that a large number of elderly women in a two-mile radius would increase strain on local social care services. Designing fully accessible buildings is expensive (New Ground is one level with unusually wide doors and corridors so residents can fully manoeuvre wheelchairs). And care homes – which, in the eyes of those with the purse strings are a perfectly adequate choice – already exist.

'The models that already exist, like sheltered housing and care homes, have not caught up with the modern older person,' says Maria. 'We have institutionalised the dependency of older people. Why not ask the people who are going to live there what they want instead? I believe models like New Ground can keep people living healthy, independent lives for longer, and less likely to need the help of public services.'

Word of New Ground has reached women in pretty much every corner of the world. Recently, Maria tells me, the block welcomed a group of female visitors from South Korea.

'They called themselves the "never-married group". They'd read about us and raised funds for a three-day trip to come and see us. I don't think they'd ever been to England before – and none of them spoke a word of English. They even hired an academic from a university to act as a translator.'

Women share a specific type of 'communality' that is rarely witnessed in groups of men, Maria has noticed. 'I don't know of any men's groups like the ones that exist for women,' she says.

Women are often struck by a desire to build confidence as we get older. We become aware of the responsibilities traditionally reserved for men – and we want to take back control.

'A lot of older women have emerged from a marriage feeling disempowered, not able at times to even write a cheque, change a plug,' says Maria. 'Either because they've always had those sorts of things done for them, they haven't had the confidence to try, or they simply weren't allowed to.'

One woman who has spent a great deal of time researching women-only living quarters is Sophie Mackintosh.

Now forty-five, Sophie has spent most of her working life as a model, offering her face to luxury fashion campaigns and travelling the world for various shoots surrounded by super-hot DJs and world-renowned photographers. These days she lives a relatively quiet life in a leafy London suburb which mostly revolves around the bustling social life of her three-year-old son.

But her ultimate goal for the future is to move to an eight-bedroom house in Hastings with her friends and their respective young children, where they'll eventually see each other through the final chapter of life, and be free of the anguish of romantic relationships. But more on that in a minute.

I came across Sophie via friends of mine – a female photographer duo who I've worked with for the best part of seven years. They've had the ill fortune of taking my picture at the pinnacles of many of my life explosions, and have never failed to cast me away from my inner turmoil for a brief moment of fabulousness. Anyway, when I told them about my book on a recent shoot they turned to each other, then said: 'You must speak to Sophie Mackintosh.'

'I guess I've got a fair few stories to tell,' Sophie responded when I first contacted her. 'When I think about my life, the only people who've made me really unhappy have been ... well ... men.'

The journey to this realisation began aged thirty-three,

amid the sabotage of her seven-year relationship with the man she imagined would be the father of her children. This would be the first shared experience we'd bond over.

The boyfriend, let's call him Frank, was an internationally known DJ. They met through the creative industry circuit and were 'intoxicated' with each other. Although they had 'absolutely no mutual interests', they'd planned a life together, fuelled mostly by 'testosterone and sexual chemistry'. They bought a large house in south London, which Sophie imagined they'd fill with a collection of little people dressed in mini quilted gilets and beanie hats. Until, that was, Frank started sleeping with his tattoo artist.

'I found out when he didn't come home until three in the morning and he told me he was "getting a tattoo". I confronted him and eventually it all came out,' she says. 'He told me he wasn't happy, he was never going to have children with me. There were all these things he'd never said before; like he wasn't happy with my career and thought I would have been more successful than I was. It was truly awful.'

She repeats one of his particularly charming leaving gambits: '"Nobody notices you when you walk into a room."'

'I think I said sorry! How sad is that.' At the time, Sophie believed that if he left her, she would die. 'I physically grabbed him by the ankles and begged him. I didn't have an identity without him.'

The break-up was the toughest thing she'd ever experienced up to that point.

'I remember sitting on the Tube sobbing and thinking that I didn't want to go on. Someone asked me if I was okay and what had happened, and I was so embarrassed to say that my boyfriend had split up with me that I said someone I knew had died. That was how it felt. Well, actually, the person who had died was me.'

A month or so afterwards, she upped and left for a job in India and did what many women do in the immediate aftermath of a break-up: she moved on to someone else. A photographer on the job, who was 'kind-hearted' and shared much of the same creative interests as her.

'But really we were bonded together by trauma,' she says. A colleague on their shoot died in 'horrific' circumstances. Witnessing the fall-out bound them together.

The photographer wasn't hugely keen on the idea of babies, but Sophie was convinced he'd change his mind in a few years. Which he did. Sort of.

'I became obsessed with the idea of having a baby. I'd managed to convince him to try with me, and we did, for four and a half years. I didn't understand why it wasn't happening – naively, I assumed I'd sneeze and a baby would come out. It wasn't until I was thirty-seven that I did any sort of fertility checks.'

Sophie's test results proved normal; she was plenty fertile. The boyfriend, on the other hand, was not. But his infertility was less of a problem than the fact he, really and truly, didn't want children. After six years together, they broke up. Sophie was thirty-nine.

'I felt like I had this watch around my neck. I had to find someone to have a baby with – and quickly. Now I know that this is not necessarily the case, of course.'

Sophie often took herself to the coffee shop at the back of the local garden centre on Sunday mornings, to journal and catch up on reading. And it was there that she met her next partner, a 'straightforward' man, nine years her junior, who worked behind the counter.

'He was very family-orientated and had this job in a beautiful, down-to-earth place – not like the chaotic worlds of previous men I'd dated,' she says. 'At first we formed a friendship. And then it grew into something else.'

She was overtly clear with her intentions. 'I said, I want a child and if you don't, there's no point in continuing this.'

Within a year of dating, she was pregnant, aged forty-two. They hadn't moved in together yet. Sophie says: 'I was transparent about what I wanted and he was cool with it, but was he ready? I don't know – probably not.

'I don't think we connected that well on a deeper, emotional level. Sense of humour isn't necessarily the same. And that's a massive thing for me.'

While her partner has been an 'incredible parent', two years after the birth of her son Sophie came to realise that the happy family she dreamed of might look different to how she imagined it.

'Will I be with this man in twenty years' time? The truth is, I don't know. I am realistic that I don't want to live in unhappiness. If you're unhappy, you have to make another plan.'

Over the past year, Sophie and her female friends have been working on exactly that.

'We're all creatives, so we're all talking about the fact we don't have pensions or much in savings, and we want to make sure we are all looked after.

'We're thinking about an eight-bedroom house in Hastings or somewhere else near the countryside where we can grow vegetables together, look after our kids together, and we know we're going to be safe.

'Some of my friends have husbands who aren't well, so they're thinking about scenarios where they might end up alone. And I know relationships don't always work out. My grandmother said you should always have £3,000 under your bed as escape money. And I guess it's this sort of idea, about having a back-up plan, that stayed with me.'

There's another reason for Sophie's motivation not to waste any time. In late 2021, when her son had just turned one, she was diagnosed with breast cancer.

Surgery to remove her breast proved curative and within a year she was cancer-free. Tests later showed that she was a carrier of the BRCA2 gene, which increases the risk of developing breast cancer by up to 85 per cent.

'My priorities changed, I was left a totally different person. And most of all I was so thankful I had my son.' (Sophie lost her fertility as a result of her cancer treatment.)

'Sometimes I lie there and stare into his eyes and I think, I made you happen. I wanted you, and I made you. And if a man hadn't been around I'd still have done it, no matter what it took.'

She hasn't 'dared' to dream of a future until the last year or so.

'I realised that, when life hands you a shit deck of cards and everything feels like it's been lost, the only thing that's generally left is a sense of humour. The ability to have a laugh. Mostly, you get that from your friends.'

Sophie's army of women have known her since she was eighteen. Now, they're 'scattered around' – from Thailand to St Leonards – and most of them have young children.

'We're all kindred spirits,' she says. 'It would be lovely to think of us growing old nearby, holding each other's hands. Now that I'm daring to dream of a future, these are the sorts of thoughts I've been having.'

She often thinks of her thirty-three-year-old self, distraught and hopeless, immersed in the ruin of the break-up that would reroute her future. 'I could have stayed on that path, and I am so glad I am not there. It was never supposed to be my life.'

I ask what she'd say to her younger self in the days after the split. Or another woman going through the same hell.

'You can't stop it. You have to go through it,' she says, through tears. 'You try to get up and, at first, you'll find your legs don't work. But then you get up on your knees for a while until one day, you'll find you are walking. I don't know how it happens. It just does.'

Chapter 14

What Now?

At the time of writing, and about six months after receiving my official 'congrats you're divorced' letter, I have just celebrated my thirty-third birthday.

It took place in an Indian restaurant on the east side of Manhattan, where fluorescent-coloured lights hang from the ceiling, the toilet is in the utility cupboard, and you must not stray from the $36 set menu which, in all honesty, is at least $10 overpriced. Around the table sat eight women – seven of whom I hadn't known longer than six months. We schlepped to a bar down the road afterwards, where there were no seats, and hovered beside a group of sweaty college grads sipping tepid lager for an hour, before deciding to call it a night. I was in bed before midnight. It was the best birthday I have ever had.

As I passed around fragments of dry naan, laughing at Ruthie's open-coffin funeral story and asking the waiter, for the third time, for more water, I was hit over the head by a moment of overwhelming happiness.

I put the plate down and looked around the table, soaking

it all in. On that exact day, two years earlier, I had been on my honeymoon, sipping Vermentino on a private wine-tasting beside my new husband. Six months later, I lay frozen on my mother's couch, stuck on a loop of traumatising thoughts about my rapidly disintegrating life. Without him, I felt rudderless. Who was I now? How would I cope? Would I ever feel anything other than relentless, spine-curdling pain?

Here I was, on my thirty-third birthday, three thousand miles from him and my comfort zone, surrounded by recent strangers, experiencing a type of joy that only happens once every so often. On that night, with those people, I felt more myself than I had done in the best part of a decade. I exhaled a sign of relief. It had taken a divorce, near financial ruin and a move across the Atlantic, but I'd done it. I had floated back to me.

A week after I wrote the above passage, I suffered what is commonly known as a nervous breakdown. Anxiety – a beast I've wrestled since I was fifteen – had been sniffing around for a couple of weeks, my torturous self-sabotaging thoughts becoming increasingly unshakable, until they meshed together like a cancerous clump, squeezing out rational thoughts.

My primary fear was one of anxiety itself. What if I was so anxious I couldn't cope? This would prompt recurring intrusive thoughts along the lines of: 'you must focus on the anxious thoughts, at all times, and nothing else.' Writing it now, I see how utterly insane it seems to give such a sabotaging idea any credence. But that's anxiety for you.

Then, one evening, I stepped away from my desk to a state of blankness similar to how I imagine it feels just before you slip into unconsciousness. It was as if my thoughts and feelings were floating in the surrounding atmosphere, totally untethered from my body and mind. I spent the subway ride home pinching my skin to remind my brain it was still connected to a body.

Within an hour, I found myself freaked out by my very existence; the subjectivity of life felt unbearable. The feeling persisted no matter how many times I told myself that seeing the world through my eyes only had been the case for thirty-three years – and I'd coped just fine until now. I attempted menial conversation with my best friend and flatmate Emma as a means of distraction, but sentences were a struggle. I told her I felt 'weird', which she guessed was down to feeling undervalued at work. I nodded, took a herbal sleeping pill and somehow managed to nod off until 3 a.m.

I lay shaking with panic, attempting to get through four episodes of Simon Schama's *The Story of the Jews* without vomiting. I peeled myself out of bed for work at 6 a.m., unsure if I was even alive. Survive one hour at a time, I told myself, over and over.

I called Mum. I needed to speak to a doctor, she said. Pills would calm me down – they'd worked before. I can't remember logging on to Zocdoc, finding a local psychiatrist and booking an emergency Zoom appointment, but I did it. I spent the day at work staring blankly at the screen, reading the same sentence twenty times, unable to shift attention from my rocketing heart and thoughts that told me I couldn't cope. I said something about diarrhoea and left at 5 p.m., clutching my bag of benzodiazepines.

My brother Sam called me. He'd spoken to Mum. 'I'm

booking you a flight home at midnight tonight. The Uber will be here at 8.30 p.m. All you have to do is chuck your stuff in a bag and get on the plane.'

And so, about eighteen months after my period of uselessness on Mum's sofa, here I was again, useless on Mum's sofa. Albeit highly medicated this time. I barely moved for forty-eight hours, unable to focus on much beside getting up every so often to pee. On the third day, I forced myself to go for a run. Somewhere between my primary school and the old Barclays bank they've now converted into overpriced flats, I saw a familiar face approaching. Patrick Hicks – an old friend I worked with at the local Waitrose in my teens who has since become the owner of a successful plumbing enterprise. Please don't recognise me, I thought. I sped up and fixated on the pavement as he flew past. I realised that, for the first time in a week, I'd thought about something other than my turmoil. It was a sign of hope.

I would come to learn that my sudden onset symptom was depersonalisation and derealisation – both very common experiences within anxiety and panic disorder.[1] The phenomenon is triggered by a delay in sensory processing signals in the brain after a period of extreme stress or anxiety. In hindsight, I experienced it once in my late teens, but assumed it was due to the fact we were in a strange place (on holiday in Turkey). The problem can present in a whole manner of ways; some describe it as looking at the world through a pane of glass, others say objects appear oddly shaped or strange in some way. Most people feel some degree of detachment from their thoughts and body. The most debilitating thing about it is that it is self-perpetuating, meaning the more you panic about it, ruminate over it, try and make sense of it, the more it sticks. As disturbing as it might feel, the trick, I've learned via various anxiety podcasts, is to live alongside it, and try as hard as you can not to prang out.

It would be five days before I'd feel steady enough to board a plane back to New York. I drifted through the airport like it was one big hallucination, periodically brought back to reality by the thumping in my chest. It turned out the drugs weren't as powerful when I was left alone with my thoughts, painfully aware that this journey back was supposed to indicate that I'd recovered.

It took about a week before I felt some semblance of normal. With every decent night's sleep my distorted world morphed into something more familiar, or at the very least, a place I wasn't scared of. I could once again adopt a laser-sharp focus to applying winged eyeliner without simultaneously tending to a catastrophe in my brain. One evening I blow-dried my hair, put on my face and stood in the mirror thinking of what a treat it was to focus on this and only this.

Apart from a slight wobble while adjusting to the pills, I was pretty much clear-headed within a month. In the interest of preventing another episode, I booked a virtual doctor's appointment – this time with someone from the UK more au fait with my medical history – about six weeks after my mini break(down). Her first question: 'Can you give me an idea of the events that happened leading up to that point, and of any difficulty in your life?' I laid it all out – the dead dad, the five years of anorexia, the hospital treatment for anorexia, the marriage, the divorce. I met her sympathetic head tilt with nervous laughter. 'I guess it's not so surprising that I get anxious,' I said.

'No', she replied. 'I'd be surprised if you didn't.'

I considered leaving this unpleasant episode out of this book. It would cast a shadow on my message of hope and resilience; assurance that it will all be okay in the end. The truth is, as you may have come to learn through reading this book, life is not a straight line. And the trauma of divorce, or ending of any long-term romantic partnership, is life-destroying for many. I believe it is crucial to acknowledge this. In fact, my failure not to, in the end, was likely what caused my anxiety to boil over. Some people can pick themselves back up and feel normal after a week or two, perhaps even meeting another partner and, in relatively little time, be living the life they were always supposed to (or so they might write in an Instagram caption). Based on the conversations with many, many divorced women I've had over the past year and a bit, I can tell you Hollywood-type stories make up a minuscule minority of cases. Most people muddle through the best they can, have a few wobbles along the way – some bigger than others – and, after many, many years, find some semblance of happiness, along with an invaluable strength.

Why am I telling you this? I guess to let you know that it's okay not to be okay. Here is permission to experience weeks of jubilant, independent freedom, followed by months of aching misery that makes you want to spend ten hours a day scrolling through videos of car repairs on TikTok. Maybe you're taking it one day at a time. Or maybe struggling through every hour. It is all perfectly acceptable.

If this is you right now, there's a few things I want you to do. The first is to tell yourself that this feeling will pass. Repeat it over and over in your head in the knowledge that nothing on this earth is for ever, especially emotions, which, according to the scientific consensus, last for a maximum of 90 seconds. The suffering is prolonged by worried thinking. Next, make sure at least one person who loves you knows how you're feeling – and try to communicate your thoughts and feelings as often as you can. We are not designed to cope with turmoil alone, and there's no use fighting evolution. If possible, remove all stress from your immediate reality. Tell work you need to duck out for a week or two and ask friends or family to help with caring responsibilities. Your brain has experienced a form of injury and rest is crucial for recovery. If several weeks have passed and you're still struggling to manage, book an appointment with your GP and talk to them about your options. A doctor can refer you for talking therapies like cognitive behavioural therapy, which might be useful for stopping a spiral of anxious thoughts. They can also prescribe antidepressant medication like SSRIs and, if you're overcome with panic (like I was), a small number of low-dose sedatives, to instantly calm you down.

I have spent many years reporting on the wonderland of concerns about antidepressants in my job as a health journalist. I've interviewed doctors who think they're the devil incarnate, responsible for everything from a spate in young male suicides to a drop in global fertility rates. I've pored over research that suggests SSRIs (the most commonly prescribed type of drug) can leave you with permanent sexual dysfunction and increases the risk of suicidal thoughts in teens.[2,3] And my conclusion is this: antidepressants are safe, effective and, in many cases, lifesaving.

The problem with research into mental health medication

is that it is exceptionally difficult to distinguish the side effects of the drug from the illness itself. Scientists have long known that depression can make it very difficult to orgasm.[4] It's also made a fair share of people suicidal too. The truth is that, at this point, several high-quality, reliable and large review analyses have shown that antidepressants work in roughly half of those who take them. Studies show that side effects – extreme anxiety, nausea, dizziness, suicidal thoughts – happen for about half of patients and most subside after the first few weeks. I recently learned that those with bipolar disorder, or with a history of the illness, are at higher risk of mania-type psychiatric symptoms when they first start the pills, so this group should be monitored closely.[5]

It is true that the long-held assumption that these drugs work by tweaking the brain hormone serotonin has been somewhat debunked;[6] no one is entirely sure how they do what they do. But that doesn't mean much in the world of medicine; the same is true for paracetamol and many of the newest, life-saving cancer treatments.[7] And it's not the case that serotonin has nothing to do with it – it's just that there may well be other brain hormones involved too.

The TLDR is this: antidepressants have got me through several unmanageable times in my life. There is no shame in taking them. There are also many, many kinds to try – as well as different doses – and I'd encourage you to push past the shit bit, at least for a month. Two, if you can manage it, and make sure you're closely monitored by healthcare professionals. For the overwhelming majority, it is worth it.

Anyway, back to my mini break(down). How did I get there?

I don't know why it happened. Perhaps it was the pressure of managing a new team with greater responsibility than I'd ever been used to. Maybe I was worried about the next step, when – if ever – I might have a family. It could have been a delayed reaction to the total and utter upheaval of everything in life that I knew to be a safe bet. I do know that when the feelings of despair crept in, I felt lonelier than ever before. I had to ride this wave without the life jacket that had been attached to me for the last decade. The precariousness of my surroundings made the prospect of losing control even more frightening; nothing was guaranteed like it had been with Ben. Until it wasn't, of course.

Moving to New York wasn't easy. I spent much of the first two weeks oscillating between crying and burying myself in bed with reruns of *Married at First Sight Australia*. I was in the most exciting city in the world at the forefront of my new beginning, with my best friend and a sparkling career opportunity. But I didn't know how to be.

I'd be introduced to new colleagues and friends of friends and find myself savaged by self-doubt, worrying I'd said the wrong thing or that I was instantly disliked. I longed for the familiarity and safety net of a romantic partner who could share in my apathy for making new connections. It was the first time in my adult life that I'd felt uneasy in social situations. And it made me very depressed. I guess it was somewhat of an identity crisis. I assumed that I'd easily slot myself into a new social life, and this would naturally define my reinvented character. I'd rely on my lifelong friend-making ability and party-girl tendencies that I'd pretty much abandoned when I met Ben. I'd learn how to have fun again.

But it turns out the transition from suburban wife to party-girl-Eve-circa-2013 was not as seamless as I'd imagined. Everything made me feel uncomfortable, or like I was somehow pretending. I felt old, past it, uninteresting. I'd sit in bars listening to my twenty-six-year-old colleagues talk about dating and group trips to Atlantic City and feel like an alien who'd recently parachuted in from its home planet. I'd make excuses and leave early, returning to my empty flat to wallow in my loneliness. The thing about divorce is, while it might take you less time than you thought to get over an ex-partner, adjusting to a new you is the real challenge. What do you like to do if it isn't ordering your favourite shared mezze platter and watching reruns of *Peep Show* nestled on the sofa? Would you enjoy tennis with a stranger as much as you did with him?

Eventually I learned the only way to discover the answers is by doing it all – everything you're invited to, even if you really and truly cannot be fucked. Most of the time I didn't like it, or didn't feel totally comfortable. But from many of those mediocre evenings came encounters with women that lifted me up and, in some cases, marked the beginning of an important friendship. I learned that, in a new environment, you need two like-minded people to make you feel safe and supported. From two comes three, and so on. After nine months, I had eight.

I moved back home to London after ten months in New York. I would have stayed, had I not been offered a job I couldn't refuse at the UK branch of my company. I worried about returning to the scene of destruction, to the same life that had once been shared and feeling like I hadn't a clue how to live it. My friends who had been single and always available for a bottle of something on Friday nights were now in relationships and rarely free. Others had grown fed up with the dire dating scene and moved to other parts of the country, or abroad. Still, when it came to my people, there were enough. I found myself drifting to a part of the city I'd never explored before and unexpectedly enjoying solo trips to neighbourhood favourite coffee shops and wine bars.

A month after I moved back, I went to view a flat in said new area, a few doors down from the UK's first cooperatively owned pub. It had one small bedroom, little built-in storage and was around twenty minutes (walking) from a Tube station. But the living room/kitchen opened up on to a boxed-in courtyard, lined with old plant pots and one wall randomly painted fuchsia. I saw myself sitting at a vintage bistro table on a Sunday morning, tapping away at my laptop, adjusting my stance to feel the strength of the morning sun on my cheeks, and wondering which cut of beef is most suitable for one person. The bare walls weren't terrifying like they used to be; now they were an invitation to my next, exciting chapter. Also, I'd already seen a sofa that I imagined would fit the space perfectly.

My offer was accepted within a week. At the time of writing, I am waiting to exchange contracts (provided the collection of flies I found recently are really just because the water has been turned off . . . not an indicator of a rotten rat under the floorboards). I am tentatively excited to resume adult life. But I am equally terrified.

I haven't a clue how I'm going to get my furniture delivered to my flat while being in my office every minute of every working day, and I'll never stop being furious that I have to pay an extra £150 to get the IKEA delivery person to put together my wardrobe (I know I don't have to, but as a result of personal growth I am now at peace with my limitations. DIY is one of many). I'm slightly concerned about getting brain cancer from the electrical substation that backs on to my patio, and I can't remember how far into the wall you're supposed to go with the power drill. Also, I hate the blinds. But whatever, I'll work it out.

I often think of the time shortly after my break-up when Mum roped me in to helping her to 'slip' a ginormous jute rug under her 100kg double bed. We spent the best part of three hours splayed on the floor, engaged in an excruciating dance of lifting and pulling, before we eventually realised it didn't fit. We immediately fell into fits of giggles. As we forced ourselves upright again, Mum hugged me and said, 'See, you don't need a man – you have me.' If she's managed it for the past nineteen years, I'm pretty sure I can too, I thought.

I was going to continue this chapter with a sunny conclusion about how I've solved the mysteries behind my shock divorce, and how the experience has made me the peaceful and enriched person I am today. But I would be lying.

Despite two years of interrogating the reasoning behind the twenty-odd break-ups featured in this book, I am no closer to understanding why Ben came to his conclusion. The way he chose to break the news, and his apparent nonchalant attitude that followed makes a little more sense now, however. But here's the thing: today, as I sit and write at my desk on a drizzly Wednesday morning, I can confidently say that it no longer matters. It is a hidden detail of the past that is no longer relevant to my present, or future. I've always hated the phrase 'everything happens for a reason'. But I can't help but shudder every time I think of the alternate world in which the women in this book don't get to discover their post-divorce lives. We'd be trucking along at bang average, completely unaware of what our worlds could be. None of the women in this book said she'd give up her current life for her former married one – me included.

The goal, I think, is to get to a place where 'the thing' is not 'everything'; when your bad mood is the result of a poorly fitting cappuccino lid or a blocked kitchen sink, rather than the sadness for a life you lost. This happened faster for me than I realised, and it likely will for you too. It took about a month for the epiphany to dawn on me: if the relationship had been right for me, I would still be in it. It was about then that my mind expanded to alternative options that I dared to feel excited about. For some people, getting to this stage takes longer. And that's okay.

It is a peculiar dissonance that, while the last two years have undoubtedly been the most unmanageable and traumatic of my life, they've also been among the best. Amid the periods of catatonic sadness has been the following: living in New York with my best friend, trips to four new towns and cities, learning to run without stopping, learning to use a corkscrew without fucking up the wine, at least ten new friends and reconnections with three old ones, one incredibly unreliable psychic reading, two work promotions, a book commission, a front-row seat at my best friend's new life in Bristol, the best sex I've ever had, the best kiss I've ever had (more on that below), reporting on a high-profile murder trial in California, driving across the state alone during said murder trial, endless cuddles with my niece, endless cuddles with two friends' babies, hundreds of Mum's homemade dinners, drunken Halloween parties, drunken New Year's Eve parties, a girl's road trip (including a *Grease* megamix singalong), a new flat (almost), a new sofa (almost), more disposable income than ever before, discovering Marmite pizza (IYKYK), a haircut that actually suits me, natural wine bar tours with aforementioned new friends, doing a cracking Shania Twain at karaoke, finally feeling comfortable in my own company. And the list goes on.

I can't offer assurances there won't be hiccups (or major spasms) along the way. But I can offer you hope. That should get you through to tomorrow, which is enough for now.

Tldr: useful stuff

20 lessons to help you survive divorce

1. Stop rushing. Whether it's finding a new place to live, a new partner or a new haircut, SLOW THE F DOWN. No one is rushing but you. When life becomes chaotic there is a temptation to quickly grab all the tumbling pieces and slot them back together again. But they'll almost definitely end up in the wrong order. Six months, a year, or even two years is nothing in the scheme of the rest of your life, and you'll thank yourself when you later end up in a place/situation that feels both right and sustainable. Remember your brain is in a state of shock and is not functioning to its full capacity; you are unable to make a fully informed

decision about whether or not you should get a fringe, or anything else that feels important.

2. Get a therapist. This advice isn't specific to those going through break-ups. It's for everyone. The world today is a kaleidoscope of awfulness and how anyone exists in it without talking at someone who is paid to listen for an hour once a week is beyond me. If you face long delays on the NHS, a GP can point you in the direction of local, affordable therapists who offer treatment at a fraction of the price of the average psychotherapist.

3. Eat and sleep. Obvious, yes, but in the immediate aftermath of heartbreak these are the first to go. You can't function without them, leading to a sense of failure which is a non-stop route to hopelessness. Set reminders on your phone to snack if you need to. If you can't stomach big meals, eat little and often.

4. This brings me on to medicine. Use it – there is no shame in getting a prescription to help you get through. Sleeping tablets can help you get a restful night, and there's a range of antidepressant medicines that work for anxiety too (as discussed earlier in the chapter). Often the physical symptoms of anxiety (racing heart, sweaty palms, hot flushes) can trigger anxious thoughts. So addressing the physical problem might be a resolution. Ask your GP about medicines like propranolol and, in extreme cases, diazepam (doctors give it in small quantities due to addiction risk) to take the edge off. Other options to help you sleep include antihistamines (the drowsy kind) and cold

and flu night medicines like Nytol (which shouldn't be used for more than a few days). Your brain is just like any other body part – when it is injured it needs medicine to make it better.

5. Time is a healer. I hate myself for saying this, but it's true. In the moments of burning hell, remind yourself of the indisputable fact that this will pass. Even if a situation isn't likely to shift for a number of months, or years, your perspective will change in ways you cannot predict. Trust the process, and go with it.

6. Just because you can't do something on your own, doesn't mean you won't get it done. I spent months obsessing over how on earth I would take on all of Ben's roles: drilling into the walls, catching rogue mice, driving on American highways without his directions. Don't bother – you'll work it out. You will be surprised how many helpful people you have around you: friends, neighbours, friends' boyfriends, friends' mums, dads, aunties, the list goes on. If you're lucky enough to afford to pay someone to do stuff for you, do it. It'll be worth it. And don't stress about not having the same skill set as your ex. He might be a dab hand with a power drill but can he express his feelings in a non-combative way? I know which strength I'd rather have.

7. Get a lawyer. Or at least talk to one. Make sure they specialise in divorce/family law. If you live in a big city like London, look for one who practises in the suburbs or the countryside, as they'll likely be cheaper. I paid mine £1,300, which I appreciate is not small change.

But it was worth every penny. It eases the sense of isolation that divorce can bring – especially when no one in your immediate circle has any experience of it. It means you don't even have to read emails or text messages from your ex if you don't want to. You have marginally more time to focus on your emotional and mental repair, which must remain the priority.

8. Delete Instagram, Facebook and TikTok. Obviously.

9. Let him have the coffee table. Or the Nespresso machine. Or whatever else it is he insists on, even if you paid for it, or it was a gift to you. Squabbling over an item you will likely grow bored of in a few years is pointless. Worse than that, it drains you of the energy you need to get up every morning and put one foot in front of the other. You might find friends and family are more insistent about physical items than you are. Tell them you appreciate their concern but it isn't helpful. I regret the hours I spent rifling through my ex's boxes in an attempt to 'win back' kitchen utensils as some sort of warped vindictiveness. Now, two years on, I can take or leave most of the furniture I fought to keep. In fact, it's still sitting in a storage unit waiting for me to decide what to do with it. If it feels worth it, and you feel strong enough, by all means put up a fight. But know that you don't have to.

10. Try not to absorb character assassinations. They often feature in big break-ups, usually as a result of one party's attempt to understand their own decision to end an objectively healthy relationship. Ask a close friend to act as a judge on your ex's opinions about you.

Everyone has their own unique experience of your character, which is, in part, a reflection of themselves. You'll be surprised at how much of your partner's personality you take on. Their opinion is not fact.

11. Don't stop working. Or at least doing something every day that requires your attention and provides a rehearsed routine. Distraction is a wonderful tool for helping you function as the trauma storm thunders. After a while you'll look up from your desk and realise you haven't thought about anything other than the words on your screen for the past five minutes. That's progress.

12. Get a lever arch file. Get several, actually. Organising the financial, property and other boring life stuff will make everything else feel slightly less chaotic. You'll get a small buzz of empowerment and reassurance that, yes, you really have got this.

13. Remember everyone on social media is lying to you at least 90 per cent of the time. None of it is real. (Of course this should be irrelevant if you've followed step 8.)

14. One silver lining of divorce is a get-out-of-friends'-weddings-free card that is valid for roughly a year after your break-up. Use it.

15. If you want to have children, the likelihood is that you will have children. Fertility doesn't fall off a cliff after thirty-five (see Chapter 4) and reproductive medicine is a thing. It might interest you to know that the reason scientists can't collect reliable data on the efficacy of egg freezing is because many thirty-something women

who undergo the procedure end up getting pregnant naturally, so don't go back for their eggs.[8]

16. The same applies to dating. There are 8 billion people in the world and you have met a thimble's worth of them. I promise that your unexpected life alteration will lead you in the direction of a new partner. But it might take a while. Also, one in two people get divorced. So half of those who are off the market now won't be for ever . . .

17. Don't go to the gym and switch to low-fat mayo if you don't want to go to the gym and eat low-fat mayo. Your relationship breakdown had nothing to do with your body or face. Your confidence will come from realising you can inflate your car tyres on your own, and not from being three pounds lighter.

18. Embrace difference, rather than attempting to slot back into your old life sans your ex. Spend time in places you've never visited before but always wanted to; try a different supermarket; try events or classes you've long been interested in but never bothered with. There are parts of ourselves we unknowingly push to the back of a cupboard when we're in a relationship. Time to dust them off.

19. I'll say it again just in case you missed it the first time: get a therapist.

20. Your friends are your airbag. Embrace them. Call them on the way to or from work (or leave long voice notes), arrange evenings to sit around and do nothing together, have boozy dinners at local mediocre restaurants, go dancing (if you can be bothered). If there is

one silver lining to come from this mess, it's the im-
penetrable union you will form with your girlfriends
after they've housed, dressed and fed you, packed up
your marital home and held you, hundreds of times,
while you cry. You will witness the astonishing extent
of their love for you, and it will grant you safety. Life
as a single woman will suddenly feel less frightening.
You know you will never be alone.

Epilogue

Some might be wondering about my post-divorce dating life. How long it took me to 'get back out there!' and how many evenings with mediocre men I had to endure before I finally met someone I didn't mind spending my Saturday nights with. Or maybe you couldn't give a shit about this at all, in which case, congrats – you've finished the book!

I debated whether to include details of my romancing in this book because, the truth is, I met someone great pretty soon afterwards. I worried that revealing this speaks to the fallacy that a new partner is the ultimate solution. It is not (need I remind you of my mini breakdown above). Also, I am well aware that my experience of dating post-divorce is unusual, and I was, for some reason, granted immense luck when I least expected it. But it would be naive of me to fail to acknowledge the natural yearning for a new relationship that is felt by many at some point after a big break-up. So here goes.

About three weeks after Ben left me, I downloaded Bumble and Hinge. It was the first time I'd properly used a dating app ever in my life, having toyed with Tinder for all of about twenty-four hours when it first launched a decade before. It was an irresponsibly premature toe dip into the dating pool, which was intended as a distraction from my exploding life. I was desperate to see the depths of hell that awaited my new single self, and imagined myself sobbing after a scrolling session in which I'd realised I didn't fancy anyone. Perhaps it was a way of justifying my loss; proving to myself that it really wasn't greener on the other side and I was right to feel like everything had gone to shit.

One evening I landed on the profile of a handsome thirty-six-year-old man who lived about two miles away. I appreciated what seemed like a genuine smile and deep, enchanting eyes. I paused to read his 'interests', which consisted of two words: 'microwaving' and 'asthma'. I laughed.

A week later, after a bit of back and forth about jobs and which photo we liked on each other's profiles, we exchanged numbers. I couldn't quite believe what was happening. It was as if I was playing the main character role in a film about someone else's life; like my hand was typing the words of another woman's thoughts. That period is somewhat of a blur. But Mum says it was the first time in weeks that she'd seen me sit upright on the sofa and express interest in something other than repeats of *Friends* on TV. She saw me laugh at my phone and thought, I don't care what it is she's doing, she must keep on doing it.

A week later, still in something of a trance, I suggested a date. I assume my eagerness was a yearning for a distraction from the flood of emails from my ex asking whether I wanted the fake Eames chair. The following Monday after work I made myself a (horrible) margarita and sipped it while I painted my face and changed my bra somewhere in the region of twenty-five times. My pathetic attempt at cleavage with my most padded bra only worked if I leant slightly to the left with bent elbows, a bit like I was riding a rollercoaster. Not sexy, I eventually decided. The reality of what I was about to do whacked me in the face in the Uber on the way to the bar. As we turned on to the high road and I clocked the shop front, pools of lime juice lurched up to my throat. *Fuck fuck fuck fuck fuck.*

I walked in to find him waiting on a bar stool at the high table closest to the door. I instantly recognised the smile from his picture. It really was an exceptionally lovely smile. As he stood up for a slightly awkward hug, I took in his handsomeness. He's pretty fit, actually, I thought. He asked what I wanted to drink. The nerves shot through my spine and I froze, staring up at him with my mouth half open. 'Surprise me,' I said. Unfortunately his surprise was an Aperol Spritz, which I hate.

I told him about the divorce as he generously took care of both Aperols. Why not reveal all to this attractive stranger, I thought. At this point, there was truly nothing left to lose. I apologised for saying too much, to which he responded: 'Why are you sorry? It's just life. People go through stuff.' He thanked me for 'sharing' with him. I told him I liked Taylor Swift and that I was aware it was an unpopular choice that made me uncool. I thought of Ben's vitriolic eye roll when she'd pop up on my 'Gals on tour 2021' playlist. But the handsome man reminded me my opinion was a popular one, and that the hundreds of millions of people who buy her records couldn't be wrong. I admitted I had a serious lack of hobbies, and if he wanted to venture into that sphere of date chat, he'd be disappointed. He was unfazed, assuring me that hobbies are mostly for people who don't love their jobs like we do. I really wanted to kiss him.

We stayed until closing, laughing about nothing and divulging some, but not all, mental health problems. We shared an Uber home and he didn't kiss me. I was so terrified that he might (and I'd fuck it up), that I stared doggedly at my phone, spouting some nonsense about the Uber driver's poor choice of route. When I walked in the door he texted me to ask when I was next free. 'I can do tomorrow or Thursday,' I replied. He texted back instantly: 'I can do tomorrow or Thursday, or both.'

Dating felt weird at first. The build-up to each one was mildly terrifying. I'd spend the hours before reminding myself of the qualities I must keep hidden – the ones that Ben had helpfully pointed out a month earlier – and the habits I knew had grated on him. I mustn't insist on getting Ubers everywhere to avoid the cold, or reveal my pathetic inability to eat spicy food. I should drink more alcohol, and faster, and be open to menu options involving red meat. I needed to remember to reciprocate compliments, and not to spend long periods of time talking about my job if he wasn't doing the same.

My ruminations would disintegrate within about five minutes of meeting my date. My brain would pivot to the thrill of his hand grazing my lower back, and the intrigue of his life story that I was desperate to absorb. It took about two weeks for me to realise that most of my above neuroses were just that – my neuroses – and he really couldn't give a shit what I ordered at a restaurant. In fact, he'd chivalrously take bites of shared dishes to 'check' for spice before reporting, 'this one is probably okay for you – but have some water with it'. Pub and dinner dates soon turned into lazy sleepovers and weekends of bingeing HBO fantasy dramas, which we'd often pause to recall a funny (juvenile) thing we'd noticed out in the wild hours earlier, and subsequently roll around laughing. We also talked, calmly, and with purpose, and listened. I'd brace myself for explosion when delving into an emotionally fraught topic, and was consistently reassured when the conversation resulted instead in a deeper connection and a big hug.

Almost two years on from our first date, and he is my boyfriend. I write this chapter from his riverside apartment in Cape Town, where he is currently working.

It hasn't been easy. We've spent the best part of our re-lationship on the other side of the world from one another. This didn't help the other major challenge: the hangover from my divorce that led to my firm expectation that he would, at some point or other, decide to leave me. There are unique elements of our relationship that I believe explain why it's survived, despite the situation I was in when it began.

First: the fact we've spent the first bit apart, for several months at a time. For most people, this might have been a recipe for disaster. But for us it meant I was forced to con-tinue to discover my independent identity, and form a life that suited me, and me only. I hoped we'd make it work, but was realistic that it might not, given the distance. Although it fuelled anxiety at times, it also offered a sense of freedom, and meant I took up opportunities I otherwise might not have (i.e. moving to New York). Second: therapy. Recalling the screaming arguments with your ex that ruined the trips to the Italian Riviera isn't cute date-night chat. It's also not nice for your new date to be constantly reminded that the person they're trying to build a connection with is still thinking about their ex. I laid all my Ben stuff at the foot of a mental health professional who was armed with evidence-based methods of helping me identify and understand my complex feelings.

I could tell Sarah (my therapist) was concerned about my rapid move to taking a lover. She asked a lot of questions about my 'intentions', 'goals' and the strength of my 'love' for Ben, if it still existed at all. I think this was intended to weed out a toxic rebound situation, which I got the impression she's seen a fair few times before. It was pretty clear from relatively early on that this was not that. The final clincher, I think, was the rather unique sensibilities of the man in question. It takes a man with record-breaking levels of emotional intelligence to see you howl in tears about an old partner, and not only say exactly the right thing, but also be confident that said hysterics have absolutely nothing to do with how you feel about him. And in today's dating landscape of ghosting, breadcrumbing and . . . benching (I think?) it is very unusual to come across a man who knows and says what he wants. And what he wants is you. But, at the risk of sounding smug, this is the man I matched with on Bumble, and the person I am lucky enough to have fallen in love with.

I know all too well that nothing is a dead cert. But I hope it shows you that falling deeply and madly in love with someone wonderful awaits you (maybe sooner than you realise, if you're on Bumble). They will be kinder, more caring, affectionate and, all in all, a far better match than your ex. I can guarantee this. Your divorce was the end of *a* relationship, not *the* relationship. You will go on to create far longer-lasting and more definitive memories with hundreds of other people you've yet to meet. In a few years, or maybe even months, the ex will fade into an amalgamation of good memories – laughing on a beach somewhere, a fun shopping trip where you bought that jacket you still love – and an appreciation of the redirection you never knew you needed. The anger may turn to a twinge of sadness, which is mostly a grief for the time you wasted fighting. For some, the trauma hangs around, but it isn't useless; it equips you with a unique appreciation for healthy connections while protecting you from emotional leeches. Your divorce is a footnote at the bottom of your life's rich tapestry. It says very little about who you are, and what you will become. My thoughts on this are neatly summed up in the obituary of Gail Ehrlich, the grandmother of my good friend Margaret who recently died, aged eighty-eight. It reads:

'Gail married George E. Ehrlich, a noted rheumatologist, with whom she travelled widely and enjoyed a wonderful life full of art and music. A previous marriage ended in divorce.'[9]

Helpful Resources

Divorce
www.familylives.org.uk
www.citizensadvice.org.uk (or call 0800 144 8848 if you're in England)
www.gov.uk/get-a-divorce
www.affordablejustice.co.uk

Religious Divorce
lighthouseforwomen.com
www.jwa.org.uk
www.shaktiedinburgh.co.uk
www.mwnuk.co.uk
www.mwrc.org.uk
www.indianladiesuk.org

Mental Health
www.mindout.org.uk
www.mind.org.uk
www.rethink.org
www.bipolaruk.org
www.youngminds.org.uk
www.samaritans.org

Financial Help

www.moneysavingexpert.com
www.themoneycharity.org.uk
www.moneyhelper.org.uk
www.turn2us.org.uk

Domestic Abuse

www.nationaldahelpline.org.uk
www.refuge.org.uk
www.womensaid.org.uk
www.mensadviceline.org.uk

Fertility

www.fertilityfoundation.org
www.hfea.gov.uk
www.thefertilityinstitute.co.uk (for Wales)

Relationships

www.relate.org.uk
www.nfm.org.uk

Acknowledgements

This book wouldn't exist if it wasn't for the twenty women and two men who gifted me their time and honesty over the last eighteen months. I can't reveal your identities but you all know who you are. Thank you for the much-needed hope of better days that you all gave me along the way. You are the heart and soul of this book.

Endless thanks to the publishing powerhouse that is Sharmaine Lovegrove. Thank you for taking a chance on me, for your inspiring words and for the invaluable friendship. The Dialogue team – Eleanor Gaffney and Gabrielle Chant – I am forever grateful for your attention to detail and miraculous sharpening skills.

The book wouldn't have been possible without the array of stellar experts who took part: Sandra Davis, David Brown, Anna Hefford, Aina Khan OBE, Shaykh Mogra, Shawn Smith, Susanna Abse, Deborah Hill, Gemma Perlin and Dr Ellie Cannon.

It also wouldn't have happened without Barney Calman – forever my biggest champion.

To my angels of New York – Tayler Steinberg, Maya Moosh, Helena Kelly, Rebecca Hoffman, Anita Franklin – who were always up for helping me hunt down obscure case studies, and happy to wait until Saturday nights to hang out.

Thanks to Grace Gabriel Stogdon, Anastasia Antoni, Emma Powell and Anjali Douglas for getting me upright (and keeping me that way), and Mum for, well, everything.

Finally, to my best friend Gabriel Henrique Gonzalez, with whom I am lucky enough to share my next chapter.

Notes

Chapter 2: The Blindsided

1. NHS Borders, *Coping With Trauma*, https://www.nhsborders. scot.nhs.uk/media/155467/trauma.pdf.
2. Steafel, Eleanor, '54 billion minutes of silence: The astonishing death of the phone call', *Telegraph*, 19 November 2023.
3. @ElectronicGround2555, 'I broke up . . .', Reddit comment, 2024, https://www.reddit.com/r/BreakUps/ comments/1azah8d/broke_up_with_my_girlfriend_today/.
4. @unofficialgirll, 'I finally reached a breaking point with my husband of 6 years. Why does leaving feel so bad?', Reddit, 2024, https://www.reddit.com/r/TwoXChromosomes/ comments/18tvspf/i_finally_reached_a_breaking_point_ with_my/.

Chapter 3: The Legal Alien

1. Zhang, Yuanting and Van Hook, Jennifer, 'Marital Dissolution Among Interracial Couples', *Journal of Marriage and Families*, 71:1 (27 January 2009).
2. Samman, Sarah, 'Why Your Interracial/Multinational Couples Might be Dropping Out: A Self-of-the-Therapist Exploration of Critical Factors', *Family Therapy Magazine*, 21:4 (July/ August 2022).
3. Bach, Deborah, 'Study finds bias, disgust toward mixed-race couples', *University of Washington News*, 17 August 2016.
4. Tweedy, Jo, '"Don't forget to have a baby!" President of all-female Cambridge University college Dorothy Byrne introduces fertility lessons telling students not to leave a family too late – after her own daughter was conceived via IVF at 45', *Daily Mail*, 10 October 2021.

Chapter 4: Children

1. Merrion Fertility Clinic, 'Science Week 2020', https://www.merrionfertility.ie/science-week-2020/.
2. Simmons, Eve, 'Fertility expert blasts celebrity mothers in their 40s who "mislead" women that getting pregnant in later life is easy though many have little problem having babies after 35', *Daily Mail*, 1 May 2021.
3. Ibid.
4. Ibid.
5. Ibid.
6. Ibid.
7. Ibid.
8. Ibid.
9. Ibid.
10. Ibid.
11. Verbanas, Patti, 'Older Fathers Put Health of Partners, Unborn Children at Risk, Rutgers Study Finds', *Rutgers Today*, 13 May 2019.
12. Stone, Bronte, Allyse, Alex, Werlin, Lawrence and Marrs, Richard, 'Age thresholds for changes in semen parameters in men', *Fertility and Sterility*, 100:4 (June 2013).

Chapter 5: The Affair

1. Perel, Esther and Miller, Mary Alice, 'In Long-Term Relationships, When Do You Find Yourself Most Drawn to Your Partner?', EstherPerel.com, https://www.estherperel.com/blog/when-are-you-drawn-to-your-partner-in-long-term-relationships.
2. Cano, A. and O'Leary, K. D., 'Infidelity and separations precipitate major depressive episodes and symptoms of nonspecific depression and anxiety', *Journal of Consulting and Clinical Psychology*, 68:5 (October 2000).
3. Sly, Kira, 'The Mental Health Impact of Infidelity in Marriages: A Literature Review', thesis (Northridge: California State University, Northridge, June 2021).
4. Moore, Marissa, 'Long-Term Psychological Effects of Infidelity', PsychCentral.com, 29 October 2021, https://psychcentral.com/health/long-term-psychological-effects-of-infidelity.
5. 'How common is polyamory in the UK?', Polyamory UK, https://www.polyamoryuk.co.uk/how-common-is-polyamory-in-the-uk/.
6. Klein, Jessica, 'The rising curiosity behind open relationships', BBC, 5 August 2022, https://www.bbc.com/worklife/

article/20220725-the-rising-curiosity-behind-open-relationships.

7. Jordan, William, '1 in 5 British adults say they've had an affair', YouGov, 27 May 2015.

8. Opie, C., 'Monogamy and infanticide in complex societies', thesis (Bristol: University of Bristol, 2019).

9. 'Monogamy evolved as a mating strategy', University of Cambridge, 29 July 2013, https://www.cam.ac.uk/research/news/monogamy-evolved-as-a-mating-strategy.

10. Smith, E. E., 'Monogamy Is Not "Natural" For Human Beings', *Psychology Today*, 20 May 2016.

11. Edgar, Blake, 'Our Secret Evolutionary Weapon: Monogamy', *Scientific American*, 1 September 2014, https://www.scientificamerican.com/article/our-secret-evolutionary-weapon-monogamy/.

12. Ibid.

13. McDermott, Rose and Cowden, Jonathan, 'Polygyny and Violence Against Women', *Emory Law Journal*, 64:6 (2015).

14. Schacht, Ryan and Kramer, Karen, 'Are We Monogamous? A Review of the Evolution of Pair-Bonding in Humans and Its Contemporary Variation Cross-Culturally', *Frontiers in Ecology and Evolution*, 7 (July 2019).

15. Zimmer, Carl, 'Monogamy and Human Evolution', *New York Times*, 2 August 2013.

Chapter 6: The Get

1. Kotecha, S., Jacobs, E. and Shearing, H., 'My husband refused a divorce for nine years', BBC, 25 August 2021, https://www.bbc.co.uk/news/uk-58334745.

2. 'Get Refusal Basics', GetYourGet.com, https://www.getyourget.com/get-refusal-basics.

3. Satenstein, L., 'How Orthodox Women Are Using Social Media to Liberate Each Other From Dead Marriages', *Vogue*, May 2021.

4. Abdul, Geneva, 'Salford man jailed after refusing to grant his wife Jewish religious divorce', *Guardian*, 1 April 2022.

5. Bristow, Collyer, 'Property tycoon jailed after refusal to grant Jewish religious divorce', Lexology, 4 April 2022, https://www.lexology.com/library/detail.aspx?g=0b886aa5-ede4-4b74-913f-3a92b99a449e.

6. Hilton, Rabbi Michael, 'Reform Judaism in 1000 Words: Bar and Bat Mitzvah', Reformjudaism.org.uk, 31 March 2017, https://www.reformjudaism.org.uk/reform-judaism-1000-words-bar-bat-mitzvah/.

7. 'A celebration of forty-five years of female clergy', Reformjudaism.
    org.uk, 22 January 2020, https://www.reformjudaism.org.
    uk/a-celebration-of-forty-five-years-of-female-clergy/.
8. Prinsley, Jane, 'Orthodox sex strike ends in New York after
    "chained woman" Malky is granted a divorce', *Jewish Chronicle*,
    12 September 2024.
9. Sash, Adina (@flatbushgirl), Instagram, www.instagram.com/
    flatbushgirl/p/C_xo6vQxg-S/?hl=en-gb.
10. Ibid.

Chapter 7: The Breadwinner . . . and an Escape

1. Collins, Lois M., 'The perils of cohabitation and why timing is
    linked to later divorce', *Deseret News*, 1 May 2023.
2. Ibid.
3. 'Rise of the female breadwinner: Woman earns the most
    in one-in-four households', Royal London, 27 May 2020,
    https://www.royallondon.com/about-us/media/media-centre/
    press-releases/archive/female-breadwinner-rise/.

Chapter 8: The Gay Marriage

1. Duffy, Nick, 'Lesbians significantly more likely to get
    divorced than gay men, according to science', *Pink News*,
    18 November 2020.
2. 'Lesbian couples likelier to break up than male couples',
    Centraal Bureau Voor De Statistiek, 30 March 2016.
3. Reality Check Team, 'Homosexuality: The countries where
    it is illegal to be gay', BBC, 31 March 2023, https://www.bbc.
    co.uk/news/world-43822234.
4. 'LGBT Rights in Maldives', Equaldex.com, https://www.
    equaldex.com/region/maldives.
5. 'May 1997 – Hawaii Becomes the First State to Offer
    Domestic Partnership Benefits to Same-Sex Couples',
    Britannica, 2014, https://www.britannica.com/procon/
    gay-marriage-debate.
6. Aguilera, Jasmine, 'What Will Happen to Same-Sex
    Marriage Around the Country if *Obergefell* Falls', *Time*,
    14 December 2022.
7. Edelman, Adam, 'Thomas wants the Supreme Court to
    overturn landmark rulings that legalized contraception, same-
    sex marriage', NBC, 22 June 2022.
8. Groppe, Maureen, 'Alito says he was right to fear that
    opponents of gay marriage would be treated as bigots', *USA
    Today*, 20 February 2024.

9. Scarcella, Mike, 'Texas justices revive lawsuit by judge censured over same-sex marriage stance', Reuters, 25 October 2023.
10. Desilver, Drew, 'In places where same-sex marriages are legal, how many married same-sex couples are there?', Pew Research Center, 13 June 2023.
11. Miller, Corbin and Price, Joseph, 'The Number of Children Being Raised by Gay or Lesbian Parents', SSRN, 16 September 2014.

Chapter 9: The Man

1. Livingston, Gretchen, *The Demographics of Remarriage* (Washington, DC: Pew Research Center, November 2014).
2. Ibid.
3. Gill, Sarah, 'Dolly Alderton on heartbreak as an inextricable part of the human experience', *IMAGE*, 10 November 2023.
4. 'Male Friendships and Mental Health: Why Men Don't Have Friends and How to Make Them', Newport Institute, https://www.newportinstitute.com/resources/mental-health/male-friendships.
5. Ibid.
6. 'Men: Why did you break-up with your ex-girlfriend or wife?', r/AskMen, Reddit.com, 2022, https://www.reddit.com/r/AskMen/comments/x5lizd/men_why_did_you_breakup_with_your_exgirlfriend_or/.
7. Smiles, Preston, '3 Reasons Men Break Up With Women', *The Preston Smiles Show*, 2023.
8. Gravningen, Kirsten et al., 'Reported reasons for breakdown of marriage and cohabitation in Britain: Findings from the third National Survey of Sexual Attitudes and Lifestyles (Natsal-3)', *PLoS One*, 12:3 (March 2017).
9. Mohlatlole, Nkuke Evans, Sithole, Sello and Shirindi, Modjadji Linda, 'Factors contributing to divorce among young couples in Lebowakgomo', *Social Work*, 54:2 (2018).

Chapter 10: The Woman Who Walked Out

1. Oppenheim, Maya, 'Divorce enquiries to legal firms soar by 95% in pandemic with women driving surge in interest', *Independent*, 8 May 2021.
2. 'Divorces in England and Wales: 2022', Office For National Statistics, 22 February 2024, https://www.ons.gov.uk/peoplepopulationandcommunity/birthsdeathsandmarriages/divorce/bulletins/divorcesinenglandandwales/2022.
3. Benson, Harry, 'Fewer Women (But Not Men) Are Divorcing

in the UK. Why?', The Institute For Family Studies, 22 January 2024.

4. Nightingale, M., Flemons, L., Bruckmayer, M., Blondes, E., Feyerabend, K., Hofman, J. and Hulme, S., *Combating Coercive Control and Psychological Violence Against Women in the EU Member States* (Vilnius: European Institute for Gender Equality, 2022).

5. Ibid.

6. Castillo, Michelle, 'Fear of being single may drive people to settle, stay in bad relationships', CBS News, December 2013.

7. Thomson, Helen, 'A third of women are more afraid of loneliness than a cancer diagnosis', *Forbes*, 18 December 2017, https://www.forbes.com/sites/helenthomson/2017/12/18/a-third-of-women-are-more-afraid-of-loneliness-than-a-cancer-diagnosis/.

8. 'The YouGov Friendship Survey', YouGov, December 2021, https://yougov.co.uk/society/articles/38491-yougov-friendship-study.

9. Cain, Sian, 'Women are happier without children or a spouse, says happiness expert', *Observer*, 25 May 2019, https://www.theguardian.com/lifeandstyle/2019/may/25/women-happier-without-children-or-a-spouse-happiness-expert.

10. Nabilah, Bilqis Nudhar, 'Happiness among Single Women and Married Women Intermediate Adults', *Proceedings of the 4th ASEAN Conference on Psychology, Counselling, and Humanities (ACPCH 2018)*, March 2019.

11. Capecchi, Susanna, 'All the single ladies: 61% of women in the UK are happy to be single, compared to 49% of men', Mintel, 13 November 2017.

Chapter 11: The Nikah

1. Sherwood, Harriet, 'Most women in UK who have Islamic wedding miss out on legal rights', *Guardian*, 20 November 2017.

Chapter 12: How Not To Get Totally F**ked In Divorce

1. 'NORTON, Caroline (1808–1877)', English Heritage, 2021, https://www.english-heritage.org.uk/visit/blue-plaques/caroline-norton/.

2. Oxley, John, 'Divorce and women's rights: A history', Vardags, https://vardags.com/family-law/divorce-and-womens-rights-a-history.

3. Bowcott, Owen, 'Prenup agreement enforced under UK law', *Guardian*, 20 October 2010.

4. Benson, Harry, 'One in five weddings now start with a prenup', Marriage Foundation, August 2021.

5. 'Child Marriage in the US', Unchained At Last, https://www. unchainedatlast.org/child-marriage-in-the-u-s/.

6. 'Child Marriage Legislation: Progress Map', Unchained At Last, https://www.unchainedatlast.org/child-marriage-progress/.

7. Steinhaus, Mara and Thompson, Lyric, *Child Marriage in the United States: A Synthesis of Evidence on the Prevalence & Impact* (Washington, DC: International Center for Research on Women, 2020).

8. Glusac, Melina, 'The most surprising divorce law in 21 US states', *Business Insider*, 1 February 2019.

9. 'Primary caregiver demographics and statistics in the US', Zippia, https://www.zippia.com/primary-caregiver-jobs/demographics/.

10. Fry, Richard, Aragão, Carolina, Hurst, Kiley and Parker, Kim, 'In a Growing Share of U.S. Marriages, Husbands and Wives Earn About the Same', Pew Research Center, 13 April 2023.

11. 'Registered Marriages in the Philippines: 2022', Philippine Statistics Authority, 1 December 2023, https://psa.gov.ph/ statistics/vital-statistics/node/1684061650.

12. Hutt, David, 'Is divorce coming to the Philippines?', DW, 10 November 2024, https://www.dw.com/en/ is-divorce-coming-to-the-philippines/a-70469717.

13. Digal, Santosh, 'Manila lower house passes divorce law', PIME Asia News, May 2024.

14. 'Saudi Arabia: Personal Status Law Codifies Discrimination Against Women', Amnesty International, 8 March 2023, https://www.amnesty.org/en/latest/news/2023/03/ saudi-arabia-personal-status-law-codifies-discrimination-against-women.

15. 'Saudi women to get divorce confirmation by text message', BBC, 5 January 2019, https://www.bbc.co.uk/news/world-middle-east-46770612.

16. Feinglos, Rebecca and Laurenzi, Sophia, '"It's hell": How divorce laws are designed to create unnecessary financial hardship for women', *Fortune*, 23 August 2018.

17. O'Hara, Karey L., Sandler, Irwin N., Wolchik, Sharlene A. and Tein, Jenn-Yun, 'Coping in context: The long-term relations between interparental conflict and coping on the development of child psychopathology following parental divorce', *Development and Psychopathology*, 31:5 (2019), pp. 1695–713, https://www.doi.org/10.1017/S0954579419000981.

18. Afifi, Tamara, 'The best possible thing you can do to help your

child through divorce', Ideas.Ted.com, 1 June 2017, https://
ideas.ted.com/the-best-possible-thing-you-can-do-to-help-
your-child-through-your-divorce/.

Chapter 13: The Woman Who Did Everything Differently

1. Williams, Sally, 'My four mums', *Guardian*, 4 July 2009.
2. Ibid.
3. Chaudhuri, Anita, '"We have brothers, sons, lovers – but
   they can't live here!" The happy home shared by 26 women',
   Guardian, 24 August 2023.

Chapter 14: What Now?

1. Ray, Sujoy, Ray, Rajashree, Singh, Neha and Paul, Imon,
   'Dissociative experiences and health anxiety in panic disorder',
   Indian Journal of Psychiatry, 15:63 (February 2021), https://
   pmc.ncbi.nlm.nih.gov/articles/PMC8106434.
2. Moncrieff, J., 'Persistent adverse effects of antidepressants',
   Epidemiology and Psychiatric Sciences, 29 (September 2019).
3. Cuffe, Steven, 'Do Antidepressants Increase the Risk of
   Suicide in Children and Adolescents?', American Academy
   of Child and Adolescent Psychiatry, https://www.aacap.org/
   aacap/medical_students_and_residents/mentorship_matters/
   developmentor/Do_Antidepressants_Increase_the_Risk_of_
   Suicide_in_Children_and_Adolescents.aspx.
4. Kennedy, Sidney and Rizvi, Sakina, 'Sexual dysfunction,
   depression, and the impact of antidepressants', *Journal of
   Clinical Psychopharmacology*, 29:2 (April 2009).
5. Simmons, Eve, '"The side effects of Prozac made me think I
   was going mad – but here's why I'm still taking it": Many say
   the risks of antidepressants outweigh the benefits. But Deputy
   Health Editor Eve Simmons has a very different view', *Mail
   On Sunday*, 18 March 2023.
6. Moncrieff, Joanna et al., 'The serotonin theory of depression:
   a systematic umbrella review of the evidence', *Molecular
   Psychiatry*, 28 (July 2022).
7. Drahl, Carmen, 'How Does Acetaminophen Work? Researchers
   Still Aren't Sure', *Chemical and Engineering News*, 21 July 2014.
8. North, Anna, 'The failed promise of egg freezing', *Vox*, 29
   April 2024.
9. 'Gail Ehrlich', Goldsteins' Rosenberg's Funeral Directors, Inc.,
   https://obits.goldsteinsfuneral.com/gail-ehrlich-2024.

Bringing a book from manuscript to what you are reading is a team effort.

Dialogue Books would like to thank everyone who helped to publish *What She Did Next* in the UK.

Editorial
Sharmaine Lovegrove
Adriano Noble
Eleanor Gaffney

Contracts
Stephanie Evans
Sasha Duszynska Lewis
Isabel Camara

Sales
Megan Schaffer
Kyla Dean
Dominic Smith
Sinead White
Georgina Cutler-Ross
Kerri Hood
Jess Harvey
Natasha Weninger-Kong

Rights
Rebecca Folland
Helena Doree
Louise Henderson-Clark
Alexis Alderton

Design
Sara Mahon
Sasha Egonu

Production
Amanda Jones

Publicity
Corinna Zifko

Operations
Jairiza Rivera

Inventory
Victoria Stephenson
Dan Jones

Finance
Chris Vale
Jonathan Gant

Copy-Editor
Gabrielle Chant

Proofreader
Clare Sayer

RAISING READERS
Books Build Bright Futures

Dear Reader,

We'd love your attention for one more page to tell you about the crisis in children's reading, and what we can all do.

Studies have shown that reading for fun is the **single biggest predictor of a child's future life chances** – more than family circumstance, parents' educational background or income. It improves academic results, mental health, wealth, communication skills, ambition and happiness.[1]

The number of children reading for fun is in rapid decline. Young people have a lot of competition for their time. In 2024, 1 in 10 children and young people in the UK aged 5 to 18 did not own a single book at home.[2]

Hachette works extensively with schools, libraries and literacy charities, but here are some ways we can all raise more readers:

- Reading to children for just 10 minutes a day makes a difference
- Don't give up if children aren't regular readers – there will be books for them!
- Visit bookshops and libraries to get recommendations
- Encourage them to listen to audiobooks
- Support school libraries
- Give books as gifts

There's a lot more information about how to encourage children to read on our website: **www.RaisingReaders.co.uk**

Thank you for reading.

---

[1] OECD, '21st-Century Readers: Developing Literacy Skills in a Digital World', 2021, https://www.oecd.org/en/publications/21st-century-readers_a83d84cb-en.html

[2] National Literacy Trust, 'Book Ownership in 2024', November 2024, https://literacytrust.org.uk/research-services/research-reports/book-ownership-in-2024